Religion and Popular Music

Bloomsbury Studies in Religion and Popular Music

Series editor: Christopher Partridge

Religion's relationship to popular music has ranged from opposition to "the Devil's music" to an embracing of modern styles and subcultures in order to communicate its ideas and defend its values. Similarly, from jazz to reggae, gospel to heavy metal, and bhangra to qawwali, there are few genres of contemporary popular music that have not dealt with ideas and themes related to religion, spiritual and the paranormal. Whether we think of Satanism or Sufism, the liberal use of drugs or disciplined abstinence, the history of the quest for transcendence within popular music and its subcultures raises important issues for anyone interested in contemporary religion, culture and society. *Bloomsbury Studies in Religion and Popular Music* is a multi-disciplinary series that aims to contribute to a comprehensive understanding of these issues and the relationships between religion and popular music.

Christian Metal, Marcus Moberg
Mortality and Music, Christopher Partridge
Mysticism, Ritual and Religion in Drone Metal, Owen Coggins
Religion in Hip Hop, edited by Monica R. Miller, Anthony B. Pinn and Bernard "Bun B" Freeman
Sacred and Secular Musics, Virinda Kalra
U2 and the Religious Impulse, edited by Scott Calhoun

Religion and Popular Music

Artists, Fans, and Cultures

Edited by Andreas Häger

BLOOMSBURY ACADEMIC
LONDON • NEW YORK • OXFORD • NEW DELHI • SYDNEY

BLOOMSBURY ACADEMIC
Bloomsbury Publishing Plc
50 Bedford Square, London, WC1B 3DP, UK
1385 Broadway, New York, NY 10018, USA

BLOOMSBURY, BLOOMSBURY ACADEMIC and the Diana logo are
trademarks of Bloomsbury Publishing Plc

First published in Great Britain 2018

Copyright © Andreas Häger and Contributors 2018

Andreas Häger has asserted his right under the Copyright, Designs and
Patents Act, 1988, to be identified as Editor of this work.

For legal purposes the Acknowledgments on p. vii constitute an extension
of this copyright page.

Cover image © dwphotos/Shutterstock

All rights reserved. No part of this publication may be reproduced or
transmitted in any form or by any means, electronic or mechanical,
including photocopying, recording, or any information storage or retrieval
system, without prior permission in writing from the publishers.

Bloomsbury Publishing Plc does not have any control over, or responsibility for,
any third-party websites referred to or in this book. All internet addresses
given in this book were correct at the time of going to press. The author and
publisher regret any inconvenience caused if addresses have changed or sites
have ceased to exist, but can accept no responsibility for any such changes.

A catalogue record for this book is available from the British Library.

A catalog record for this book is available from the Library of Congress.

ISBN: HB: 978-1-3500-0147-3
        PB: 978-1-3500-0148-0
        ePDF: 978-1-3500-0371-2
        ePub: 978-1-3500-0149-7

Series: Bloomsbury Studies in Religion and Popular Music

Typeset by Integra Software Services Pvt. Ltd

To find out more about our authors and books visit www.bloomsbury.com
and sign up for our newsletters.

Contents

Acknowledgments — vii

Introduction *Andreas Häger* — 1

Part 1 Artists

1. Metaphors and Symbols in Popular Music as Exemplified in Katy Perry's Music and Music Videos *Adrian-Mario Gellel* — 11
2. CeCe Winans, Black Gospel Music, and the Ambivalence of Stardom *Angela M. Nelson* — 29
3. Judas Priest and the Fury of Metal Redemption *Brian Froese* — 47
4. The Art of Darkness: On Biblical Language in Ozzy Osbourne's Solo Albums, 1980–2010 *Michael J. Gilmour* — 65

Part 2 Fans

5. Consecrating an *Extraordinary Being*: Fan Culture among Gilda's Followers in Argentina *Eloísa Martín* — 79
6. God is in the House: Nick Cave, Religion, and Serbian Fandom *Sabina Hadžibulić* — 95
7. I'm Your Messiah and You're the Reason Why: Para-Religiosity in the Fandom around Prince *Carla Schriever* — 107

Part 3 Cultures

8. *My Pravoslavnye: Russkii rok*, Orthodoxy, and Nationalism in Post-Soviet Russia *David-Emil Wickström* — 123
9. "Can I Take My Dog with Me to Heaven?" Swedish Country Music and Religion *Thomas Bossius* — 137
10. Punk and Religion in Indonesia *Jim Donaghey* — 151
11. Dylan Goes to Church: The Use of Bob Dylan's Music in Protestant Churches *Andreas Häger* — 167

12 Theater in Search of a Storyline: The DJ as "Technoshaman" in the Digital Age of EDM *Melanie Takahashi*   185

Notes   201
Bibliography   239
Selected Discography   250
Contributor Biographies   252
Index   254

Acknowledgments

This book has its origins in an effort to publish a second edition of the book *Call me the Seeker: Listening to Religion in Popular Music*, edited by Michael Gilmour, who is a contributor to this volume. In the end, it turned out as a different book, with some of the authors from the previous book contributing new chapters, and with some new contributors.

I would like to thank Lucy Carroll, Lalle Pursglove, Chris Partridge and many others at Bloomsbury for the invitation to edit this book and for their vital assistance. I also want to thank my colleagues at the Department of Sociology at Åbo Akademi University, with a special thank you to Tatu Terävainen for invaluable technical help. And not least, I thank all the authors who have patiently worked to contribute chapters to the book, as well as those scholars who came along for the journey for a while but for various reasons did not have a chance to finally write a chapter.

Lastly, a thank you to the readers, who invest time and money to take the opportunity to learn something new on the fascinating topic of religion and popular music.

Andreas Häger
Turku, Finland, September 2017

Introduction

Andreas Häger

This book looks at the relations of religion to popular music, primarily through the prism of the artist. The individual chapters study the relation of different artists to religion. A starting point for the book is that the meaning of popular music does not reside only in the works, or in the artists' biographies, but is constructed in a web of discourses and practices involving artists, works of different kinds, media, fans, as well as various aspects of music industry.[1] Fans, but also critics and scholars, make their own interpretations of the works and lives of popular music artists. These studies are therefore not limited to looking at the works or biographies of the artists, but at least as important is the context in which these artists and their works are interpreted and used, and more specifically how their relation to religion is constructed.

The study of religion and popular music is a small field with a relatively short history. It has reached a certain level of consolidation, for example with a few anthologies such as this one, with this book series at Bloomsbury and the handbook by the same publisher.[2] There is also an increasing number of scholars—including authors in this book—for whom this field is a central research interest, rather than an amusing side project. The field is part of a more general study of religion and popular culture, sharing issues and concerns as well as theoretical approaches with research on other popular expressions.

In this introduction, I will present some theoretical issues regarding religious change which I find relevant for this volume and for the field of research on religion and popular music in general. One perceived result of such change, discussed at the end of this chapter, is the permeation of the boundaries between religion and popular music.

The chapters

Before moving on to the theoretical discussion, the chapters in the book are presented in a short overview. The book is divided into three parts, under the headlines "Artists," "Fans," and "Cultures."

The first chapter, by Adrian-Mario Gellel, discusses symbol use in popular music through the analysis of a video by Katy Perry and of how her fans use Perry's work as a symbolic resource in their own lives. The chapter shows how symbols from different sources are mixed and that the symbol use does not always have to be very conscious on the part of the artist or the fans. The second chapter, by Angela M. Nelson, analyses the frictions between stardom and faith in the music and biography of the African American gospel artist CeCe Winans. The classical discussion on the tension between Christ and Culture, as presented by Richard Niebuhr,[3] is used as a starting point. The final two chapters of Part One are dedicated to analysis of heavy metal lyrics, as Brian Froese discusses the lyrics of Judas Priest, and Michael J. Gilmour studies those of Ozzy Osbourne. Both of these authors study traditional themes in heavy metal lyrics—the nature of evil, the apocalypse, individualism, etc.—partly from the perspective of how these themes tie into biblical texts.

Part Two of the book discusses three cases of popular music fandom. The chapter by Eloísa Martín talks of a case of fans of a dead artist, the Argentine singer Gilda, and how the fan activities have made her a star and an "extraordinary being" after her death. The chapter shows how practices related to saint devotion within Roman Catholicism, and not least its material dimension, are used as a model for Gilda fandom. Sabina Hadžibulić discusses the interpretations of the religious aspects of Nick Cave's work by Serbian fans, looking at how fans from a post-socialist society interpret the religious aspects of the works of an international Anglo-Saxon star from the perspective of their own experiences of religion.

Carla Schriever devotes her chapter to the exploration of what she describes as a para-religious relation which Prince's fans have to their idol, both before and after his death in April 2016. Central in Schriver's interpretation of Prince fandom is the tension between a physical relation, as being present at concerts, and a metaphysical relation, to the fan object.

The third part of the book is titled "Cultures" and looks at relations between religion and popular music in different cultural—national or institutional—settings. David-Emil Wickström's chapter looks at the role of the national and political context in his study of the hard rock band Alisa and its relation to nationalism and the Orthodox church in contemporary Russia. Thomas Bossius discusses the views on religion among three major stars of Swedish country music. The chapter analyzes religious and existential aspects of song lyrics and biographical material, in the framework of Swedish secularization. Jim Donaghey's chapter is a study of punk rockers in Indonesia, who identify as Muslims while being repressed by the Muslim establishment. The two final chapters discuss relations between popular music and religion in two different institutional settings. Andreas Häger's chapter studies the use of Bob Dylan's music in church services in mainline Protestant churches in Scandinavia and North America; while Melanie Takahashi discusses the role of the DJ as spiritual guide within electronic dance music (EDM) and the concept of "trance" in EDM in light of the digitalization of DJing.

The three parts of the book are centered on artists, fans, and cultures, respectively. However, all chapters in the book discuss an artist (or artists), with the exception of the final chapter, which rather focuses on the role of a particular type of artist, the DJ. The fans are especially emphasized in the second part of the book, but they are also present among the interpreters of Katy Perry's videos in the first chapter as well as among the participants in the Dylan masses or the EDM crowd of the last two chapters—and of course among the authors of the book, as most of us write about artists and music we enjoy. The last part of the book, "Culture," focuses on religion and popular music in relation to particular cultural settings. But of course these settings are also very relevant in the chapters on, for example, African American gospel, British metal, or Argentine cumbia.

Changing religion

The connections between religion and popular music are examples of how religion is changing. In research on religion, there are a number of concepts describing various aspects of how religion and its relations to society are changing. The most fundamental of these concepts is secularization.

This is not the place to go into an extensive discussion on secularization. Perhaps it is helpful to note one classical typology of secularization, by Karel Dobbelaere,[4] which talks of three aspects of secularization: institutional differentiation, as when the church loses domains such as education; religious decline, in membership, practice, and belief; and religious change. The latter aspect is most important here,[5] describing the changing content in the practices of institutionalized religion, using popular music in church—but also the fact that the religious institutions are facing increasing competition, for example from popular music, in formulating their "own" tradition. The intersections of religion and popular music could also be viewed as an example of institutional differentiation, as the church loses its control over religious music—and indeed over the religious texts and traditions. Institutional differentiation implies an increased religious pluralism, and religion appearing in popular music is part of this pluralism.

A process of change in religion that also has received a fair amount of attention is the privatization and individualization of religion. This is an effect of institutional differentiation and the general individualization that follows, as well as an effect of the increased pluralism in the sphere of worldviews. Religion becomes a concern for the private sphere, and religious views become more individualized. Drawing on popular music in one's religious views and practices, or using religion as a resource in personalized and idiosyncratic ways in works of popular music, are two central aspects of how privatization of religion is relevant in the relations of religion and popular music. Both these aspects are studied in many of the chapters here, as is the often strong rejection of institutional religion closely linked to privatization of religion.

Another important process of change is the mediatization of religion, which is part of both institutional differentiation and religious change. The concept describes the influence of media on the ways religion is practiced.[6] Popular music is a mass medium per se, and also depends on many different media and technologies. One aspect of the mediatization of religion is that media are the central means for many people—and at least in Europe most people—to get in touch with religion; one example of this is discussed in Chapter 6 on Nick Cave fandom in Serbia. In addition, religious institutions must adapt to the terms of media in many ways, from using popular music in church to putting services on YouTube; the chapters on popular music and institutional religion (Chapters 2, 8, 10 and 11) all provide examples of this.

One could also speak of an aestheticization of religion. Borrowing from Featherstone's[7] discussion on the aestheticization of everyday life, I list three aspects of aestheticization of religion. First, the boundary between art and religion is blurred as religious practices can be interpreted as works of art. Secondly, religion can be turned into art and practiced with an aesthetic intention. Thirdly, aestheticization of religion can take the form of saturation of religious practices with multimodal signs, images, and impressions. These facets of aestheticization of religion are easily perceivable in the use of popular music within institutional religion. In addition, as people to a greater degree come across religion through various forms of media and popular culture, their experiences of religion are going through a process of aesthetization, not least in the form of an increased barrage of visual and audial material—a prime example of which is the encounter with religious symbols in music videos (see Chapter 1).

These changes in religion are not a one-sided process; there are other social processes at play and religious institutions resist some of the changes. Woodhead and Heelas point out that a process of sacralization is going on parallel to secularization[8]; and Partridge has conducted an extensive investigation of sacralization within popular culture.[9] Woodhead and Heelas talk of three processes of sacralization: an increase in the number of religious adherents; a growing public role for religion; and increased intensity in religious involvement. The aspect of sacralization they speak of that has the most obvious relevance here is a growing public visibility and role for religion. The increased connections between religion and popular music can be understood as examples of an increased public visibility and importance of religion. Increase in numbers as well as in intensity can be related to fandom, in understanding fans as "worshippers" (as in the study of Prince fans in Chapter 7), and taking into account the strong emotions expressed by fans of popular music at least since the days of Elvis and the Beatles.

In addition to the three aspects of sacralization discussed previously, the sacralization of popular music can also be understood as giving it a seal of approval, a religious legitimacy. This is done through bringing music into institutional religion, but also when artists are constructed as religious figures. It is a form of sacralization to use religious language in describing a certain artist, for example talking of an "idol" that is "worshipped". It is a different form of sacralization to more explicitly tie these artists to a specific religious tradition. Such attempts at sacralization are questioned by those who prefer to keep religion and popular music apart. Both those who attempt to give popular music religious legitimacy, and those who resist this, are reacting to religious change.[10]

Sacralization in the sense of religious approval of, for example, popular music is one way institutional religion comes to terms with secularization, increased pluralism, and mediatization. Religious institutions can give a seal of approval to a whole musical genre or to individual artists, defining them as carriers of a religious message. But this goes both ways, as artists performing and producing popular music outside an institutional religious context—as do almost all artists discussed in this book—appropriate religious material for use in their works, making for example the Bible a resource for the writing of rock lyrics, or fans and media use religion in their interpretations.

Writing on religion and popular music, including research, can also function as part of the sacralization process, bringing attention to the connections of popular music to religion. At times, this form of research has veered close to Christian apologetics, attempting to interpret every form of popular music as proclaiming a Christian message.[11] In this collection, we have made a conscious effort to avoid this form of scholarship.

Boundaries

In framing the topic of this book, indicated already in the title, as a discussion on "religion and popular music," it is rather presupposed that they are two different and distinct entities. But the relation between religion and popular music is one of not only connections, or entanglement, but sometimes of a merging or at least near merging. Therefore, a central aspect of the relations between religion and popular music can be described as negotiating boundaries. The way I understand the category of dialogue in Forbes's typology of relations between religion and popular culture,[12] boundary negotiation and maintenance are crucial in this dialogue. In all the cases studied here, religion and popular music are involved with each other in different ways, and in all of them, the issue of boundaries is present if not necessarily explicit.

The negotiations of boundaries between religion and popular music can be described in terms of the processes of religious change discussed above. Secularization decreases the sphere of religion and tightens the boundaries, as it were, while sacralization moves the boundaries back out. There is a process of mutual appropriation between religion and popular music: popular music borrows from religion, and vice versa. When religious institutions appropriate a musical genre and an artist, they contest the boundaries of religion and popular music, stating that certain parts of popular music belong within a religious sphere; and when popular music appropriates religious expressions, these become part of popular music. As stated above, the aestheticization of religion blurs the boundaries between religion and art, as religious practices are interpreted or even intended as works of art, and there are many examples of this not least in the use of popular music within Christianity.[13]

The studies show several examples of how religion and popular music merge and how the boundaries are blurred. Religion becomes a resource for popular music in many ways, as religious elements are appropriated. The lyrics of heavy metal, and in a sense the whole genre, depend on religious material, as shown in Chapters 3 and 4. The video by Katy Perry analyzed in Chapter 1 is another example of how religion is an inevitable resource for popular music. In these and other instances, religion becomes integrated in the expressions of a genre or an artist to the extent that a genre such as, for example, heavy metal would not exist as it is without its religious elements. The Argentine Gilda fans use religious tools in their popular music practices, and their fandom and their devotion of Gilda are completely entwined with religion. But for the Serbian Nick Cave fans, his religious references rather cause confusion, and they see them as foreign elements both to rock music and to Serbia.

The two spheres may also merge in the sense that popular music may be a way of practicing religion. This is the case for a gospel artist such as CeCe Winans, and for the participants in the Dylan masses. Especially in the case of gospel, as in contemporary Christian youth culture, practicing one's faith is hardly possible without the music. As is shown in the chapter on Winans, this may lead to issues regarding clashes between elements of the two cultures, and coping with these clashes is part of the negotiation of the boundaries between religion and popular music.

In the studies in Part Three of the book on various national contexts, the relations between religion and popular music take on a different twist. The study of Russian hard rock shows how both religion and music are subsumed in the discourse of nationalism. In both Sweden and Indonesia, the national context means that the boundaries between religion and popular music are kept more intact, but in very different ways. In Sweden, the secularized culture makes fans ignore or reject the religious aspects of (particularly American) country music; and the Swedish country artists are using religious elements in their lyrics while maintaining a critical stance towards institutional religion. In Indonesia, the conservative Islamist and nationalist forces resent the presence of punk culture; and to the punks, their music is a sphere of freedom from religion.

In fan studies, seeing fandom as a form of religion is not unusual.[14] The same perspective is employed in Chapter 7, on Prince fandom, as evident already in the chapter title, quoting Prince describing himself as a Messiah. Uses of religious metaphors in describing and interpreting popular music are common. One example is the use of the term "trance" within EDM. Chapter 12 in this book shows the limitations of such use, and questions the extent to which religion and popular music are merging on the dance floor.

The study of religion and popular music is a small research field dedicated to a vast topic. These two spheres of contemporary culture exist in a complex relation; at times mutually repellent and at times closely intertwined to the extent that it is impossible to know where one ends and the other begins. Many people encounter religion through popular music, and popular music can be an essential form of religious practice. It is the hope of the authors in this volume that the studies presented here may be useful contributions to the ongoing discussion on this topic.

Part One

Artists

1

Metaphors and Symbols in Popular Music as Exemplified in Katy Perry's Music and Music Videos

Adrian-Mario Gellel

Homo symbolicus

Alongside the labels of *homo faber, homo politicus, homo religiosus*, and so on, it has long been acknowledged that humans may also be understood as *homo symbolicus*.[1] Maybe more than any other cognitive tool, the ability to perceive and create symbols is not only pervasive in all human activity but it is also responsible and co-responsible for the development of other major human characteristics, namely the development of language, religious thought and behavior, as well as the development of culture. Through our symbolic ability, we are able to perceive and construct a reality that is not physically found in nature. Thus, for example, I cannot find any concrete object in nature that we call love but I know and perceive what it is when I experience it or observe it in the interaction with or between others. Above all I am able to communicate it to myself and to my community symbolically through narratives, poetry, art, or even rituals.

It is with and through this ability, or rather tool, that we have been able to heighten awareness of our existence, make sense of our surroundings and our experiences and communicate with our selves and with others. However, as Barrett has aptly argued, this tool would have been useless, had humans not been able to share thoughts about thoughts (what he refers to as "metarepresentation") and, as a result of this ability, be able to transmit those thoughts and knowledge through a cumulative form of culture.[2] Indeed, what humans have been able to transmit was not only knowledge about the physical world, such as for instance how to use a tool, but more importantly thoughts about thoughts. Most of the time, this latter type of knowledge has been passed on through symbols. Thus, for instance, the reflection on the experience and definition of love has for generations been passed on through beautiful symbolic language in literature from the myth of Eros and Psyche to the Biblical book of the Song of Songs (8:6–7):

> Place me as a seal upon your heart,
> like a seal on your arm;
> for love is as strong as death,
> its ardour endures to the grave.
> It burns with blazing flame,
> a raging fire.
> Torrents of rain cannot quench love;
> nor floods sweep it away.

to St Paul's reflection in the thirteenth chapter of his first letter to the Corinthians:

> [1]If I speak in the tongues of men or of angels, but do not have love, I am only a resounding gong or a clanging cymbal.[2] If I have the gift of prophecy and can fathom all mysteries and all knowledge, and if I have a faith that can move mountains, but do not have love, I am nothing.

to the most famous love story of all: William Shakespeare's *Romeo and Juliet*.

> Did my heart love till now? Forswear it, sight! For I ne'er saw true beauty till this night.

The list of examples is of course endless. Through such literature, it becomes apparent that although the experience of love is a human universal that has been experienced since the appearance of homo sapiens on earth, the way we have come to understand it has not only been communicated through symbolic activities (narratives, prose, art …) but it has also been shaped by these activities. Indeed, it should be noted that the employment of symbols is not in itself an activity that tends to simply read and thereafter permanently crystallize reality but, since the symbolic logic is intrinsically related to meaning making, it requires a fair amount of plasticity. Thus, while the communitarian aspect contributes to a reasonable degree of stability, the successive interpretation and re-reading of the symbol, a process that includes the possibility of its mixing and amalgamating with other symbols, makes it possible for the symbol to be flexible. This has allowed us to not only access, perceive, communicate, but also, to a considerable extent, to shape the reality we live in.

However, even though human beings have become symbolic creatures, it should not be assumed that symbolic activity has always been present. Although modern humans seem to have evolved some 200,000 years ago, scholars normally agree that symbolic behavior seems to have appeared somewhere between 135,000 and 70,000 years ago.[3] However, it took us another 20,000 to 60,000 years to start to exhibit symbolic thinking in a consistent and prolific manner through artefacts such as statuettes and painting. Current archaeological evidence seems to suggest that the concretization of symbolic thought appears to have been learnt over a long period of time. Like any other tool that humans have invented, once the ability to construct and concretize symbols has been mastered, it shaped the reality in which humans lived and opened the possibility for new discoveries and new inventions. In this sense, this type of knowledge is as important, if not more important, as any other form of knowledge since it precedes, and gives access to, all other forms of knowledge.

Nevertheless, in a world that highly values positivistic logical knowledge and hard facts, there is a tendency to undervalue knowledge obtained from symbolic activity. It may be argued that in our hypermodern culture where knowledge has never been so accessible, and is indeed over abundant, we seem to be losing the ability to discern wisdom from knowledge, which weakens our ability to make proper use of cumulative culture.

Popular music and symbols

Popular music is a powerful cultural artefact that reflects and contributes to the shaping of ways of life. The lyrics and music are powerful tools that make use of poetry and narrative and that foster personal and group rituals. With the advent of music videos, the symbolic power of popular music has been boosted by visuals. The accompanying video with all its theatrical re-enactment and dance provides ample symbols that shed light on the meaning of the lyrics. Indeed Beaudoin noted that young people make use of accompanying videos to interpret lyrics.[4] Furthermore, with the advent of the internet and social networking in particular, the stage of popular music was set to change. With a wider availability of the product, which can be easily viewed and downloaded either legally or non-legally, the industry has resorted to new means to produce revenue and to ascertain industrial viability. Thus, for example, taking cue from the entrepreneurship of Jennifer Lopez, it almost became standard for female pop singers to be involved in fashion and to launch their own fragrance products.[5] As Vesey has aptly noted, the fragrance itself operates as "a celebrity intertext" that extends the narrative that the pop artist wants to communicate through brand cultivation.[6]

Thus, while the music and lyrics are at the center of the symbolic activity, there is a whole range of other cultural materials that amplify the original product—the song. In today's globalized society, the media and a capitalistic economy have become not only the medium but also the shaper of the narrative/s and symbols that the pop artist and his/her entourage want to convey. Thus, for instance, Lady Gaga does not solely rely on her music to construct her image; music is just the hub of a larger reality where art, fashion, concerts, live musical/theatrical performances, digital media and social networking, as well as social activism, form an intricate network. This network ascertains the construction of an icon as well as contributes to the formation of her message. Furthermore, the interaction of the audience through social media continues to consolidate, interpret, and shape the message.

The complexity of the relationship between popular music and symbol construction of each individual artist, along with the conveyance of these messages, should not be underestimated. Within this context, it would be useful to imagine a three-dimensional web with different levels where the levels are all connected to each other and yet where each product (lyrics of an individual song, an album, a music video, fragrance …) endorses its own narrative and symbols. Thus, it is as if there are clusters of symbolic materials which are connected to each other in a complex manner with one cluster being more intimately connected than others and with clusters that do not have strong symbolic depth.

The phenomenon surrounding Lady Gaga seems to currently epitomize this complex web. As I have argued elsewhere, Lady Gaga makes a conscious and strategic use of symbols, metaphors, and life experiences which she draws from a vast repertoire of cultural and symbolic baggage.[7] She strategically chooses to employ religious symbols, symbols derived from myth, and those developed by pop culture during these past years, mostly through theatre, music, art, and fashion. The strategy is further enhanced by her ability to point to the potential of her work as symbolic resources for individuals. That is, she points to her audience that the symbols that she makes available to them may be used to generate meaning in specific moments of rapture of their ordinary experience in order to "enable them to make a new adjustment to the situation or to 'resolve' the problem."[8] Lady Gaga not only provides the imagery, music, text, and rituals but she uses different media, in particular the new media, together with fashion and her activism work, not only to relay her message but above all to amplify it. I have argued that through a mindful use of symbols, Lady Gaga consistently pushes an immanent message which centers on the importance of self, love of self, uniqueness/originality, creativity, and the potential for every individual to be at the top.

However, while admitting that not all, and not even most, popular music has a deep symbolic value or makes use of religious symbols, it is still very possible to listen and view popular music in the top twenty charts that makes use of symbols and that strikes a chord with the audience. This seems to be the case with Britney Spears's single *Dance Till the World Ends* which was released in 2011 and which was tied with the hype about the end of the world supposedly predicted by the Mayan calendar. The message of the music video was very immanent within the central idea that dance and music help one escape from any eschatological thoughts.

Although western societies are said to be secular, yet myriads of religious symbols still abound in the media, including in popular music. Music frequently deals with deep personal experiences that are most of the time fundamental to our being human. Consequently, the richness of the symbol systems provided by religions, which for millennia have dealt with the same issues, becomes an inevitable source for the symbols adopted by the music artist. Yet not all artists adopt the same conscious strategy or philosophy when drawing from religious symbol systems. In this sense, Lady Gaga intentionally adopts symbols eclectically in order to answer her own questions in her own way. Her music video *Judas* (released in 2011) exemplifies her strategy as well as her mastery of drawing and reinterpreting religious symbols in order to develop her own parallel narrative and answers.[9] However, one must concede that Lady Gaga's interest in art and fashion makes her more prone to being consciously symbolic. Other artists, such as Katy Perry, who is the focus of this chapter, while still making use of symbols and metaphors are not necessarily so intentional when developing their image.

Katy Perry

Katheryn Hudson, known as Katy Perry, was born during the first half of the eighties during the Reagan administration at a time when the United States was experiencing an economic boom and at the height of the Cold War. As an American millennial, she experienced the two wars on Iraq and the changing world scenario especially with terrorist attacks and the environmental crisis. She forms part of an American generation that is more racially diverse, highly molded by the internet and social networking, as well as influenced by media and a consumerist culture.[10] Perry also forms part of the least religious American generation, with a tendency to distrust religious institutions and to construct their own belief system.[11] However, religion and her immediate family played an important role in shaping her life and, consequently, her symbolic repertoire. Unlike most American millennials, 74 percent of whom are the children of either divorced or of a single parent,[12] she was raised in a traditional family. Katheryn was brought up by non-affluent born again Christian pastor parents who became itinerant evangelists during the nineties, with young Katheryn changing home seven times before settling in Santa Barbara, California.[13]

After the huge popularity that she received through the release of her third album, *Rolling Stone* magazine defined her as follows:

> Goofy, sexy and above all else a savvy marketer of herself, Katy Perry has made herself both relatable and completely out there. She's girlier than Gaga and edgier than Beyonce—the kind of suburban superstar who probably still has all her Lisa Frank gear in a box at the back of her very insane closet.[14]

Up till now Perry has released five albums. The first was realized under her real name of Katy Hudson when she was still a Christian music singer. From a sales point of view, this album was a complete failure and spurred Katy to reconsider her persona and music genre. The song which launched her to notoriety was *I Kissed a Girl* (2008). The song was released in 2008 and dealt with homosexual experimentation. Apart from being very well received by the audience, it created controversy especially among conservative Christian groups. The song became a sign of her definitive break from her previous music style and was the beginning of the creation of hostility with the conservative Christian audience. Although her relationship with religion is definitely different from when she was younger, she may still be considered to be religious in that she uses religious language for her own spiritual quest. Up to 2010, Perry considered herself a Christian, claiming that she believed that Jesus is the Son of God and that

> God is very much still a part of my life ... But the way the details are told in the Bible—that's very fuzzy for me. And I want to throw up when I say that. But that's the truth.[15]

Yet by 2013, she drifted away from formal religion, claiming that

> I don't believe in a heaven or a hell or an old man sitting on a throne. I believe in a higher power bigger than me because that keeps me accountable. Accountability is rare to find, especially with people like myself, because nobody wants to tell

you something you don't want to hear ... I'm not Buddhist, I'm not Hindu, I'm not Christian, but I still feel like I have a deep connection with God. I pray all the time—for self-control, for humility.[16]

She further claims that she is still into Transcendental Meditation and that she is influenced by the writings of Eckhart Tolle.[17]

As with other pop singers, she was deemed by conformist Christians to be associated with the so-called Illuminati, a purportedly secret society that holds influence over the music industry with the aim of creating a new satanic world order. However, in an interview with *Rolling Stone* magazine, she categorically denied any such involvement especially since, as she stated, she does not know whether it really exists.[18]

The accusations against Perry started with the release of the music video *Dark Horse*. In this video, which is set in an ancient Egyptian context, she depicts herself as a sorceress. The images of pyramids, the eye of Horus, as well as the concept of "playing with magic" attracted the attention of many social networkers to the possibility that the video might be an Illuminati video. Indeed many started to point to different signs and symbols in her videos and concerts that supposedly refer to Satanism and/or to the Illuminati cult.[19] However, even though there are a number of signs that seem to make use of masonic, witchcraft, and Satanic symbolism, it is more probable that the use of such glaring signs are none other than a marketing ploy to increase audience attention and discussion on social media. In fact, these symbols, although used in a consistent and frequent manner, do not seem to connect to form intricate narratives or messages. It could well be that she and/or her entourage make sure to insert signs that purportedly refer to the conjured Illuminati sect in her videos and concerts in order to attract attention and create controversy. It is after all the able use of media, both traditional and the new social media, that exposes the artist in order to increase sales of music and his or her merchandise.

Perry's *Wide Awake*

The song *Wide Awake* forms part of her re-issued third album, *Teenage Dream*. The first edition of the third album was an acclaimed success. Five of the thirteen featured songs reached number one on the American Billboard Hot 100; a feat that had only previously been achieved by Michael Jackson. A few weeks after the release of this album, she married Russell Brand in a

Hindu ceremony. Both the tabloids and Katy Perry herself in her biographical documentary film *Katy Perry: Part of Me* (2012) depicted the relationship as a fairy-tale type marriage. It was only a few months after the end of their relationship that she released the second edition of her third album. Two of the six new songs, *Part of Me* (2012) and *Wide Awake* (2012), were related to the end of her love story. When she re-released her album, *Teenage Dream: The Complete Confection* she claimed that she needed to move forward and that she "had a few things to get off my chest …."[20] Indeed she intended the music video *Wide Awake* as the final chapter of her *Teenage Dream* phase. Perry claims that through this music video she "knew I wanted to put my one last exclamation mark on everything."[21] It seems obvious that this was a way for her of closing a chapter and making a fresh start.

Wide Awake is one of Perry's music videos that makes the most use of symbolism. In contrast to Lady Gaga, who is more intentional about the use of symbols in most of her work, Perry's music videos either do not include symbols or are very much less explicit. The video opens with the last shooting scene of *California Gurls* (2010) and closes with Katy going up on stage facing the audience and starting to sing *Teenage Girls*. *Wide Awake* (2012) is thus sandwiched between her backstage work of preparing music for consumption and the courage she finds to continue moving on and face the audience. Consequently, as she herself acknowledges, the narrative told in the video is mainly presented as a journey.[22] Indeed, in an interview to MTV, Katy claims that the music video represents "the labyrinth of my life for the past two years."[23] This would refer to the period from when she first released the third album, which includes the time when she got engaged to, married, and divorced Russell Brand. However it should be noted that the video makes allusions to instances that occurred before 2010.

It thus seems that for Katy Perry, the lyrics of her music as well as most of the symbols present in her music videos served the purpose of a symbolic resource in the way Zittoun has defined it.[24] In other words, in this music video, Perry intentionally sought to construct meaning for herself through the lyrics while, with the help of her collaborators, she chose the narrative through which the visuals would better communicate and help her explore her intended meaning. In so doing she was purposefully making use of her cultural elements in order to make sense of the positive and negative experiences that she underwent during the previous two years. Furthermore, she was able consciously to develop a means to move forward, that is, she adopted music as a means to help her transition to a different phase in her life.

When speaking of the dynamics of transitions, particularly in young people, Zittoun mentions "three interdependent streams of processes," that is (i) the change in one's social and symbolic fields, (ii) which consequently might require new skills or knowledge, and (iii) the engagement in meaning-making.[25] Through the information available in interviews as well as in the music produced for *Teenage Dream: The Complete Confection* and *Prism*, it appears that Perry fulfils the first and the last of the three processes. Through her intense, yet short-lived relationship with Brand, Perry moved from the life of a single woman, to that of a married woman, to that of a divorced single woman. There does not seem to be enough information for one to claim evidence for the second process, although given that there were reports that Perry was "devastated" from the breakup of the relationship and that she sought help through therapy,[26] it is possible to assume that she had to learn new skills and knowledge conceivably through cognitive restructuring. Lastly, the writing of lyrics and the making of a video contribute to "the narrativization of experience and the semiotic elaboration of its emotional and nonconscious prolongations."[27] Furthermore, as an artist, she intentionally offers her own music as a potential symbolic resource to her fans. For instance, in a recent interview she claims

> You know it's funny, I think I have a really hard time writing super sexy songs. The other day I was like, "I'm going to write a song about sex!" I did it, and I think it's really great, because I still have sex and I like to write about all my life experiences. But I think I was put on this earth to lift people up and elevate people and do that through my messages, quite frankly.[28]

The symbolic repertoire available in *Wide Awake*

The individual experience of the artist seems to be at the center of the whole process in the construction of a symbolic repertoire for the audience. As will be argued later on, it seems that in constructing symbolic repertoire, the individualization process is accentuated in Perry's music. This leads to a number of consequences that need to be investigated further.

The imagery adopted in the video makes use of three categories of symbolic repertoires. The first category of symbols used are what may be termed as classical symbols, that is, symbols that derive from mythology, religion, or philosophy. These symbols are mainly used to frame the basis of the narrative told by the video. It should, however, be noted that even though these constitute a foundational element of the narrative, it does not necessarily mean that Katy Perry is consciously aware of their original or full significance. For instance, in an interview on MTV, she refers to the two minotaurs that appear toward the end of the music video as demonical figures.[29] It appears that she is not aware of the relationship between the Minotaur and the labyrinth. The second category of symbols, which are also used to develop and enhance the narrative, are derived from fairy tales, children's narratives and popular culture television series. The last type of signs/symbols are drawn either from her own experience or from signs/symbols adopted in her second and third albums. Table 1.1 outlines the main, but not all, visual symbols used in the music video.

Table 1.1 The three categories of symbols used in the music video

Classical symbols	Symbols from narratives	Self-referential symbols
Labyrinth	Mirror/Looking glass	Strawberry
Caterpillar	Freddy Krueger	Light from the chest
Darkness	Alice in Wonderland type of land	Cat
Lantern	Prince on a unicorn	Young Kathryn
Light		Wheelchair/Hospital
Mountain with light shining on it		
Eve and the forbidden fruit		
Two Minotaurs		
Butterfly		

The main narrative of the music video is sandwiched between the last shooting shots of *California Gurls* and Perry being lifted on stage to start her performance.[30] While the beginning and end of the video make reference to Katy's experience as a public persona, the main narrative of the video occurs in private. Indeed, as she herself disclosed, she intended the narrative of the video to represent a journey.[31] As soon as she is on her own in her dressing room taking off her wig, she looks into the mirror from which a labyrinth, made of dead branches of a creeping plant, extends into a different dimension. As Katy, who is now robed in a dark cloak, claims that she is wide awake, the door of the labyrinth appears in the background and a caterpillar moves over dead branches that form the shape of a heart. The camera moves up the walls so as to show the intricate labyrinth and a mountain with moonlight shining through the clouds.[32]

The symbols that the music video makes use of in the first minute are already dense. There is a reference to Lewis Carroll's *Through the Looking Glass* narrative. Like Alice, Katy is moving into a different dimension. Yet, while Alice seems to have been moving in her cat's dream, by stating that she is wide awake, Katy makes it clear that she is not dreaming at all and that this parallel/symbolic dimension is the true reality. Darkness, the dead branches, and even the labyrinth all signify death while the shape of the heart seems to suggest a dead love. The caterpillar could be initially mistaken for a worm and therefore understood as a reference to the underworld and death. However, identifying it as a caterpillar would imply the hope of rebirth or afterlife.

Furthermore, the moonlight shining on the mountain at the end of the labyrinth contrasts greatly with the darkness that dominates the rest of the labyrinth. The mountain may be understood as the prize at the end of the journey. In antiquity, the labyrinth was synonymous with the idea of a journey. The greenery on the plateau of the mountain once again refers to life. On the other hand, in Judeo-Christian language, the mountain is the place of transcendence where one encounters the Spirit. The latter meaning of the symbol does not seem to tally with the intended meaning adopted in the video, although it may well refer to the concept of self-transcendence.

As Katy moves through the labyrinth with a lantern in her hand, she finds and eats a strawberry that is protruding from a dead branch.[33] The image of Katy moving with a lantern in her hand refers to her search. While Diogenes walked through the streets of Athens, as a cosmopolitan (citizen of the world), with a lantern in full daylight to search for an honest man, Katy moves through the darkness of her own private life in search of light, truth, resilience to move on, and of her true self.

It is interesting to note that Katy picks the strawberry with her left hand which puts into evidence the tattooed word "Jesus".[34] The action does not seem to be coincidental since Katy is wearing one lace arm sleeve only on the right arm. The lace sleeve covers her right arm while at the same time highlights the tattoo on her left arm. The picking of the fruit from a high branch is suggestive of the biblical narrative of Eve who transgresses God's command and eats the forbidden fruit. It seems that the strawberry does not only refer to the biblical narrative but concurrently it also seems to refer to the second album, *One of the Boys*, released by Perry in 2008. Indeed an image of a strawberry was impressed on the CD of that compilation. Through this image, the narrative told by the music video is pushed back by a further two years. Just as the forbidden fruit led humanity to sin and to be wounded so much that it needed Divine intervention and redemption, so Katy poisons herself with the strawberry. Indeed, as the narrative unfolds, it will become clear that the strawberry that Katy ate was poisonous and that she too needed some form of intervention and redemption.

After eating the strawberry the walls of the labyrinth start to close in on her. At this point, sparks of light come out from Katy's hand as she pushes the walls apart and a firework shoots from her chest into the dark sky.[35] This seems to call a little girl from a place whose background is full of light. The glow that magically surrounds the hands of Katy and the young girl suggests that the two are connected to each other.[36] The reference to the spark and to the fireworks that comes out from Katy's chest remind the viewer of the music video *Firework* from the third album *Teenage Dream*. It is thus evident that help does not come from the outside but from within. The call comes from Katy's chest which in the previous music video *Firework* referred to uniqueness of the human person. Furthermore, the girl, as will be revealed later on, is none other than her young self.

Katy, who is no longer clad in dark robes, and the little girl move through a hall of mirrors, at the end of which is a large mirror where Freddy Krueger is amongst paparazzi shooting photos of her. On breaking the mirror, hundreds of butterflies fly from the shattered glass.[37] The scene suggests that back in the "real" dimension, nightmarish people are waiting for her, while the fact that the image of the child is not visible on the mirror seems to indicate that the child is either a spirit or an imaginary figure in her psyche. On the other hand, the use of butterflies at this point of the narrative is not altogether clear since the butterfly is normally understood in terms of rebirth. Indeed, as it shall be evident later on, moving through the shattered glass does not lead Katy to a redeemed situation.

Whilst going through the interpretations attributed to this scene by bloggers, one notes how the Illuminati narrative is used in order to interpret this scene in a different manner. For instance, Vigilant Citizen claims that the mirror, butterflies (particularly monarch butterflies), and the labyrinth "visually represent the inner-world of Monarch slaves."[38] According to Vigilant Citizen, the video makes reference to the Monarch programme which is supposedly used by politicians, the military, and some elite groups to control the mind of people. The site claims that "some celebrities are actual victims of mind control" and that "entertainment is used to subtly normalize and glamorize this awful practice through symbolism."[39] For Vigilant Citizen, the music video is none other than a narrative about Katy's useless attempt to break free from the alleged Monarch programme. This and similar interpretations were put forward by a number of YouTubers.

As the two Katies continue their journey through the shattered mirror, one notes the little girl Katy pushing the older Katy in a wheelchair, while a butterfly is following them. Katy is seen trembling with the poisoned strawberry in her hand. Two Minotaur guards block their way but the little girl goes up to them and stomps her foot emitting magical waves that send the Minotaurs flying while at the same time cure Katy.[40] It is thus the young self that saves Katy.

The doors open to reveal a beautiful labyrinth full of light and flowers while a mechanical cat made of grass stares at the girls with psychedelic, swirly eyes. The two girls are welcomed by a Prince Charming who appears riding a unicorn. He flatters Katy while crossing his fingers behind his back but Katy proceeds to punch him so hard that he flies into the bushes. Katy can now move through a heart-shaped hole that was formed by the fallen prince.[41] If she passes over the prince who is still on the floor, Katy will be able to exit the labyrinth. It is here that the little girl places a gift in Katy's hand.[42]

While Katy is waving goodbye to the girl, she becomes aware that the little girl is none other than her young self who is now identified as Katheryn by the license plate on her pink bike.[43] Back in her dressing room Katy is ready to go on stage for her *California Dreams* tour. As she opens her fist, a butterfly flies away and follows her up on stage.[44] Contrary to the images of the butterfly used in the shattering of the mirror scene, the butterfly that followed Katy through the mirror on to the stage connects in some way to the caterpillar that was originally seen at the entrance to the labyrinth and refers to Katy's new beginning. Like Theseus she was able to come out victorious from the labyrinth. Similar to Theseus, it was love that guided her on her journey out from the labyrinth. While in the Greek myth it is Ariadne's love that saves Theseus and in the biblical narratives it is the love of God that saves humanity, in *Wide Awake* it is the love of self and one's own innocent self that saves the adult from the deceptions, wrong choices, and poisons of life.

Beyond *Wide Awake*

The message of self-love, self-empowerment, and resilience is not totally new to Katy Perry. Besides exploring issues of romance, sex, and love, Katy Perry has always promoted the need of being authentic to oneself. However the complexity of interpreting her message in its totality arises from the, at times, contradictory stances that she takes both in her music and in the messages that she posts. Going through her singles and albums one could note two different phases of development which should not, however, be understood to be linear and are completely separate from each other. There is the initial phase when she is being noted and rises to fame while the second phase starts with her divorce and the re-issue of her second album under the name *Teenage Dream: The Complete Confection* (2012).

In the first two albums, there is hardly any material that is pregnant with symbols. With the exception of the music video *Firework* (2011), which emphasizes the uniqueness and special character of each individual as well as the fundamental duty to be true to oneself, and *Who am I Living For?* (2010) which for the first time makes explicit use of Christian religious language, the other music videos and lyrics have no particular symbolic depth, even though conspiracy theorists read *E.T.* (2010) through the Illuminati lens.

The start of the new phase coincides with the breaking of her "fairytale" relationship, which led her to require therapy and consequently made her consider a number of aspects of her life. The devastating experience of her divorce with Russell compelled her to soul search through the writing of lyrics. She claims that *Wide Awake* (2012) and *By the Grace of God* (2013), which were released in the subsequent album, were gifts from God.[45] In the last two albums, *Teenage Dream: The Complete Confection* (2012) and *Prism* (2013), as well as the recently released single *Rise* (2016), there are more songs that are explicitly autobiographic and that make more use of symbolic language and imagery. The explicit use of Christian religious language at the end of the first phase (*Who am I Living For?* 2010) as well as in the second phase (*By the Grace of God* 2013) demonstrate that Perry never completely left behind the religious language that she had acquired when she was younger. Given their similar upbringing, even though in a slightly different manner, this compares to the way Lady Gaga draws from her own symbolic resources.[46]

If one were to compare the symbolic repertoire of Lady Gaga and Katy Perry, one immediately notes that the former is more intentional and deep in the use of symbols in both lyrics and visuals of her music videos. This is due to Lady Gaga's interest in art and fashion as well as the influence that Andy Warhol has on her works. On the other hand, the works of Perry do not always exhibit such intentionality or depth. Notwithstanding this, however, given that in a number of her songs she explores issues related to relationships and personal struggles, there are many who find that the lyrics resonate with specific periods of their lives and therefore become a symbolic resource. Such was the case for Deftly who in her comment on *Wide Awake* said:

> I just got dumped by my boyfriend of about a year and four months. Basically, I got played. This song makes so much sense to me in that context. I was delusional, I would make up excuse after excuse for questionable things he did in the relationship because I was high on the good feelings he gave me. It seems to me like Katy may have written this song about a similar relationship. Now that I know I got played and that he never cared, it hurts so bad. I "read the stars so wrong" but now I'm "wide awake" to what really happened and I almost feel like a new person ... "born again out of the lion's den."[47]

Conclusions

Once life becomes a story to be told, it automatically becomes potentially metaphoric and symbolical due to its allegorical power. This is especially true of poetry and consequently also for music lyrics. However, when analyzing Perry's own music repertoire, one notes that there are various levels of depth that can be explored. On a purely superficial level, any song has the potential to become a symbolic resource for any person who is passing through a similar situation or is asking similar questions to the ones that are dealt with by the music and/or the images present in the music video. On a deeper level, connecting the issues dealt with by the song with symbols present in other works, particularly classical or religious works, results in a more refined and profounder understanding. This may be obtained either through the lyrics alone or more effectively through both lyrics and imagery. Such was, for instance, the case with Lady Gaga's *Judas* (2011) or Madonna's *Like a Prayer* (1989). In the former, in both lyrics and video one could note, among other things, an exploration on the relationship between flesh and the spirit.[48] Likewise in the music video *Like a Prayer* (1989), issues related to social justice, sex, and spirituality were investigated.[49]

It perhaps needs to be said that the way symbols are being understood in this chapter is definitely closer to the idea of Open Symbol as defined by Häger[50]; that is, a symbol that is open to interpretation by respecting the plasticity of the sign representing the symbol whilst at the same time acknowledging its origin and conventional understanding. In a globalized world that is brought together by the internet, in particular by social media, the hegemonic power of institutional communities, such as churches, has been greatly diminished. For instance, commenting on the interpretation of *Wide Awake* (2012) Anikabritt stated:

> I am very glad people can relate to this song in many ways.
>
> having said that ... I do seem to believe it is about her struggle surrounding her faith and how her divorce has caused her to rethink them.
>
> I understand many people believe it is insane to see the song from a Belief perspective and I think that is totally okay to differ in opinions.[51]

The point is illustrated much more clearly in the comment made by Spirityvoice on *Who am I Living For?* (2010), which makes use of biblical and Christian language, where s/he states:

> I think that this song means to be true to yourself. There are religious references in the song, which I think are meant to be taken in a spiritual manner rather than in a religious sense. A spiritual teaching in Christianity that comes through in this song for me is the personal victory in faith, in heeding how one is chosen or called. She is called to the road less travelled, to strive in making a real difference in originality. It seems she feels that to be true to herself, she lets go of any control others may have on her art, be it organized religion, or the music industry itself, though none of us live in a vacuum or are completely alone and these people exist in relation to the artist ...[52]

Moreover, as a globalized society we are moving more into a post-secular age where there is an acknowledgment of the power of the wisdom of age-long religious traditions, language, and symbols. This seems to be the reason why the music industry continues to make use of religious symbols in both lyrics and videos. A case in point is the recent release by Daft Punk's *Starboy (feat. The Weekend)* (2016). While there is no Christian language in the lyrics, the song, which is a personal protest, is accompanied by a music video where the artist makes use of a neon light cross to destroy his "old self's" apartment. The symbolic power of the imagery is powerful yet it only tangentially uses the conventional meaning of the Christian symbol.

A third element that emerges from this analysis is the danger of a reductivist use of symbols. Humans, by nature, are symbolic. It is the main way through which we relate to the world around us. Throughout the millennia we have created symbols which have been defined and refined through narratives, rituals, and art. These have been filtered within communities and have been passed on from one generation to the next. Yet it seems to me that within a more individualistic culture, there is the risk that the deeper meaning of a number of symbols, as well as the symbols themselves, will fade away. This will be further accentuated by the development of self-referential metaphors and symbols. Even though by their very nature symbols are malleable, they still require a community that receives them, connects them with other symbols, and interprets them. One needs to wait and see if and how the internet may be able to develop and sustain a community of individuals able to connect with the symbols used by past generations in order to answer the same fundamental questions and respond to the same fundamental experiences.

2

CeCe Winans, Black Gospel Music, and the Ambivalence of Stardom

Angela M. Nelson

Introduction

This chapter engages in the debate about the role of the Christian religion in daily life and the extent to which Christianity is compatible to and aligned with culture. Although these debates are evident in the New Testament of the Holy Bible (which is the sacred text of Christianity) by such writers as Paul and John, academically they have been brought to the forefront by theologian H. Richard Niebuhr's *Christ and Culture* typology explored in the book of the same title in 1951. Although Niebuhr's argument has been challenged and contested by theologian D. A. Carson in his *Christ and Culture Revisited* (2008), Niebuhr's typology is a good framework to explore a dichotomy that is still very relevant to Christians today. Specifically, this chapter examines the idea of stardom as representing "Culture" and its impact on the black gospel singer represented here as "Christ." This chapter addresses the ambivalence associated with American stardom and the black gospel singer with special attention to the life, faith, and music of Priscilla Winans Love, or CeCe Winans, formerly of the popular gospel music siblings duo, BeBe and CeCe Winans. Although black gospel stars were in place long before the 1980s—Arizona Dranes of the 1920s and 1930s, Rosetta Tharpe and Clara Ward of the 1950s, and Mahalia Jackson of the 1960s[1] are good cases in point, BeBe and CeCe Winans illustrate a shift to a different level in the process of becoming and of remaining a black gospel star in the late twentieth century. This different level is television: the single most important medium that catapulted the siblings duo toward celebrity and stardom.

I examine Winans's autobiography *On a Positive Note* (1999), two recordings by BeBe and CeCe Winans, Winans's debut solo album *Alone in His Presence*

(1995), her album *Throne Room* (2003) and companion book *Throne Room: Ushered into the Presence of God* (2004), and Black Entertainment Television's *Journeys in Black* documentary series installment about Winans (2003) in order to show the black gospel singer's priority of proclaiming the Gospel of Jesus Christ while at the same time accommodating the requirements of being a celebrity in American popular culture. This chapter, by closely examining the ambivalence of stardom in the black gospel singer's life, sheds new light on the role of celebrity in black popular culture in particular and African American culture in general as well as shedding light on the debates within the Black Church about its ritualistic expression of black gospel music outside of its walls. Further, CeCe Winans demonstrates both the problematic and transformative role celebrity plays in the lives of black gospel singers into the twenty-first century.

I discuss black gospel music as it relates to Winans's rise to and current status of stardom and juxtapose this condition against the "Christ and Culture" dilemma that black gospel singers in particular and Christian singers and westernized Christians in general experience. Black gospel singers are participants (voluntarily and involuntarily) in three social processes—standardization, celebritization, apostillization—that impact significantly on their ability to exalt Christ and to downplay Culture. Together, these social processes support the black gospel singer's stardom (Culture) confirming their role as stars (Culture) of religious song (Christ) and hinder and veil the black gospel singer's role as Ministers of the Gospel of Jesus Christ (Christ). I argue that black gospel singers employ specific rhetorical strategies and cultural practices to clearly mark their sacred ground of being on the side of Christ (apostillization) while being aware of Culture (standardization, celebritization) and its demands on them. These strategies and practices safeguard black gospel singers from and mediate the negative effects of stardom in their personal lives and validate their sincerity and authenticity as believers (a term that Christians, especially Protestant Christians, use to identify themselves). This study is important because of its exploration of how black gospel singers demonstrate a thoughtful, reflective, and practical response to Christ, going outside of the walls of the Black Church, and carrying with them in black gospel music a hope and belief that an identity and peace, power, preservation, and prosperity can be realized in the lives of all people in all Cultures through knowing Christ.

Considering the black gospel singer in relationship to stardom, Niebuhr's Christ–Culture typology is a useful, beginning framework to understand the problematic nature of their co-existence. Niebuhr argues that Christians (particularly westernized Christians) have come to terms with Christ and Culture in five ways: Christ against Culture, Christ above Culture, Christ of Culture, Christ and Culture in Paradox, and Christ transformer of Culture. In broad terms, "Christ" is the Church of God and "Culture" is the World (or Culture) of Man. Theomusicologist Jon Michael Spencer argues that the "entire history" of black gospel music (up to the timeframe of his analysis) is an "anticultural *movement*" where "all but a few gospel songwriters of the modern era are of the 'Christ against Culture' type."[2]

The catalytic moment when the black gospel singer engages the Christ and Culture dilemma is when they are: doing the work of the Lord outside of the place of the Lord. The work of the Lord is singing black gospel music. The place of the Lord is the Black Church. If one is "outside" of the place of the Lord, then one is in the world. Culture is of the world and Christ is of God. Celebrity is Culture; it is of the world and outside of the Church (or Christ). Celebrity and stardom is a concern of Christian singers and gospel singers and their observers and listeners because of this seemingly impossible alliance. The alliance cannot peacefully co-exist because celebrity is a cultural and social problem connected to the secularization of society. Secularization is a social process representative of the world encroaching upon that which is sacred. Therefore, *where* the black gospel singer sings gospel music (and the context, rhetoric, and practices of the *where*) is one point of contention and an influential source for the basis of ambivalence explored here. Before discussing the role that standardization, celebritization, and apostillization play in the black gospel singer's life, I will provide a brief overview of CeCe Winans's personal and professional background.

Winans's background

CeCe Winans's musical start is with her immediate family of twelve (which includes her parents and eight siblings plus BeBe) and her church in the city of Detroit, Michigan. BeBe (Benjamin) and CeCe (Priscilla) Winans became National Professional Gospel Singers when they joined *The PTL Club* in 1981 as a part of the PTL Singers.[3] *The PTL Club* was a religious talk-variety-music show co-hosted by evangelists Jim Bakker and Tammy Faye Bakker broadcast on the PTL ("Praise the Lord" or "People That Love") Television Network. The Winanses were two of the first African Americans to join the group. African American Howard McCrary, friend of BeBe and CeCe's parents, David and Delores Winans, and musical director for *The PTL Club*, invited the siblings to go to North Carolina to audition for some openings they had.[4] At that time, BeBe was nineteen years old and CeCe was seventeen. CeCe was a recent high school graduate[5] and both were barely adults. As Winans remembers it, McCrary was "hoping to recruit new black talent to infuse the television show with more soul, and he thought BeBe and I would fit in well with the group."[6]

Winans began singing professionally alongside of her brother BeBe. Winans noted that singing together was the "furthest thing" from their minds when she and BeBe moved to North Carolina.[7] A song, as opposed to a well-planned marketing strategy, was responsible for this new union. The song which birthed their union as a duo was "Up Where We Belong," a religious version of "Love Lift Us Up" by Jack Nitzche, Buffy Sainte-Marie and Will Jennings from the Taylor Hackford 1982 film *An Officer and a Gentleman*. The song was first sung by the Winanses together on *The PTL Club*.[8] CeCe recounts that it was "one of the most frequently requested songs by *PTL* audiences … It was an instant hit on the *PTL* broadcasts."[9] BeBe, in Black Entertainment Television (BET)'s *Journeys in Black* about CeCe, said that they sang "Up Where We Belong" "every day for a couple of years. It's all he [Jim Bakker] wanted to hear."[10] CeCe notes that she and BeBe "ended up singing duet because requests started pouring into the station" for them to sing together.

> People liked to hear that brother-and-sister pair sing together. Churches throughout the country started calling the network inviting the two "colored" singers, BeBe and CeCe, to come to their church to sing together for one or another of their church programs. Pretty soon, we couldn't get through a day of broadcasting without singing that song. People in the audience, people throughout the country, especially Jim and Tammy Faye—everyone was always asking us to sing that song together.[11]

We should not miss the significance of this moment in their careers: BeBe and CeCe Winans sang a song on national television (PTL Network) that, in its original version, became a national and internationally award-winning song ("Love Lift Us Up (Where We Belong)") from an award-winning film (*An Officer and a Gentleman*). In Winans's poem "PTL," she writes, "'Lord Lift Us Up Where We Belong' was the song we sang, it gave us national exposure and led the way to fame."[12] Tammy Faye Bakker created a religious version of the song by changing some of the words to include reference to Christianity and Christian themes. The song was taught to the PTL Singers but BeBe and CeCe were chosen as the lead singers.[13] In the film, "Love lift us up" was sung by Joe Cocker and Jennifer Warnes (two white pop singers). The song performed very well with American and international audiences.[14] A Platinum-certified song, "Love lift us up" hit Number 1 on the US *Billboard* Hot 100 chart on November 6, 1982, and it won the Golden Globe Award for Best Original Song and the Academy Award for Best Original Song in 1983 and the BAFTA (British Academy of Film and Television Arts) Film Award for Best Original Song in 1984. It is possible that the general popularity of the song with the American popular music audience contributed to the song's popularity with PTL's Christian audiences. Being a hit song with the Winanses, the popularity of "Up Where We Belong" touches on the cultural process of standardization.

Standardization

Standardization is a social process that has been imposed upon the black gospel singer because of traditions within the Black Church and the popular music industry in America. I use standardization here to mean the ways that black gospel music conforms to standards of performance, beliefs, and sound. Sociologist Theodor Adorno argued that in "the advanced industrial countries pop music is defined by standardization" and that the "'standard' song … must stick to an unmercifully rigid pattern."[15] Black gospel music is in a sense standardized and sticks to a "rigid pattern" because it encompasses styles, beliefs, and sounds that are recycled by its creators and these components are already known by its audience. The Black Church is the birthplace of black gospel music, the space and place of its primary audience: African American Christians. Black gospel music is standardized in its theology and music. In the Black Church, the black gospel singer is trained in theology and music. Pearl Williams-Jones contends that the "greatest gospel artists are usually those who were born nearest the source of the tradition."[16] The source of which Williams-Jones speaks is the Black Church. From the Black Church, the black gospel singer gains techniques from the free-style collective improvisation of the congregation and the rhetorical solo style of the black preacher.[17] This standardization of music and theology brings familiarity to the singing of black gospel music. Familiarity allows believers to join together to practice and proclaim the beliefs and values they share. Winans's commitment to black gospel music and its beliefs and values is in part due to her upbringing in the Pentecostal-Holiness tradition through the Church of God in Christ denomination and due to the upbringing of her parents and the influence of her entire family: "Church is where I was surrounded by friends and comrades who had similar interests and values. By the time I entered high school the family had joined a new church, Shalom Temple, a nondenominational Pentecostal church in West Detroit."[18]

Winans describes in detail how the Black Church trained her to be a gospel singer.

> Choir singing was our delight because it was the one place in the church where we enjoyed an element of independence. The adults permitted us, for the most part, to do what we pleased in the choir: we chose what music we wanted to sing. They ... permitted us drums, guitars, and organs, which we used to pump up the beat. As we matured, the lessons we've learned from singing matured. We learned how to sing four-part harmony, how to blend our voices without losing our own special timbre, how to appreciate the talents of a good accompanist because of his or her ability to help you pace yourself. Best of all, we learned the creative, artistic, and heartfelt aspects of singing: if you don't feel what you're singing, neither will your audience; always give your best when you're singing to a "packed house" or to a "slack house."[19]

Concerning the theologies of black gospel music, which is standardized in many of its themes, CeCe Winans is well-versed. During her time with her brother BeBe, CeCe Winans and her brother featured tracks about heaven as well as themes of struggle and suffering on their first two albums. Heaven as a transcendent reality is a popular theme in black gospel music and Christian music in general. In "Heaven," from their third album *Heaven* (1988), BeBe and CeCe Winans sing of heaven as being the place for which they long. In their next album, *Different Lifestyles* (1991), struggle is evident in the "long hard" days, keeping their heads up, the presence of war, and in their endurance of "nights." Contrariwise, they refer to heaven as a "better place" that is full of love and peace. Heaven is a place that is blessed and where they will find rest.

CeCe Winans records a great deal of songs that praise and worship God, another one of the standard dominant theologies in black gospel music. Her first solo album *Alone in His Presence* (1995) and her 2003 album *Throne Room* demonstrate this fact. Each song on *Alone in His Presence* has a biblical scripture reference noted with it. God and Jesus are cast as Father, Provider, Redeemer, Comforter, Protector, Healer, and Deliverer. The album contains no songs that focus on heaven or struggle or suffering as a part of daily life. The focus is on God and that is what makes the songs on this album praise and worship. Winans includes three traditional (or standard) hymns on the album: "I Surrender All," "Great is Thy Faithfulness," and "Blessed Assurance." Winans fondly speaks about hymns such as these being sung in her church, in her home by her parents, and in annual concerts her family held during the Christmas season: "Back then some of the songs we all sang were rearrangements of traditional church hymns."[20] Hymns such as these were songs of uplift and assurance in Winans's life: "We could always depend on an uplifting favorite hymn, like one my grandmother sang at church, to lift whatever cloud loomed over our heart."[21] Winans includes two medleys on her *Alone in His Presence* recording—one focusing on praise and the other on the blood of Jesus. Medleys are a standard practice in Black gospel church choirs and with Black gospel singers. Both medleys are a combination of songs popular with Pentecostal-Holiness congregations and contemporary gospel songs and praise songs. Winans co-writes three of the praise and worship songs on the album: "Alone in His Presence," "Because of You," and "He's Always There."

Worship and praise of God is the main focus of *Throne Room* (2003) as well. These foci are the foundation of the album. Each song has a biblical scripture reference noted with it and there is no focus on the individual except when the individual wants to be like God. Like *Alone*, this album has no themes of heaven as an afterlife reward or songs that discuss struggle or suffering as a part of daily life. Worshiping God first and only is the main theme. Winans includes one traditional hymn on her *Throne Room* album, "How Great Thou Art." "How Great Thou Art" as sung by singer George Beverly Shea was Shea's signature song heard during the Billy Graham Crusades from the 1940s to the early 2000s. The hymn is a standard in Protestant churches and exemplifies what it means to worship God with one's mouth. Winans co-writes seven of the praise and worship songs on the album: "Throne Room," "You're So Holy," "Oh Thou Most High," "No One Else," "Hallelujah Praise," "Just Like You, Jesus," and "A Heart Like Yours."

In addition to theology, Winans's songs are standardized in terms of musical structure, vocal techniques, and instrumentation. Rhythm, percussiveness, and call-response are key features of black urban/contemporary gospel music in particular as well as in black popular music and black folk music in general. CeCe Winans's sound and style were first influenced by her family and church upbringing. BeBe and CeCe Winans's music was in the urban/contemporary style, very much similar to the sound of their brothers Ronald, Marvin, Carvin, and Michael of The Winans. Vocally, Winans was influenced by Tremaine Hawkins[22] and Gladys Knight.[23] Because of these two women, she "learned that singing with passion was just as important, if not more important, as vocal ability."[24] Winans's recorded sound first began with the "BeBe and CeCe sound."[25]

Many of the songs on our debut album were written and produced by BeBe and producer (and friend) Keith Thomas. The two of them created the BeBe & CeCe sound. BeBe's lyrics and background vocals arrangements combined with Keith's hit making genius for pop music combined to successfully arrive at a sound that was contemporary, hip, smooth, and striking. Compared with the three days BeBe and I had spent in the studio years earlier recording the *PTL* album, months went into making this album. They wouldn't release it until they were sure the sound coming out of the speakers was the same as what they were hearing in their heads.[26]

Standardization is a way of organizing a cultural art and ritual form. Standardization sets the stage for another cultural process—celebritization. A celebrity is known for their "well-known-ness." A star is a celebrity who is proficient or skillful at doing some particular thing. The black gospel singer's ability to conform to the standards of black gospel music and the black gospel singers who came before them is important in demonstrating this proficiency or skill.

Celebritization

Since singing with *The PTL Club*, recording with an American record label (Sparrow Records), and participating in many of the practices associated with the American popular music industry, BeBe and CeCe Winans were thrust into the world of celebrity culture. Since these aspects of their lives were occurring outside of the Black Church, it is considered to be the "Culture" side of Niebuhr's Christ–Culture dichotomy. From a Christian ethos, celebritization is a secularized activity that replaces the fame, name, iconic status, stardom, and celebrity of God through, Jesus Christ. Secularization is problematic because it is "of the World" (or its source is Culture) encroaching upon that which is sacred (or Christ). Celebritization is a social process imposed upon black gospel singers in particular and Christian and gospel singers in general and the Winanses were not left untouched by it. Simply by living in the United States of America during the late twentieth century guaranteed their immersion into celebrity culture. It is with this meaning that I use celebritization here: the societal and cultural changes implicit by the concept of celebrity.[27] In other words, the fact that black gospel singers are considered to be stars and celebrities has been a significant cultural change within the Black Church and African American culture that has been received with highly mixed reactions.

In her 1999 autobiography, *On a Positive Note*, CeCe Winans discusses celebrity and stardom and its problematic nature. Winans clearly has a personal understanding of stardom and fame: "I know firsthand how easy it is to become so drunk by this carousel called stardom, so dazed by your own ambitions, hungry for the next conquest, that you lose sight of what's really important …".[28] When discussing her and BeBe's first tour of the PTL studios back in 1981, Winans remembers that people "crowded into the state-of-the-art television studio just to get a chance to glimpse the famous Jim and Tammy Faye Bakker and the famous celebrity Christian guests who came daily on the show."[29] She also notes that black "celebrity singers and ministers were always being invited onto the broadcast."[30] In another section of her autobiography, Winans specifically discusses the problem with stardom. Winans's discussion is connected to her being at a church in Atlanta in 1996 along with Jim Bakker, the person who gave Winans and her brother BeBe their first professional jobs as gospel singers in 1981. By 1996, Jim Bakker had long resigned as President of the PTL Television Network, had been released from jail, and had divorced his wife Tammy Faye. Winans describes Bakker's status at that time: he "had gone from being blessed to being broken, to seeing all the ministries and fortunes he'd amassed lost and given away, to then being blessed by becoming a blessing to God's people by sharing his broken experiences as a lesson for all."[31] Being there with Bakker reminded Winans of "why I have always insisted upon catching a red-eye flight back home after all the awards ceremonies are all over."[32] Relationships are important to Winans. She views her intimate, personal relationships as the ones that help to protect her from falling head-over-heels into celebrity culture: "I've always been afraid that if I ever … get caught up in the glitter and glamour of being … a star, then I might lose my way and my purpose … I pray to God that before that ever happens, I can get on a red-eye and come home to my family."[33]

Winans met and became good friends with black pop music star Whitney Houston in 1988. Winans is much more direct in her autobiography when describing the problems with celebrity, stardom, and fame as it relates to Houston, saying: "Until I met Whitney I didn't know how much I did not want to be famous. She has to worry about people with cameras in her front yard and backyard. I don't know how she deals with it."[34] Further on, Winans describes how she and Houston met and a few of the "celebrity" inconveniences that Houston had to deal with. She resolves that "stardom can isolate you and insulate you from good friendships. I look around at some of the bad choices, ugly attitudes, and competitive streaks of others in the field and I see how the desperate wish to be a star can also insulate you from good, sound, sisterly advice."[35]

Driessens considers mediatization as a prerequisite and catalyst for celebritization.³⁶ Mediatization, or media as a social institution, contributed to the Winanses' rise even in the late 1980s and 1990s. That is, the *where*, the *when*, and *what* type of media the Winanses were connected to, contributed to the Winanses' prominent place in American popular culture. After BeBe and CeCe's first album on Sparrow Records was released in 1988, Winans began the journey of being "in the news": appearing on magazine covers, co-hosting television awards programs, performing on television programs and awards programs, being talked about or interviewed in news articles, and participating in ministry, or service, to others. The work of mediatization in Winans's career is particularly shown through television, records, sales charts, and awards.

As mentioned above, television was the critical component to the rise of BeBe and CeCe Winans to celebrity status. When the Winanses joined *The PTL Club* in 1981 the latter was already a very popular religious program. So, when BeBe and CeCe Winans joined the PTL Singers, they were stepping onto a national arena with exposure that exceeded records, radio play, live concerts, and newspaper and magazine articles. This national televised exposure is critical to understanding the building of their celebrity status in the late 1980s and beyond. *The PTL Club* (only rivaled by the programming on Christian Broadcasting Network, CBN, and Trinity Broadcasting Network, TBN, at that time) was a part of the PTL Television Network which began in 1974 along with Jim Bakker being hired as its president.³⁷ Within five years, the network, based in Charlotte, North Carolina, was carried by satellite twenty-four hours a day to cable systems across America. *The PTL Club* was a very popular daily television program carried on 200 affiliate stations, on 3,000 cable systems throughout the United States, and aired in a number of overseas countries.³⁸ As popular as *The PTL Club* was, neither BeBe and CeCe nor their family had ever heard of Jim or Tammy Faye Bakker in 1981.³⁹ Winans went on to state that "if I had known of *PTL*'s immense fame and popularity as a Christian broadcasting satellite I probably would not have found the nerve to go out and audition for it."⁴⁰

CeCe Winans's mediatization has been facilitated by her appearance on television programs related to gospel music. Winans has appeared on numerous awards programs either as a host or performer. For example, Winans co-hosted the Gospel Music Association's 26th Annual Dove Awards on April 27, 1995, with contemporary Christian music star Steven Curtis Chapman. For the week ending May 13, 1995, on the *Billboard* Top Gospel Albums chart, BeBe and CeCe Winans's album *Relationships* was Number 8 on the chart. It had been on the chart for 23 weeks. This was two weeks after Winans co-hosted the Dove Awards.

CeCe Winans also co-hosted the 29th Annual Dove Awards on April 25, 1997, with Gary Chapman, another contemporary Christian music star. More recently, on August 10, 2016, Winans participated in a press conference announcing the nominees for the 2016 Gospel Music Association's Dove Awards.

Although television can help a black gospel singer or Christian singer move into celebrity status, what television appearances do ultimately is to help sell the records of the featured singers. Therefore, records are a marketing tool as well as a central component of how mediatization acts as a social institution for Christian singers and gospel singers. Winans describes the first album she and BeBe recorded in this way, as well as sharing some background information about the recording process for the album.

> We made an independent album with *PTL* called *Lord Lift Us Up*, which came out about the time I was returning to Detroit [in 1984]. We completed the album in three days … The album capitalized on our popularity on the *PTL Show* and was a [success] …, there was still plenty of interest in booking us, despite my leaving *PTL*. There were always invitations coming in for us to sing at some church or concert hall.[41]

Winans's statement that their album "capitalized" on their "popularity on the *PTL Show*" is the hint that mediatization was at play in 1984. This is a strategy commonly used in the American popular (secular) music industry.

The Winanses' climb to celebrity and stardom began with *The PTL Club* and continued with many recordings that placed on *Billboard* music charts from 1984 and beyond. Chart ratings are a central part of the American popular music industry but they are very important in the world of the black gospel singer as well. Winans's mediatization continues through rating how her recording "charts" as compared to the recordings of other black gospel singers or Christian singers. By the time the Winanses released their first album in 1984, black gospel music (including Christian) album performance had been tracked by *Billboard* although not always published consistently in the printed weekly periodical.[42] The popularity of BeBe and CeCe Winans's albums and songs is evident in the chart standings from listeners, record stores, and urban (read: black) radio stations. Both *Heaven* and *Different Lifestyles* charted on the *Billboard* magazine Top Gospel Albums chart at Number 1 in 1988 and 1991, respectively. Winans's solo effort, platinum-certified *Alone in His Presence* reached Number 2 on the *Billboard* Top Gospel Albums chart during the week of October 28, 1995. Winans's chart performance has been impressive. Her gold-certified *Throne Room*, released September 9, 2003, reached Number 1 on the *Billboard* Top

Gospel Albums chart, Number 1 on the *Billboard* Top Christian Albums chart, Number 21 on the *Billboard* Top Hip-Hop/R&B Albums chart, and Number 32 on the *Billboard* 200 chart on September 27, 2003. The longevity of Winans' (as well as most national, professional black gospel singers) artistry and ministry is illustrated in the duration that their albums are on the *Billboard* charts. By February 26, 2005, *Throne Room* remained on the *Billboard* Top Gospel Albums chart at Number 11 for 76 weeks.

Although year-end chart performance based on Nielsen data for sales, number of downloads, and total airplay ratings as a criterion for qualifying to be a finalist for an award, were not in practice during the Winanses' early recordings (for certain, the concept "download" was not in circulation in the 1980s!), today it is commonplace. The popularity of BeBe and CeCe Winans's albums and songs is evident in the awards from the gospel music industry. Both *Heaven* and *Different Lifestyles* won Best Gospel Album at the Soul Train Music Awards in 1990 and 1992, respectively. *Heaven* was voted Pop/Contemporary Album and "Heaven" was voted the Pop/Contemporary Song in 1990 by the GMA Dove Awards. The popularity of BeBe and CeCe Winans arises from the songwriters' and the singers' ability to capture the convictions, contradictions, values, beliefs, performance practices, and theologies of its fiercely loyal community: African American Christians and believers in general. Individually, CeCe Winans has won many awards over the course of her career. One significant award in particular she won was from the Gospel Music Association. Winans was the recipient of the Female Vocalist of the Year at the 1996 Dove Awards.[43] Winning this award established Winans as the first African American woman to receive this particular honor from the GMA.[44]

Apostillization

Although singing an urban/contemporary style of black gospel music which some believers describe as representing the World, or Culture, in Niebuhr's typology, in CeCe Winans's solo albums she has always included songs which represent a process that I call "apostillization." Apostillization is the cultural process where the black gospel singer most represents the Christ of Niebuhr's typology. Apostillization is taken from the role of the Apostle in the New Testament of the Bible. A detailed, representative description of the Apostle is chronicled in the Book of Acts. The twelve men Jesus handpicked to "follow" Him were called his "disciples." After the death and resurrection of Christ, disciples were referred to as "apostles." Apostillization is the impact of the gift and office of Apostle on the black gospel singer. The primary pillars of apostillization, which were leading principles of the Apostles in Acts, are worship, prayer, intercession, warfare, and prophecy. These pillars are anti-Culture at their foundation.

In the songs and performances of CeCe Winans since separating professionally from her brother, BeBe in 1995, there is a strong emphasis on worship. Several of Winans's albums could be considered worship albums because they include songs that focus only on God and not on the believers' life. Winans wrote a book to accompany her *Throne Room* album. It is clear in the book that Winans is talking about worship because of references to two concepts: "throne room" and "presence." A "throne" commonly refers to the seat of a king or queen. It is a chair, a three-dimensional object that symbolizes their power and authority. Winans is describing the throne room of the Most High King, God, and what believers should do when they arrive there. The subtitle of the book is "Ushered into the Presence of God." Presence is an important concept in Judaism and Christianity: the "presence" of God is everything. The Presence of God, assures believers that they are spiritually protected, provided for, accompanied, and enabled to live productive, peaceful, and prosperous lives. The presence of God is fully realized in His throne room. Winans wants listeners and believers to know that *there*, the throne room, is an important place for them to be.

Prayer can happen in the throne room. Prayer is important to Winans. She views prayer as a "rich heritage" that the people "who were before" her gave to her.[45] Winans opens *The Throne Room*, the companion book to the same-titled album, with a prayer:

> Jesus, awesome Lord and Savior
> I want your name to be the first Word in this book
> Just like you are the first Love in my life
> The first Song on my lips
> The first and only Hope in my heart.
> Lord, I ask you to lead everyone who reads these pages
> To see you as you are—
> So beautiful, so powerful, so worthy of our worship.
> I pray all of these things in your precious, holy Name,
> Amen.[46]

This is typical of a prayer that a believer (or Christian) might address to Jesus, the Son of God, or God, the Father of Jesus. Winans magnifies his name (which worship does) by relating it to ordinary circumstances and conditions in her life.

She declares that Jesus is the first word, love, song, and hope in her life. From God's perspective, He and Jesus are "everything" and Winans acknowledges this "everythingness" in the opening prayer above. Worship is an expression orally, physically, and relationally that demonstrates that God is "everything" in a believer's life.

Prayer encompasses two additional pillars of apostillization: intercession and spiritual warfare. In this opening prayer of *Throne Room*, CeCe Winans intercedes for others by asking Jesus to "lead everyone who reads these pages [t]o see you as you are." Intercession is one person or several people praying for another person or group of people. The intercessor stands in between the person being prayed for and God. When a person takes time to pray for others (Christ), they are demonstrating the unselfish nature of their divinity. In so doing, they are pushing back on the selfish nature of humanity which is not to help others—a characteristic exemplified in the world (culture).

In her autobiography, Winans shares her belief in the importance of prayer, intercession, and spiritual warfare especially during the time when her older brother Ronald was hospitalized with a ruptured heart in 1997. "I am convinced that our family could not have survived the trauma of watching Ronald's life hang in the balance had we not had church families across the country praying and interceding to God on our behalf."[47] Winans says, "I could feel the spiritual warfare … We were warring with demonic forces for my brother's life … We were fighting for my brother's life with the only thing that we knew worked, namely prayer and pleading the blood of Jesus over him. It was such a team effort."[48]

A believer who engages in spiritual warfare is both a pray-er and an intercessor. They are warring and fighting for the victory and success of other people. Winans has definite thoughts about spiritual warfare and its role in the believer's life as well as the concept of prophecy. Prophecy, another pillar of apostillization, is a theological concept well-known and referred to in black Holiness-Pentecostal churches. In the most basic sense, prophecy is a form of discourse inspired by God that declares the purposes of God for an individual, family, group, city, or nation, especially declarations foretelling future events.[49] It is within this setting that Winans came to know what prophecy was. Concerning her brothers, The Winans' first contract with Light Records in 1981, Winans notes, "God had upheld my grandfather's prophecy that our family would spread God's Word through song."[50]

For Winans, prophecy is a Word from God. Because of her belief and trust in God, Winans allows this type of God-inspired word to guide her in the decisions she makes regarding her musical ministry. As much as she is thankful for this word, because of traditions surrounding her gender, Winans held herself back for a time: "Singing, recording albums, and traveling around the world spreading God's word through music were things I dared not dream for myself. I was content to retreat into the background, out of the spotlight, where good, modest Pentecostal girls like myself were expected to dream and live out their existence."[51] As important as Winans's belief in and experience with prophecy, it does not materialize as a significant theme in either *Alone in His Presence* or *Throne Room*. Winans does the ultimate diminishing of herself as a star. In these albums, God is *the* star. Together, worship, prayer, intercession, warfare, and prophecy are used by the black gospel singer to demonstrate and express their belief in Christ.

Rhetorical strategies

Standardization, celebritization, and mediatization have shaped the twenty-first-century national professional black gospel singer. Black gospel singers employ specific rhetorical strategies and cultural practices to clearly mark and secure their sacred ground of being on the side of "Christ" while at the same time being aware of the demands of "Culture" on them. The black gospel singer utilizes at least four rhetorical strategies. These rhetorical strategies are the statements the black gospel singer makes when they speak about their music and life in interviews, during performances, in writings, and on social media posts. These strategies reinforce their stand as Ministers for Christ singing the Gospel to the Culture of Man. The four rhetorical strategies are (1) awareness of their purpose; (2) their primary role as a worshiper; (3) humility when receiving recognition related to their singing (award nominations, awards, and sales ratings); and (4) dependence on and deference to God when others describe them as having "success," "fortune," or "fame" or when the black gospel singer (or someone close to them) sees the impending opportunity to have success, fortune, or fame.

When Winans talks of having a purpose for her life and the "special gift"[52] God had given her, she is employing a rhetorical strategy to stake her claim as a Minister for Christ as opposed to being a Celebrity for Culture. Reflecting on the myriad emotions she experienced before and during her first solo at age seven, Winans says:

> Looking back on it, I know now that my own personal, individual ministry as a singer was born that day, but I didn't know it back then … I didn't understand anything about purpose. Purpose is the reason for you to be here, the something

you have to do that will matter. Purpose is what gives your life meaning and significance. All I knew at seven years old about my purpose was that God was with me, and with God, all things were possible ... that day ... I learned that I was born to sing.[53]

Reflecting on the meaning of her time as a *PTL Club* singer, Winans says:

"I realized that being paid for singing and having the opportunity to sing before a national audience were not validation that I was living my purpose. My real validation was in enjoying my work and finding joy and contentment in it. I knew that when these two were gone, it would be time to go—despite a salary and television audience."[54]

Winans demonstrated the rhetorical strategy of deference to God when recounting the feelings she experienced while flying to North Carolina to audition for *The PTL Club*:

I didn't want to be off to North Carolina to chase after some glory for myself. I wanted to go home. I'd seen all the hard work my older brothers had put into their work ... I didn't want any part of that. All I wanted to do was sing for Jesus. If the Lord was in fact beckoning me to come out to North Carolina to sing for Him, I was prepared to give up everything I had planned for myself to do what God wanted.[55]

Winans expressed deference to God in terms of doing what He had planned for her life when dealing with her "growing weariness" of the "resentment" she sensed from other *PTL Club* singers during the time when she and BeBe were repeatedly asked to sing "Up Where We Belong": "I tried not to notice the resentment I was sometimes feeling from some of the members. I had learned long ago from singing in church that you can't apologize for God's plan. You can't explain why and how God uses you to communicate to an audience. It's the Lord's work."[56]

Cultural practices

In addition to rhetorical strategies, the black gospel singer employs several cultural practices to downplay the negative and ungodly effects of stardom and to magnify the importance of Christ in their lives. These cultural practices are ritualistic activities that the black gospel singer performs and participates in in their daily lives. These practices center on relationships and values that are described by the black gospel singer and by others about the black gospel singer. The black gospel singer's cultural practices may include (1) personal worship;

(2) personal prayer; (3) group prayer; (4) intimate, personal relationships; (5) corporate relationships; (6) separation of sacred and secular lyrics; and (7) multiple album concepts. The black gospel singer's intimate, personal relationships include God, spouse, children, extended family, friends, and spiritual coaches, mentors, and parents. Their corporate relationships include church membership and, in many cases today, church leadership. Church leadership, for example, relates to Winans because she and her husband Alvin Love started a church in 2012.

Personal worship is important to Winans as an identity and practice. In the opening of her book *Throne Room*, she declares, "I've been a worshiper most of my life."[57] Winans self-identifies with worship. She has chosen to lead a lifestyle of intimate worship to God and encourages believers to do the same. Further, Winans has kept a strict separation of the sacred and the secular in her music. Her Pentecostal-Holiness upbringing is the chief cause of this.

> Given my deep roots in the Holiness church, it should come as no surprise that only one kind of music was permitted in David and Delores's home: gospel music. Raised in the Pentecostal tradition, my parents were determined that they would raise their children in the way of holiness and sanctification. This meant no parties, no clubs, no smoking, no drinking, no makeup, no jewelry, no finger popping, and above all no secular music … Both parents threatened to brand us if they ever caught us playing "worldly music" in the house or even in the car. "Holiness or hell" was the way they put it …[58]

Beyond the threats often heard as she was growing up, Winans's parents were supportive of her and BeBe's recordings although members of their church were critical of the sound and style because it was not "Christian enough."[59] However, the sound and style of the music was not her parents' major concern. CeCe's father said "music to me is based on lyrics. You can have a fast tempo and can be saying 'Yes, Lord, Yes.' You can have a fast tempo and be saying 'baby, baby, baby.' So, it's the lyrics that you sing."[60] In other words, "it's the lyrics" that matter to Winans' parents and she learned well, committing to only song lyrics that relate to God. When BeBe and CeCe recorded and released *Different Lifestyles*, their producer Keith Thomas said "they were afraid the church was going to kick them out."[61] The Winanses were concerned about being "kicked out" of their church because the sound, style, and recording practices of their recording were *so* close to the secular style, sound, and recording practices of the time. Thomas says about Winans and secular lyrics: "I have called CeCe here a few times to do demos for me. And she's turned me down twice now because maybe one song would have the word 'baby' in it or it was kind of geared towards the secular marketplace. It tells you how strong her conviction is about the Christian marketplace and what she says and what she's all about."[62] Thomas's remark about a song being geared towards the "secular marketplace" is telling of the power of commodification and the American popular music industry. What components must a song have to be geared towards the secular marketplace? In Winans's mind (and heart, no doubt), the secular marketplace wants songs that include the word "baby" (culture). She would not agree to sing those kinds of lyrics because "baby" would be focused on a person rather than on God (Christ).

Conclusion

CeCe Winans illustrates the ambivalence black gospel singers experience regarding stardom and celebrity in America. In the culture of black gospel music, stardom and celebrity are regarded with disdain and in a negative light. Overall, however, her life and music show how black gospel singers are navigating the waters of celebrity culture and its impact on the world of black gospel music. While the black gospel singer as star may not be an icon shaping American political discourse (as black film stars did during the Civil Rights Movement[63]), the black gospel singer is an icon representing Christian discourses calling for, encouraging, and pleading for man (Culture) to reconcile to God (Christ) and to live a purpose-filled, peaceful, and prosperous life on earth through. Standardization and celebritization are products of Culture that typically do not connect to Christ. On the other hand, apostillization is a product of a deep and intense, personal relationship with Christ. Apostillization is the demonstration of Christ in the black gospel singer's life. In sum, the black gospel singer's personal relationship with Christ is the foundation and the impetus of the rhetorical strategies and cultural practices black gospel singers use to proclaim Christ and downplay Culture. In so doing, ambivalence may still exist but it is ameliorated through the black gospel singer's daily words and actions.

3

Judas Priest and the Fury of Metal Redemption

Brian Froese

In 1988 and 2005, Judas Priest produced two biographical accounts of the band's early days in the songs "Monsters of Rock" and "Deal with the Devil."[1] Both iterations of their origin story emphasize their emergence from the "Black Country" region in central England, combined with a slow start and eventual global significance.[2] There are a couple of significant differences. "Monsters of Rock" places an emphasis on birth imagery, "The seed became the embryo," and the industrial rugged nature of their home, through images of smoke and dirt.[3] Whereas in 2005, "Deal with the Devil" retains the industrial founding and the global spread of Judas Priest metal, but it also embedded—instead of organic images—a more infernal root: A deal with the devil. Insinuating their rise and energy to a devilish arrangement, Judas Priest makes clear that despite origins of a foul nature, their power is also intimately tied to their uniform of leather, whips, and chains.[4] It is a rags to riches tale told with the coupling of organic birth and growth to hellish energy.

Outside the metal community Judas Priest was known largely for two highly publicized events that caught them in the maw of the highly charged American political-cultural environment in 1985. In 1985 the Parents Music Resource Center (PMRC) formed as a committee to help parents acquire influence, even control, over the access children and teenagers had to music deemed overly violent, sexual, or satanic. Known as the "Washington Wives," as several members had high-profile husbands in Washington, including Tipper Gore, then wife to Democrat senator Al Gore, and Susan Baker, wife to then Republican Treasury Secretary James Baker, they succeeded in having a Senate hearing over the issue—leading to the creation of warning labels for offensive lyrics. Releasing a list of the "Filthy Fifteen," the PMRC highlights fifteen especially offensive songs. On the list were eight heavy metal/hard rock bands. Though mostly cited for explicit sexual or violent lyrics, two were thrash metal bands singled out for satanic/occultist lyrics. Judas Priest made the list for the explicit sex in the song, "Eat Me Alive."[5]

Though Judas Priest was cited for sex, they would find themselves ensnared in accusations of Satanism resulting from the 1985 suicide and failed suicide of Ray Belknap and James Vance, respectively. The ensuing court trial in Reno, Nevada in 1991 centered on the issue of subliminal backward messages inserted in their albums to "mesmerize" listeners. It was a trial Judas Priest won.[6] Lead singer Rob Halford was bewildered by the trial, saying, "the prosecution … tried to paint this picture of drug crazed Satan worshipers and nothing could be further from the truth. It's absolutely ridiculous and bizarre. People just don't appreciate that, you know, we're humans with feelings like everybody else, and we don't all sing about love."[7] What he may not have been aware at the time was the long history Satan and satanic panic had in American culture. Following a brief contextual look at the role Satan plays in American culture and Judas Priest's place therein, I explore their quest for redemption as articulated in songs pointing to a selective, creative, and transgressive use of Christian concepts, concerning especially mortality, messianic creatures, the Devil and abyss, individualism and sex.

Devil, devil everywhere

Though it seemed as if something pernicious had descended into the bedrooms and Walkmans of 1980s youth, the cultural apparatus, or architecture, around Satan's presence in American metal into the early to mid-1980s had been long in place. Throughout the history of the American republic, Christianity has always been in company with the non-Christian, quasi-Christian, and anti-Christian— sometimes in harmony and sometimes in hostility. Thus, despite congressional hearings, wrongful death litigation and satanic panics, the convergence of Christianity, Satan, occultist religion, and popular entertainment already occurred centuries ago.[8]

The history of Satan in popular music goes back far, though we do well to begin in America's Deep South. The story of Robert Johnson in the 1930s is legendary, drawing together elements of regional, religious, and racial significance. It is the tale of a young restless African American itinerant musician. Although the details vary according to sources, it remains the legend of a Faustian bargain made in Mississippi at the crossroads. There young Johnson, the story goes, handed his guitar to the devil who tuned it, played some songs, and returned it in exchange for his soul. That he died at the young age of twenty-seven leaving behind a corpus of highly influential songs at times exploring satanic themes which later fed a popular imagination gripped by the thrill and terror of the Dark Lord coming to claim his payment. In the few years of his young life, Johnson became the father of the blues. Without the blues and gospel there would be no rock music and without the importation of African American blues music to Britain in the 1960s, fused some say with Richard Wagner, or Gustav Holst's *The Planets—Mars, The Bringer of War* (1914–16), there would be no heavy blues and thus no heavy metal.[9]

Popular culture for much of the twentieth century enjoyed the vital presence of Satan. In the 1930s, one could hear a bluesman moan about hellhounds and devils, sermons on hell and devils, or, in the early 1940s, enjoy the comics of sultry femme fatale *Madam Satan* luring men to erotic destruction. Throughout the twentieth century, one encountered the Evil One by simply being in the culture. The Dark Lord was ubiquitous. An entire cultural apparatus existed to sustain the devil in every medium over the decades. Pulp magic books, for example, were very popular, including a "boom" in the 1920s and 1930s significant enough to be called a "menace" by educators. Throughout the 1960s and 1970s, there too was great interest in things magical and occultist as tarot cards and ouija boards became popular entertainment purchases.[10]

In the 1970s and early 1980s, a witchcraft panic swept Britain, and evangelists brought the concern across the ocean influencing, for example, American revivalist Morris Cerullo to criss-cross the country in his "Witchmobile," warning the youth of "dabbling in Satanism, blood-drinking, and perverse sex."[11] With the devil woven through virtually all segments of popular culture, that history's ultimate villain emerged as bandleader for heavy metal is hardly a surprise. Satanic panics continued through the 1980s, often relating to heavy metal, and Judas Priest was caught in the slipstream.[12]

Yet, within the lengthy span of their career, the band explored many themes from astral plane metaphysics to decadence. Within their corpus from 1974 to 2014, they articulated a vision of muscular spirituality that takes seriously questions of violence, alienation, and the atrophying of modernity though a lens that transvalues Christian imagery, including that of the devil, and icons mixed with rough sexual desire. Judas Priest were not breaking icons; they were repurposing them. The name itself, drawn from the Bob Dylan song, "The Ballad of Frankie Lee and Judas Priest," also represents a "mild exclamation" of good and evil duality where the betrayer and proclaimer of Christ is found in one.[13]

Call for the Priest

In the 1970s, Judas Priest was part of the heavy metal process breaking away from hard rock, spending their time playing in "workingmen's clubs."[14] Financially the band was strapped and they slept in their van while recording in Notting Hill, and cleaned their teeth with snow in Holland and Germany.[15] They hailed from Birmingham, where employment for young men was found mostly in the metal foundry, and Judas Priest marks their metal identity through a working-class origins tale. Guitarist Glenn Tipton described it, "'Where we lived, you could always hear the foundry, the big steam hammers. Day after day, when that's pounding, you've got some sort of heavy metal rhythm in you from the word go.'"[16] Singer Rob Halford reflected that as a boy walking the one to two miles to school, everyday passing by "melting, iron-metal works factory," the presence of its smoke, smell and taste was a constant.[17] Indeed, Birmingham was the "Black Country" and "by its very nature, breeds heavy metal … [a place] of steel, car parts, burning rubber, metal stamping tool and die, and early death from blackened lungs."[18]

On April 16, 1974, Judas Priest signed their first recording contract with Gull Records. With Tipton signing on soon after, the metal quintet Judas Priest, with record contract in pocket, was formed, and consisted of Halford, Tipton, K. K. Downing on guitar, Ian Hill on bass, and John Hinch on drums.[19] Tom Allom, their producer during the 1980s, described metal as "'always bigger than [life]; by definition, it's bigger than big. That's why you have to strive to make it sound impossible large … To me, heavy metal is about the unreal and the unobtainable.'"[20] And so it was with Judas Priest.

Mortality

On Judas Priest's early albums, reflective lyrics on mortality came strongest, beginning with their 1974 self-disclaimed debut, *Rocka Rolla*. Their initial foray into existential rumination occurs on the three-song progression, popularly known as the "Winter Suite." These songs, "Winter," "Deep Freeze," and "Winter Retreat," follow the progression of the cold season and the overwhelming sense of mortal dread in the protagonist. As winter "gets stronger," the narrator, filling with angst, speculates whether he is dying and as the snow falls he has a growing and deepening "awful feeling."[21]

While "Deep Freeze" re-iterates the dread of snow, "Winter Retreat" brings the listener to the dawn of spring, as the cold winds and icy formations on his face and eyes recede and "Warmth eases back to my soul."[22] Winter's other reference in their corpus occurs three years later on "Last Rose of Summer." A song redolent of a pining love, "Last Rose of Summer" takes us softly from the waning days of August to the growing darkness of fall and winter. Having given his lover a rose signifying the end of summer, it will become in the cold of winter a reminder that they will reunite and the warmth of summer will soon come again. The season of death is impermanent, and as the ardor of spring will return—so will the narrator.[23]

Winter is a natural season in which to reflect on one's life. On "Run of the Mill," the narrator asks someone if their life was fulfilling, if their dreams and ambitions were met and then caustically needles, "Should I give sorrow, or turn 'round and sneer." Thus scolded, the listener did not have great prospects in life nor sought improvement, resting on the ideal of a common humanity. This humanistic observation of the mediocre life concludes with a dismissive account of hobbling about with a cane. Finally, it is revealed that the person rudely spoken to was the narrator himself repeating, "I can't go on." Similarly, on "Let us Prey," we hear the plaintive cry: "Call for the priest, I'm dying."[24]

The rhetorical strategy employed in "Run of the Mill" reoccurs in "Epitaph." Halford commented on "Epitaph," in 1976, "'As there are no places for children in our modern cities, there's also no place for the old.'"[25] On *Sad Wings of Destiny*, "Epitaph" is a forlorn piano piece where we hear the story of an old man in his last days. A life of pain is behind him as mortality awaits, and lastly, "A lonely grave," visited only by wind and leaves. Again, the ending reveals an epitaph of the one who passed as the listener.[26] These ironic shifts take on a more self-reflective tone forty years after *Rocka Rolla*, with, "Beginning of the End." The poignant theme of loneliness at one's end, "Walking alone into the dying mist ..." is paired with Christian allusions to resurrection and an enduring love. Understanding that death has arrived, the narrator prays, "lay me to rest" that they will "rise by the grace of God."[27]

In the dark ballad, "Beyond the Realms of Death," mortality and agency coincide in the lamentation of a depressed individual entering into a catatonic state. While others washed and dressed him, his mind was his haven until, "The wind kissed him," and he died. Upon his death the narrator exclaims that not only did he reject the world—made of sin—but it was his decision to end his life in a potent action against it. Wondering how many more thousands have lives like this, the song argues for agency and hope in a dismal existence.[28] As Ian Christe observes, "the mission of heavy metal: to confront the big picture—to create a connection between life and the cosmos."[29]

The anti-war song, "Dying to Meet You," is the first Judas Priest song to articulate a clear religious theme image while unpacking the hypocrisy of wartime killing. The soldier opens the song observing the surroundings and in the bucolic context of a sunrise and bird's song, notes how easy it is to rape and kill the enemy. He asks the warrior if, after repressing thoughts, killing is fun. Sensing the hypocrisy he continues, "But you wouldn't lay a finger on your mother" and the killer "won't go to hell," instead be awarded a medal. The raconteur surmises such accolades are a balm for the "pain and sin" they feel inside.[30] This moral evaluation of one's work vis-à-vis another more conventional context is also made regarding contract killing. In "Killing Machine," the narrator is a contract killer reflecting on his work, "What manner of man am I?" but sees others hurting others too, especially friends betraying friends as everyone is simply taking care of their own needs.[31] Along with these early ruminations on mortality and deadly vocations, Judas Priest presents their audience with a visual and lyrical purpose to much of their career: The Fallen Angel and a passel of sky-born saviors.

Fallen Angel

The cover art of four albums is significant to the religious themes and identity of Judas Priest. The painting, "Fallen Angel," by Patrick Woodroffe, was commissioned for *Sad Wings of Destiny*. It depicts a sorrowful angel kneeling on the ground in a hellish landscape, head lowered, around its neck a medallion the band called "the devil's pitchfork"; later, "the devil's cross." We see the devil's cross next, on the back cover of 1984's *Defenders of the Faith*, where the epigraph describes the creature, the Metallian, as the enforcer of the metal faith. We read of the Metallian, "Rising from darkness where hell hath no mercy and the screams of vengeance echo on forever, only those who keep the faith shall escape the wrath of the Metallian … Master of all Metal."[32]

The angel is next prominently featured in 1990, on the *Painkiller* album cover. Here, the Fallen Angel of 1974, now in robotic form, rides a metallic steed over the smouldering ruins of a city as the devil's cross emerges in its center.[33] On the album's back is printed: "As mankind hurled itself forever downwards into the bottomless pit of eternal chaos, the remnants of civilization screamed out for salvation—redemption roared across the burning sky ... The Painkiller!"[34] The Fallen Angel now rides as *Painkiller*, from hell to urban dystopia. The story of Fallen Angel/Painkiller continued in 2005 on *Angel of Retribution*. Both Tipton and Halford say the cover image of *Angel of Retribution* is the angel from *Sad Wings of Destiny*. No longer in a place of despair and gloom, it now rises optimistic for the retribution it will soon enact. Significantly the image presents the angel from hell with a Christian halo appropriated from medieval iconic art. In fact, the resurrection of the Fallen Angel is foreshadowed on "Solar Angels" through such rich imagery as "Golden halos radiating" with wings outstretched.[35]

Following the angel's rise in 2005, it graces the cover of *Redeemer of Souls*, bearing the devil's cross medallion and a fiery countenance. It is now a fully developed creature of hell and savior: "Death, doom and destruction rain down upon the forsaken. One being stands alone to save humanity / A solder born from the past on sad wings of destiny / Powerful, unflinching and bearing the eternal force / That will proclaim and assert metal's deliverance / The Redeemer of Souls!"[36] From 1974 to 2014, Fallen Angel evolved from a hell-bound lament to savior of humanity through the cult of heavy metal.

Such a claim by Tipton and Halford is warranted considering the song "Angel." As Fallen Angel/Painkiller transforms into Retribution, we have the only metal "gospel" song in Judas Priest's corpus. The Angel comes to us fallen in hell, the metallic savior of a desiccated hellscape finally realized and fulfilled in steel resurrection. Transvaluing such points of orthodox Christian theology as deliverance and salvation, Judas Priest after forty years introduces us to Angel. The song works as a petition to the title character as we hear, "Angel—put sad wings around me now/Protect me from this world of sin." A clear reference to *Sad Wings of Destiny*, this thread from 1974 is pulled further with the reference to finding "A better place and peace of mind."[37]

Recalling the cosmic journey of "Dreamer," on *Sad Wings of Destiny*, Angel takes our petitioner on a space journey to "chase the sun" while "reaching for the stars." Furthermore, to underscore the repurposing of Christian imagery, Angel is a savior—though unlike the metallic and brutal saviors from throughout their career, Angel comes with "velvet wings" shining a light on the saddened, and as the sadness becomes the very wings themselves, the narrator declares, "When all my sins are washed away/Hold me inside your wings and stay." The embrace is to last until the final resurrection.[38] The cleansing remission of sin, resurrection, and an Angel reminiscent of Christ himself who declared his love for those who rejected him saying, "How often I wanted to gather your children together, just as a hen gathers her brood under her wings."³⁹

Metallic eschatology: Saviors from the sky

Related to the Fallen Angel motif is one of the most prominent themes in Judas Priest's oeuvre: The metallic savior from above. Related closely to the Fallen/Risen Angel motif, the sky descending savior is woven throughout their four decades of work. In his analysis of ancient apocalyptic religious faith, Norman Cohen argues for the centrality of the "combat myth," where a god defends the ordered world against chaos.⁴⁰ This narrative is found throughout the ancient world, and in Christianity, its fullest expression is found in Revelation 12–13. Cohen observes combat myth, "in all its forms is the same: that cosmos has always been threatened by chaos and always will be, yet has always survived and always will."⁴¹ Judas Priest through much of their career used combat myth and such classic mythical tropes as Chaos and Cosmos.

Conrad Ostwalt has described traditional popular cultural apocalyptic traits as on one level apocalyptic symbols and narrative devices that provide "meaning to chaotic existence."⁴² However, as Elana Gomel argues, apocalypticism is also an attempt to escape time and history—to look for the future beyond our constraints. And we see this at work in Halford's approach to lyric writing. In 1976, he described his lyrics as "'firmly bound to the present,'" though mixing with elements of fantasy, and mentioned "Tyrant," on *Sad Wings of Destiny*, as an example. In "Tyrant" he shifts the lyrical voice from the oppressed to the oppressor, thus presenting both points of view without reconciliation or deliverance for the tyrannized. It ends in dread. Three decades later when asked a similar question, he responded, "'I am talking about real issues in fantasy time … ambiguous time, smoke-screen time.'"⁴³

As Gomel argues, the escape sought in much apocalyptic writing is from history itself and it needs to be read as well in secular terms where society is under siege and emerges reconstituted, more pure, primitive, and natural.⁴⁴ In the apocalyptic tale of "Rapid Fire," Judas Priest describes a direful world crushed under the weight of great violence. The violence here is described as "pounding," "final grand slam," and "fast devastating." Then the purifying purpose of the ferocious rampage is announced where deliverer wields an axe to slash against greed.⁴⁵ It is not only purifying, it is reflecting the purifying images that Christ used describing the final judgment in the parable of the wheat and tares: "Sifting the good from the bad."⁴⁶

The first instance of a savior-from-the-sky is in the song, "Dreamer Deceiver." In a pastiche of images from space travel to drugs to gnostic progression, "Dreamer Deceiver" offers deliverance. Within the context of daily life, the narrator by a window in a dreamy summer day "Saw a figure floating" who asked the confused onlookers if they were happy and then took them by the hand up into the air. From their ascension they traveled through "purple hazy clouds" as Dreamer Deceiver controlled their "sense of time" and told them that "in the cosmos is a single sonic sound" and to focus exclusively on its note, then "We would see our minds were free." The peace and freedom which comes to the mind when separated from the body—focused on the single controlling note—is short-lived. From this state of cosmic blissful harmony, Dreamer Deceiver becomes simply Deceiver. Chaos follows order. Shifting quickly from "floating way up high" our cosmic travelers find themselves in a galactic storm where "All is lost, doomed and tossed."[47] Powerful external forces supplant the euphoria of a false deliverance as they are buffeted by meteors and dying comets confused if they can remain eternally.[48]

As the Dreamer Deceiver took those who came under its spell for a cosmic journey, another character, "Starbreaker," performs a similar act. Unlike Dreamer Deceiver, Starbreaker comes to town as a heartbreaker. His "Star voyage to a new world" has the appearance of a seduction, though it retains the cosmic journey motif as it takes one "up so high" to a "Paradise … /For the chosen few." Those gathered by Starbreaker ask it to understand them and to lead them onwards. It is a savior of only a few chosen returning only once in a lifetime.[49]

Similar to Dreamer Deceiver and Starbreaker is the "Evening Star." The protagonist travels to a "distant shore" to which he was called by an "inner voice." Again, we have the quiet call from an outside force where the people involved follow without knowing why. While "Dreamer Deceiver" pointed out celestial harmony in a single sonic note, the rising of the Evening Star removed the "haze" from his mind and now with clarity and inspiration, the stumbling of his youth has given way. After his time at the distant shore he returns home, following his celestial guide, the Evening Star.[50]

Moreover, Judas Priest created several metal messiahs over their lengthy career that simply came to earth without any galactic description. These characters include Sinner, Exciter, Hellion, and Metallian to name a few. To illustrate, the album epitaph on *Screaming for Vengeance* exclaims: "From an unknown land and through distant skies came a winged warrior. Nothing remained sacred, no one was safe from the Hellion as it uttered its battle cry … Screaming for Vengeance."[51] Sometimes the saviors from the sky were mythical and alien. On

"Riding on the Wind," Mars, the god of war is glowing as the "demons yell" while blasting through space blinding everyone—powerful as a "thunderbolt from hell."[52] In 1990, Halford growls, in the song "All Guns Blazing," that the coming salvation will be made through immense "bone crushing" violence. He sacralizes the violence by linking it to heaven-sent "sad wings," recalling Fallen Angel.[53]

In 1976, we were introduced to Exciter, a cosmic creature traversing the universe whereupon his arrival to earth "The age of fire's at hand." Clear in its purpose, Exciter came with a soteriological task possessing the immensely dangerous power of deadly fire by his touch. Humanity is nonetheless drawn towards him despite pronounced sufferings wrought by his fiery power so that "the very soul of your being will cringe." Though he is unseen, he comes in the imagery of fire of the Spirit in Acts chapter two: "suddenly there came from heaven a noise like a violent rushing wind, and it filled the whole house where they were sitting. And there appeared to them tongues as of fire distributing themselves, and they rested on each one of them." Or, in the song: "you will taste the fire upon your tongue."[54] His purpose is to "snap" humanity out of complacency and self-indulgence creating only lost vision and lies. No one encountering the salvific fire of Exciter goes unmarked, "All shall bear the branding/Of his thermal lance."[55]

In the band's later years, characters like Painkiller (1990), Judas (2005), and Dragonaut (2014) also descend from the heavens. Painkiller descends with a "terrifying scream" as a transgressive incarnational figure that is "half man and half machine," while Sinner came on a demonic steed, and Painkiller rides the "Metal Monster/Breathing smoke and fire" and with "Planets devastated," humanity falls to its knees echoing Exciter from an earlier era. Painkiller comes in tremendous fury, noise, and violence with evil its target destroyed by "boiling clouds of thunder/Blasting bolts of steel" as evil is mangled under "deadly wheels." More powerful than any earthly force, including an atomic blast, Painkiller completes the metallic overhaul of Christ in both power and soteriology. He resurrects from the grave, "Flying high on rapture," and "Returns from Armageddon to the skies" to bring forth humanity's resurrection.[56] The theme introduced by Exciter, the metallic messiah, is completed.

As a composite, adding Judas to Painkiller and Exciter adds a layer of transvalued Christian mythology, reminiscent of John Milton's *Paradise Lost*, where the descent from heaven to earth is precipitated by the battle in heaven where, in Judas Priest's telling, order then comes from chaos. As their Judas, and namesake, the "Eternal betrayer/Ice cold and evil … /Dark prince of the world" arrives and like Exciter and Painkiller, "Humanity trembles" though in this soteriology, "none will be saved." Judas continues down to hell to resurrect and evangelize the new true faith emanating from his "crucified steel." Judas became the satanic deliverer of humanity. We tremble, are enslaved, never saved but destiny replaces chaos from a fractured heaven and empowered hell.[57]

The Abyss

Mircea Eliade argues that within mythologies of death the element of a journey to or through spiritual worlds are important signifiers of the separation of body and soul. Furthermore, while on such a journey a state of ecstasy may exist where one can observe the superhuman. These elements are certainly present in the visions and journey of St. John in "The Revelation of John."[58] The taking on the role or identity of evil or Satan or a satanic follower has its social value. Clifford Geertz explains, "But whether in the form of a trickster, a clown, a belief in witchcraft, or a concept of original sin, the presence of such a symbolic reminder of the hollowness of human pretensions to religious or moral infallibility is perhaps the surest sign of spiritual maturity."[59] Religious stories and symbols are powerful as they summarize how the world is and how one should live in it; symbols have power because they order experience and symbols of evil are attempts to reconcile us to the presence of evil and the destructive forces within ourselves.[60]

Judas Priest's first song to foreground the Devil is "Sinner." Harkening to the horsemen of the apocalypse in Revelation, it arrives on a steed with fiery eyes and a blazing mane as mountains turn dark and the sun goes black with mayhem ensuing. It is the end of time itself. Sinner is not only the personification of war but also arrives with an impressively demonic posse escorted by vultures with the odor of battle all about. He "roams the starways" and calls humanity to vice and damnation as they fall by his hand. Those caught in his wake suffer a torment of boiling blood "setting them alight."[61]

Descent into hell is also important. In an early song, "Saints in Hell," a story of self-declared saints descending to hell to reclaim a stolen bell is told. Although it is unclear whom the saints and wannabe martyrs are, a reasonable interpretation, the "8000 years" reference notwithstanding, is that of crusaders. The crusading imagery includes the quest to reclaim a stolen relic "With their banners held high," the promise of likely martyrdom and city streets flowing with blood in the French lyric, "Abattoir, abattoir, mon Dieu quelle horreur." The saints, however, do not die in hell, though there was carnage. Despite the onslaught of fists, spears, "wild cats," "scream eagles," "king cobras," and "blood sucking bats," the saints make it out, but then it is announced that the war has ended and the saints survived.[62] The saints, not martyrs, restored their world. Similarly, another conflict with demonic forces, in "Demonizer," is a much simplified story where demons are exorcised in a quest to ascend to Satan's throne challenging for sovereignty.[63]

Sometimes hell wins. "Night Crawler" explores the nature of hell and its creatures where "sanctuary" cannot be found and prayers are simply whispers of "last resort." Using stock horror film imagery of dark night rain and evil creatures descending staircases to prey upon helpless victims, Judas Priest holds up Christianity for its emptiness, "Their last rites echo on the wind." Although their last rites become lost in a windy rainy night, they return to orthodox Christian teaching upon the quick dispatch of the victims; "Souls ascend to heaven" in Eucharistic imagery of consuming flesh and blood.[64]

In a further forceful reconstitution of the Eucharist, in "Devil's Child" Judas Priest combines Christian imagery, violent desire, and heartbreak in a heart-pounding, angry song. As the narrator loses willpower and submits to the dominant the realization dawns that despite the passion, he is with the one "so dammed wicked." The assailant's fingers clutching the singer's throat, he cries out, "Oh no got your claws stuck in me" seeing clearly the attacker as the Devil's child. The end point of the encounter is one of smashed dreams, lies, and a torment "Fit to snap my soul." At the song's climax, as the guitars snarl, Halford's voice reaches towards its legendary heights, "You took my heart/And left it blown to smithereens" and then the sacrifice of his body to his betrayer takes on images of the Lord's Supper, "You cut my flesh/And drank my blood that poured in streams" and the humiliation intimated by crucifixion. Christ's execution by crucifixion is transvalued into a song of heartbreaking torment and intimate betrayal—as Jesus too was betrayed to death by his friend Judas.[65]

Judas Priest's re-inscription of Christian texts and practices includes the Lord's Prayer in "White Heat, Red Hot." This song, about gladiators, is introduced with a parody of the Lord's Prayer following its cadence and phrasing to exalt ecstatic experience in the gladiatorial arena, concluding with, "Give to us this day of glory the power and the kill." The Lord's Prayer, of supplication and devotion to God's will, is here transvalued into a creed for gladiator combat and lethal victory.[66]

Muscular individualism

As is found in theatre, there is a "rhetoric of vengeance" that has as its basis movement towards increasing dislocation and injustice, "[the] tragic revenger whose actions, motivated by a growing recognition of the lack of innate social justice, traditionally move the revenger away from the culturally sanctioned. This process of alienation has long been recognized as integral to the revenge process."[67] In fact, "the revenger may very well act outside of the legal structure of his society, his vengeance by necessity assumes a structure of its own that must subsequently find license as a legitimate discourse."[68] Judas Priest's privileging of strong individualism was also articulated through cries of youthful alienation and rebellion. There are contexts given such as unemployment, frustration, alienation, youthful anger at the world, and a suffocating home life. In this vexation rests the justification to break the law, break out of a dead-end neighborhood, running away from home seeking freedom.[69]

On songs like "Heading out to the Highway," the lone individual, rejecting peer pressure, growls with the strength of going it alone and learning from mistakes. The virtue on the road is found on the curve, the straight, wain or decline, and while, "everybody breaks down sooner or later" (the elements of the highway that knock one down), the choice to rise up remains. Alternatively, as in "Reckless," the strong individual is a "real survivor," "indestructible," "radioactive," and rockets through the upper reaches of the atmosphere.[70] This emphasis on solitary explosive force is merged with the religious expectation of kneeling, akin to the "Exciter," though in "Hard as Iron" the kneeling is out of fear—to beg for safety.[71]

A subset of songs about the strong loner concerns the stoic individual that simply stands strong and resolute towards the world without any motive other than self-determination. There is "Grinder," where the narrator traverses earth and its open landscapes, empowered by a strong sense of self-reliance; he then takes his leave of the monotony of life with the majesty and power of a "mighty eagle."[72] This conceit includes the call to take one's share in this world filled with sorrow, remaining perpetually strong, focused on "new tomorrow," as in "You've Got Another Thing Comin'," or simply to vanquish all challengers in racing hard.[73]

Closely related is isolation. In "Stained Class," the one separated from society sees his position in the community as estranged by the world which created him. It is a type of confessional statement expressing disgust towards a faithless society given to apathy and deceit.[74] Similar protest at the isolating effects of a corrupt society is "Screaming for Vengeance," where the cloistered are hopeful that in biding one's time revenge will come. Patience mixed with vengeance is the virtue of metal redemption.[75]

Judas Priest's corpus is rife with the strong individual facing immense odds, embroiled in intense conflict. Always victorious, the powerful individual warrior, as in "The Sentinel," acts from a sense of pride and duty, "Sworn to avenge/ Condemn to hell."[76] For the Sentinel, victory comes in an apocalyptic landscape where "Dogs whine," and the streets are laden with "upturned burned-out cars." The church itself has abandoned this hellscape, as "From deep inside its empty shell/A cathedral bell begins" and the storm gathers. The Sentinel in this context, with the ringing of a church bell, in a landscape devoid of people, except the unnamed challengers, is the new savior. As the bell falls silent the brawl ensues with great violence and sharp weaponry as the street fills with the blood from slain bodies. In this carnage the Sentinel remains aloof despite casting about seeds of death.[77] Unlike established religion, having left the decaying urban landscape, the lone savior is a warrior condemning his rivals to hell in their violent deaths. The motive was vengeance constructed through rhetorical discourse.

Sex and the sacred

Sex and the transvaluation of Christian images also runs through Judas Priest's career. Our initiation into the sexual world of Judas Priest begins early. In the song "Rocka Rolla," we meet a "Man eatin' momma" that culls men from boys. Connecting her to the metal foundry of their youth as a "steam driven hammer" adds a poignantly powerful sexual image to a woman clearly in control of the world around her. She mixes a sadomasochism, "She's a grip and choke ya," with a party-hard lifestyle, "Barroom fighter/Ten pint a nighter/."[78] The Rocka Rolla woman is soon followed up by the "Whiskey woman" of *Sad Wings of Destiny*. She is caught in a liminal state, figuring her way through life at a key point of transition in the context of excessive alcohol use and losing her man to another woman, all while ageing with no one around to care.[79] The narrator of "Victim of Changes" is strongly attracted to her, and seeing that she is with other men, cries out, "good God pluck me." He is in pain that she does not notice him as she has aged to a maturity that now overlooks him.[80] Ageing alienates others and ultimately herself; and all are victims.

The sadomasochism theme hinted at in *Rocka Rolla* returns in "Island of Domination." Here we come to it through images of the Christian apocalypse where an invasion under cover of night came on the horses of "destruction and doom."[81] Recalling the horsemen of the apocalypse of Revelation 6:1–8, here people are taken to the Island of Domination where "Nightdriver demon of desire" embodying sexual want descends taking on roles of "Spinesnapper" and "Throatchoker" in an attempt to break the captives down. Finally, the prisoners meet "Lashing of strappings with beatings" and in the heat of lashings and strappings the great mess of domination is accepted as blessing.[82]

Halford is a gay man and his identity caused him much anger and isolation in the strongly heterosexual metal culture of the 1970s and 1980s. For the *Hell Bent for Leather* album Halford brought leather studs to the band's look. The S&M look came from a visit to the shop Mr. S in London where they were outfitted, and for Halford this evolution represented the coming together of his two worlds. The tough leather, studs, and spikes look, including caps and whips, was soon adopted by many metal bands, and it became a sort of uniform, though most who embraced it had no idea from where it came. It did mesh, however, seamlessly with their "tough, angry, aggressive, and extreme" music. This sartorial turn also made public, without words, Halford's sexuality. He officially came out in the early 1990s, but by then it was metal's worst kept secret. As the leather and whips were adopted, Halford began to ride his Harley Davidson motorcycle on stage, cracking a whip, and the tough metal image was fully put together. In an endorsement deal with the Harley Davidson Company, he purchased the bike for a dollar.[83]

On the *Hell Bent for Leather* album, two songs convey the new, rough sexual image. In "Burnin' Up" after a back-and-forth of sexual teasing, promise and withdrawal, the narrator declares, "And as you lose control, of your very soul/ Your desire takes over." Then, much darker, in "Evil Fantasies," a sexual encounter, described as a seeming mix of reality and imagination is not only violent, but "evil" as only a thought. In the expression of deep sexual desire, cast in desires of control and being controlled, subservience, nails cutting skin, a feared "dark side" dissmissive of "compassion," the composer asserts that from this evil the other cannot hide and his dark side will be well fed. Thus, as their new sartorial image was released, so too a powerful synergy of rough sexual energy and transgressive spirituality.[84]

Although there are allusions to religious idioms, such as "You put me back to promised land" and "You've really got what it takes to make a bad man better," on "Troubleshooter," the sadomasochist and rough sex theme is largely agnostic.[85] Otherwise, over the course of several albums a song or two is devoted to this theme resulting in a mélange of whips, dog leashes, domination, joyous suffering, oral sex, and by the time of *Defenders of the Faith* in 1984, graphic violence and lusty vampirism melding the draining of one's blood with the promise to "trap and devour," claiming ownership over one's soul.[86] The violence of *Defenders of the Faith* is a crescendo on this theme as the return to descriptive accounts of rough sex and loss of autonomy in the presence of great and powerful lust return.[87]

Judas Priest had their tender moments of love, heartbreak, and loneliness. The ache of a lonely heart comes to us in "Here Come the Tears" where a deep craving for love gives way to loneliness when a romantic connection is made, "Take me now, in your arms/Let me rest, safe from harm" and then the tears fall. This is similar to the reunion of lovers in "Desert Plains" some albums later.[88] "Desert Plains" is rich in imagery as the lone traveler on his motorcycle rides through the night, lit by a full moon and "Quartz light to guide me" until sunrise when the two lovers are reunited. The love and sexual tension are strong with the traveler whose body aches and heart bleeds with passion. This is an epic and heroic journey, guided by light from the cosmos and fulfillment reached. Of the myriad of songs Judas Priest has about strong individuals, this is the one example of the heroic trope in a context of romantic passion.[89]

More typical is a mixture of tender affection, obsession, and fear of abandonment. Halford sings of a broken heart in "Before the Dawn" as one's lover leaves just as the early morning birds start to call and what seemed like a lasting relationship dissipates with the sunrise. The similar cry to a lover departing of "Don't Go" is found again on *Point of Entry* where the now broken connection brings loneliness and a resolution to take care of one's self.[90] These concerns of abandonment coupled with powerful desire are made vivid with a heart restrained by chains, a feeling of enslavement, and projection that the other "turned mean overnight."[91]

Captured by the painful clutch of lust and desire is a soul filled with "darkness" where home is like a "cell" while "living through this hell." As if stricken with a fever, the besotted sees one's object of desire exclaiming, "I heard your body talk," and the effect was apocalyptic with a "shooting star," "magnetic trance," a "crash down from afar," a "strange fate," "destiny," and then in realized consummation (or imaginary, it is not clear): "we were like angels in the night." This is an eternal rapture where from the vicissitudes of mundane reality albeit tortured existence, comes a life giving lust granting angelic bliss.[92] A similar tale of erotic desire and passion with redemptive quality is "Out in the Cold," where the narrator, plagued with sleepless nights carried by longing and regret, calls out to his lover in a quasi-gospel plea: "Please rescue me." Regretting pain caused when together, and a developing sense of neediness, the cries continue for rescue: "I wish you were here/Takin' good care of me/I want you."[93]

Conclusions

Judas Priest projects dislocation, isolation, and oppression onto Christian imagery and key theological teachings in a re-animated mythology that recasts them into a fantastical framework characterized by individual heroism and redemptive violence. In particular the band works with Christian redemption and eschatology through an industrial working-class appropriation that sacralizes both Chaos and Cosmos in a reconstructed, though metalized, tribal rewriting into post-Christian stories.

Despite a rejection of Christianity, Judas Priest presents a sacralized universe, even if evil seems triumphant and redemptive. Thus, in protesting their own sense of marginality, Judas Priest, in a post-Christian age, called upon their own trinity of sky-saviors, heroic warriors, and resilient individuals to set things right.

In their rejection of institutional Christianity, Judas Priest uses images of mortality, supernatural beings, sky-born saviors, violence, sex, and evil to present not only their socio-religious critiques, but also to suggest that in transvaluing Christianity the alienated may find power in their own dislocation and encounter strength in their own minds: the inverted role of Satan. Following Clifford Geertz, Mircea Eliade, Norman Cohen, Conrad Ostwalt, and Elana Gomel, we see how the violent and, for a time, allegedly satanic imagination of Judas Priest articulates mythic strength to their listeners, offering hope through the salvific power of metallic fury. Judas Priest expresses a desire for marginalized individuals to rework repressive icons of Christian deliverance, resurrection, Christlike rescue, apocalyptic transformation, and journeys to hell to find the power they already possess in their imaginations ripe with vitality.

The symbols, as Geertz asserts, "synthesize a people's ethos—the tone, character, and quality of their life, its moral and aesthetic style and mood—and their world view ... their most comprehensive ideas of order." Moreover, here the idea of order was to actually enter into the disorder, depression, and anger.[94]

In 2008, with the release of the double-album biographical study "Nostradamus," Judas Priest encapsulated their decades-long career in one shot. "Nostradamus," over the course of ninety minutes, brings together the powerful individual, spiritually in tune, a human but also existing in another dimension, where apocalyptic, violent, providential themes co-mingle. Here told is a tale of love, pain, and metaphysical transcendence. "Nostradamus," though not their final album, exists in its progressive musical ode—recalling 1970s musical conceits—and lyrical summation of their key themes. In "Nostradamus," chaos, order, and destiny weave their way through. It is as it was at the conclusion of *Defenders of the Faith*, where extolling the virtues of heavy metal pieties of strength, individualism, grand themes, and apocalyptic vision of that appropriating English royal title, Judas Priest declared: "We are the defenders of the faith."[95]

4

The Art of Darkness: On Biblical Language in Ozzy Osbourne's Solo Albums, 1980–2010

Michael J. Gilmour

On January 27, 2016, Black Sabbath brought the bluntly named "The End" tour to Winnipeg, Manitoba, Canada. After opening with "Black Sabbath" and whipping the crowd into a suitable frenzy, Ozzy Osbourne's first words of greeting elicited audible groans from the faithful (and I happened to have my cell-phone video recorder running):

> You know, people have been asking me, they say, "Is it *really* the end of Black Sabbath?" It's true. I gotta tell ya, it is. So I hope you enjoy the show tonight. I hope you're having a good fucking time. We're gonna carry on with a song called "Faeries Wear Boots."

The frank finality of the moment jarred, as did earlier announcements that *13* (2013) would be the band's last full studio album.

There is also an air of finality about Osbourne's latest (at the time of writing) solo album. The last track on 2010's *Scream* (just 1:02 in length) plays like a doxology, closing with thanks for all those standing with the singer over the years: "God bless/I love you all."[1] Whether or not this is actually "The End" of solo-Osbourne remains to be seen but the song does serve as a convenient frame for thinking about Ozzy Osbourne's art of darkness because it suggests a contemplative mood, an encapsulation of a career ("for all these years"). This brief consideration of Osbourne's work considers some of the explicitly religious language of the songs from "I Don't Know" (*Blizzard of Ozz*, 1980, UK; 1981, US) to "I Love You All." What does it signify (if anything), and how does it function?

We still await a major study of religious dimensions in Osbourne's music. This short chapter is emphatically not it. My aim here is less a formal argument than an attempt to capture something of the atmosphere of this music and offer a modest call for more robust and systematic theological treatments of Osbourne's work.² What we find in the music from *Blizzard of Ozz* to *Scream* is a playful openness to the otherworldly, a curiosity about an indefinable something over the mountain.³ At times, this consciousness of the ineffable terrifies, with demons and devils populating the lyrics, and yet there are moments that are strangely comforting. Utopian dreams accompany the jeremiads and the longed-for something on the other side.⁴ Faith and creed, submission to higher powers and moral platitudes have nothing to do with it, of course. Never these. Yet, there is a vague sense of the uncanny in the music. There is also catharsis. The songs rage against injustice, hypocrisy, and violence. They also mock convention and ethical banalities, even normalcy itself; and all of this gains poignancy by constant appropriation of religious language and symbols. This style lends *gravitas* but also a mischievous air as Osbourne evokes sacred themes that ought not—or so our culturally and socially constructed instincts lead us to suppose—be part of a rock concert.

Ozzy the prosecutor

At the beginning of the book of Job, the Lord holds court with an assembly of heavenly beings. The *satan* is among them. This is neither a proper name nor the personified embodiment of evil known from the New Testament Gospels and later folklore. This *satan* is a member of the celestial council functioning as prosecutor or accuser in the forensic sense.⁵ He has a job to do. When the Lord asserts that Job is an upright man, the *satan* tests the claim. "'Does Job fear God for nothing? Have you not put a fence around him and his house and all that he has, on every side?'" (Job 1:9–10). The *satan* interrogates divine pronouncements, scrutinizing the ways of God. From a literary point of view, he also pushes the narrative forward. There is no story without the devastations he unleashes on the wretched Job. He also asks questions readers inevitably ponder. Since few enjoy the same extraordinary wealth and good fortune Job does (1:1–5), they quite reasonably wonder about fairness. *Why do some have peace and prosperity but not others?* Ultimately, whatever theological insights we gain from the book of Job result from the *satan*'s words and actions. Without this character, there is no approach to the mysteries of theodicy or the ways of God considered throughout the book.

Use of such a literary device as the *satan* is hardly unique to biblical literature. Dark figures lurk in the human imagination and their presence is both necessary and constructive. Antagonists and sceptics, the monstrous and the disenfranchised, villains and outcasts are all as necessary to storytelling as their heroic, pious, or praiseworthy counterparts. There is no knight-errant without an obstacle-strewn quest, no real virtue without temptation, no certainty about truth claims until someone posits alternatives. Wherever there are stories to tell, the negative side of binaries plays a necessary part. There is no heaven without hell, no victory parade without a battlefield, no Shire without Mordor.

Fascination with dark themes and manifestations of our deepest fears are ubiquitous and timeless in the arts, giving expression to the chaos lurking beneath the surface of the individual psyche and ordered society. The ancients were no strangers to this; ancient mythologies often included the monstrous and horrific.[6] The same is true for modern societies. Representations of the tragic and terrifying give shape to our apprehensions. They also help us process the nature of both imagined and real hostilities. Is chaos "out there," beyond the borders of civilized society? An external threat? Or is it "in here," lurking within the human heart? Perhaps the best answer is both/and, which explains why we tell stories of foreign invaders like H. G. Wells's *The War of the Worlds* (1898) but also others such as Robert Louis Stevenson's *The Strange Case of Dr. Jekyll and Mr. Hyde* (1886) that remind us we are our own worst enemy.

Like Job's *satan*, Ozzy Osbourne cross-examines truth claims and scrutinizes the ways of God, orthodoxy, authority, and social normativity. What is more, his defiance of social convention—evident in his speech, dress, lifestyle, irreverence, and more—involves relegation to the fringes.[7] His interrogation of traditional values thus comes from the margins. He is a voice crying in the wilderness rather than the *agora*, a prophet not welcome in his own town, simultaneously addressing the very society he eschews.[8] This posturing as outsider involves regular identification with the dark alternatives, with the negative side of various binaries, and these often derive from biblical sources.

Ozzy Osbourne songs are regularly first-person narratives with the singer identifying with madness[9] over sanity; death over life; nightmares over dreams; darkness over light; self-destruction[10] over self-preservation; irreverence and heterodoxy[11] over piety and orthodoxy. The narrator in "Let It Die" (*Scream*, 2010) combines a number of these polarities in one place. Frightening descriptors in a process of self-revelation (the repeated "I'm a …" formula) include sinner, killer, loser, liar, oppressor, coward, and bringer of a death kiss. Collectively, these overwhelm their positive counterparts like servant, leader, and savior. After all, evil potentially contains *some* deceptive trace of the good, or at least the appearance of it—the wolf in sheep's clothing (Mt. 7:15), Satan masquerading as an angel of light (2 Cor. 11:14). A little yeast works through the whole loaf (see

1 Cor. 5:6; Gal. 5:9). On the other hand, biblical discourse insists true goodness cannot contain *some* evil (e.g., Rev. 22:15). Be perfect, Jesus says, just as the heavenly father is perfect (Mt. 5:48). Osbourne narrators drift constantly toward the tainted, the ruined, the imperfect, and the corrupted.

In "Let It Die" and throughout the Osbourne catalogue, we hear the ramblings and confessions of all manner of scoundrels and ne'er-do-wells: a hit man; a spook of children's nightmares; a tempting devil; a demon-possessed man; a serial killer, and many more.[12] There is, to be sure, some evolution in lyrical style across the decades. With reference to the early albums, one commentator observes that Osbourne's lyrics treat "the grimmest of subjects, including the agony of insanity. In later years Osbourne has kept to more contemporary issues, rejecting to a certain extent the satanic, werewolf image he constructed around himself during the early 80s."[13] Even with a writing style tempered in some way across the decades, the evocation of biblical and religious language and symbols remains a constant across his solo career.

Sacred imagery in heavy rock/metal is routine. Ozzy Osbourne's particular contribution to a musical aesthetic employing a biblically- and religiously-informed lexicon—from 1970 to 2016, from Black Sabbath's eponymous debut to what is announced to be the band's final recording—is both persistent and inventive. All the solo albums include examples, both lyrically and visually through the inclusion of provocative images in liner notes. Angel wings in the album art for *No More Tears* (1991) and *Scream* (2010); crosses in hand and around the neck for *Blizzard of Ozz* (1980), and hanging on a wall upside down on the cover of *Diary of a Madman* (1981); an alien-like crucified figure on the cover of *Down to Earth* (2001), and so on. Obvious allusions to biblical passages and motifs abound as well, as in the 1986 album title *The Ultimate Sin* (cf. Mk 3:22–30; Mt. 12:22–32) or 1988's *No Rest for the Wicked* (Isa. 57:20–21). Always, though, that preference for darkness over light, an artistic and aesthetic preference that allows interrogation of his subjects from the margins.

Ozzy the outsider

In 2010, during the week John Lennon would have turned seventy (born October 9, 1940), Ozzy Osbourne released a recording and video of "How?" in tribute to the fallen Beatle and in support of Amnesty International. This song from Lennon's *Imagine* (1971) presents Osbourne in a very interesting light. The lyrics and accompanying video complement each other in such a way that they reinforce the artist's embrace of an outsider status.

Osbourne walks through the streets of New York, seemingly disoriented. Swirling camera shots heighten this impression. He strokes his chin as though wondering what way to go ("How can I go forward when I don't know which way to turn?"). He walks through crowds but the gawking passers-by are not helpful; many pull out phones to snap pictures of the out-of-place celebrity. No one approaches to offer assistance. His appearance—long black coat, tattooed fingers, black painted nails, dark purple glasses, long hair—contrasts sharply with the tidy, formal attire of those in the middle of their work day, and the casual dress of tourists. Osbourne is conspicuous, a spectacle, an interloper, an unlikely presence trespassing on a busy sidewalk.

He searches for something and though he does not know which way to go, he keeps moving just the same. He buys flowers and holds them carefully as he walks the streets. Perhaps significantly, he passes what looks like a church. *That* sacred site is not the one he wants. The song ends when he arrives at Strawberry Fields, the "Imagine" memorial in Central Park that celebrates the memory and music of John Lennon. *There*, Osbourne lays down the flowers. *There*, he finds what he seeks.

Biblical authors tend to idealize those keeping to the fringes. They are the devout who resist the permissiveness of the majority. They take the narrow road few others choose. They are countercultural, turning the other cheek when an enemy strikes and aspiring to moral integrity even behind closed doors (Mt. 5:39; 6:6). Osbourne is an outsider in a very different sense. He walks past the famous "LOVE" statue in New York and places flowers respectfully at the "Imagine" memorial and in so doing, claims John Lennon's vision of peace and love. Imagine there are no wars, no religion to divide, no reason to kill. In a world scarred by division, dislike, and death, to embrace nonviolence and love is to be out of step with the majority. Perhaps ironically, Osbourne chooses the road less traveled (Mt. 7:13) but it leads to rock and roll, not religion.

Faith is a recurring subject in Osbourne songs but he typically abandons religious categories in favour of a trinity of substitutes: sex/romance, music, and self. Mere assertion of "belief" in these things is not enough, however. Rock and roll needs a foil. Rebellion and the flaunting of convention require some notion of order and normalcy to exist, and so the song lyrics must reject something (usually God or organized religion) before asserting belief in some shocking alternative. This is not unusual in popular music and perhaps "God" by Osbourne's hero John Lennon (*John Lennon/Plastic Ono Band*, 1970) provides a useful model illustrating the pattern: "I don't believe in Bible/ ... Jesus/ ... Buddha/ ... Gita/ ... I just believe in me/Yoko and me."[14]

Osbourne follows suit, as the sequence "You Can't Kill Rock and Roll" and "Believer" on 1981's *Diary of a Madman* illustrate. The first involves rejection of an unidentified "they" who fill his head with lies. They twist truth, do not have answers, make promises they cannot keep, tell stories that are untrue, and apparently harass him ("Leave me alone"). They seem to represent organized/conventional religion but the singer rejects what they have on offer and chooses rock and roll instead. It, *not what you're selling*, "is my religion and my law." This is very much what we see in the "How?" video, with Osbourne walking past a church and directing his devotion instead toward Strawberry Fields and all it represents.

The second song in this *Madman* sequence also turns away from one thing toward another. He mentions mountains moving before his eyes, a subtle allusion to Mt. 17:20: "if you have faith the size of a mustard seed, you will say to this mountain, 'Move from here to there,' and it will move" (cf. Lk. 17:6). The object of faith referred to in the Gospels is obviously God but in "believer" it is the self: "You've got to believe in yourself ... I'm a believer."

We see this redirected faith again in "Revelation (Mother Earth)" (*Blizzard of Ozz*, 1980), which also adapts the language of the Gospels: "Mother please forgive them/For they know not what they do" (cf. Lk. 23:34). Like Christ on the cross, the narrator is in a desperate situation, with death the inevitable outcome. The "death" awaiting Osbourne is humanity's destructive ways. History books tell the story of empires falling. He expects children "of the future" to suffer the consequences and they too are likely to behave the same way, unless Mother (addressed again in the sixth verse) teaches them to "fight all the hate." The song is darkly apocalyptic. The singer's dystopian vision includes a vision of the world burning and seas turning red, imagery taken from John the Seer (compare Rev. 16:3 with 16:8).

"Revelation (Mother Earth)" resembles "Dreamer" from *Down to Earth* (2001) in some respects. That song also refers to history repeating itself and Mother Earth but this time, there is concern *for* her, not a plea for help from her. Her survival is uncertain owing to humanity's abusive treatment of the environment.[15] The singer also despairs over the violence that suffuses society and wonders if an end to anger, hate, and bigotry is possible. At the bridge of the song, we also find Osbourne turning away, in effect, from traditional religion. "Your higher power," he tells the listener, "may be God or Jesus Christ" but for my part, I do not really care what you choose. This is an interesting remark in that he does not condemn religious belief, even if he does not claim it for himself. He does not call out to "Mother" or "Father" but instead clings to what he describes as a fantasy, a dream, in much the same spirit as John Lennon's "Imagine"—"you may say I am a dreamer but I'm not the only one."

Ozzy in the first-person singular

The arts frequently incorporate embodiments of cultural defiance, anti-social behavior, rebellion, and transgression. From the Serpent to Sauron, rogues are a storytelling convention, pervasive in both literature (the antagonist opposing the protagonist/hero), and religious discourse (devils, demons, fallen angels, embodiments of chaos). We do well to ask what "transgressive" characters contribute and what purposes they serve. At minimum, they permit self-definition, aiding in constructs of social cohesion ("We are not that"). They also function prophetically, challenging hegemonic values, social mores, institutions, and conventions. In the arts, transgressive characters enact a *carnivalesque*, a permitted overturning of the rules. Sanctioned misbehavior is something we expect of rock stars. Their job is to be extravagant, to defy the humdrum monotony of routine their audiences experience. And like Lear's fool, such characters are potential sites of wisdom because they have permission to speak. Osbourne plays the part. He is a clown and jester wearing a broken crown.[16]

Ozzy Osbourne is, of course, the quintessential rock star whose unlikely rise from rags to riches includes all the cliché trappings of destruction and excess. The harsh realities of his childhood and youth are important themes in the "official" biographies and these inevitably contribute to the fan experience. Think of his memoir *I Am Ozzy* (2009) or the documentary *God Bless Ozzy Osbourne*, co-produced by son Jack Osbourne (2011). In both, there is attention to his struggles in school (owing in part to dyslexia), petty crime and a brief stint in jail, poverty, and the bleak outlook facing youth in postwar Birmingham.

After achieving success with Black Sabbath, substance abuse emerges as a dominant motif in almost all discussions of Ozzy Osbourne. So too are the personal tragedies of his life, among them the death of close friend and guitarist Randy Rhoads in 1982 and the attempted murder of wife Sharon in a drug-induced haze in 1989. Rightly or wrongly, many hear Osbourne songs as (entirely) autobiographical, taking them to be the confessions of a survivor.

Ozzy Osbourne the man and "Ozzy Osbourne" the construct are, in effect, a modern enactment of the antimasque. The masque was a performance art popular in the early seventeenth century in England, "an elaborate form of court entertainment that combined poetic drama, music, song, dance, splendid costuming, and stage spectacle. A plot—often slight, and mainly mythological and allegorical—served to hold together these diverse elements."[17] (There is something very rock and roll about this multi-layered art form.) The poet Ben Jonson wrote poetic scripts for court masques. One of his innovations to the form was the addition of the antimasque. Such "characters were grotesque and unruly, the action ludicrous, and the humor broad; it served as a foil and countertype to the elegance, order, and ceremony of the masque proper, which preceded it in performance."[18] By juxtaposing the two, by presenting the sharp contrast of dignified court behavior with anarchy and absurdity, we see the former all the clearer. Embodiments of dissent and departure from established values allow greater clarity about what those values are. Osbourne's Prince of Darkness/wild man/werewolf personae function in similar ways.

Along with this posturing as antisocial nonconformist is the tendency for Osbourne narrators to be damaged antiheroes. One moment king, the next moment clown; he is, as one song puts it, a broken-winged jester with a broken crown.[19] There is a fall from grace, from royalty to court buffoon. It is from the position of shattered outsider that Osbourne's commentary on social mores, religion, politics, and more is most poignant. Positioned as an unlikely, broken-winged prophet, embracing his antisocial behaviors, insanity, and buffoonery, he emerges as a forceful example of popular music's potential as unlikely moral authority. Strange as it sounds, Ozzy Osbourne is weirdly conservative. Though telling the stories of/giving voice to the bogeymen of children's nightmares, killers, psychopaths, occultists,[20] serpents in the garden, and more, the songs are not nihilistic. A longing for peace, understanding, love, and the wellbeing of individuals and the planet pervades the music.

Having said that, what does wellbeing mean? Ambiguities exist and the moment we try to define it and impose it on others there is the potential for coercion. A striking example is "Latimer's Mercy" from *Scream* (2010). Robert Latimer is a Canadian farmer who killed his severely disabled daughter in 1993 out of a desire to end her pain. The courts convicted him of murder. "When you see a kid go through pain and agony," Osbourne said of the story, "I don't know whether I could do that to my kid, but I'm not in that position."[21] He does not condemn or praise the girl's father but tries to capture the emotional motivations behind the act: "Your eyes shine as I turn on the motor/The tears fall as the mercy gets closer."[22] Goodness exists though it is ambiguous. A murderer is a potential saint in Osbourne songs and those we expect to maintain high moral standards (politicians, the military, religious leaders) are potential warmongers and charlatans. Hypocrisy is arguably the greatest evil in Ozzy Osbourne's music.

His alignment with dark characters and themes is occasionally reactionary, part of a critique of hypocritical religion in particular. This is the case with "Miracle Man" (*No Rest for the Wicked*, 1988), which mocks duplicitous televangelists. The video for "Miracle Man" parodies Jimmy Swaggart, who went through a widely publicized fall from grace following sexual indiscretions in the late 1980s and early 1990s. The greed signified by stacks of dollar bills and pigs at troughs apply to others as well, such as (at the time) Jim and Tammy Faye Bakker. In remarks introducing that song during a concert, he also mocks Oral Roberts who, in 1986, claimed God intended to kill him if he did not raise eight million dollars from his followers:

> You know what really pisses me off, man? I don't get this, why you have to pay to see God, man. You know, I'm gonna die tomorrow so if I don't get seven [sic] million dollars, I'll die. Well I always fucking say, fucking die asshole. And these are the kinds of guys that say, if you listen to the likes of Ozzy Osbourne, you're sure … gonna go to hell. Well if that's the case, we're gonna have a fucking good ol' time down there![23]

Such criticisms do not target religion *per se* but rather those who impose their views on others, those claiming the moral high ground even as they fall short of the very standards they demand of their congregations. They conceal their crimes "behind a grandeur of lies" and what is more, they claim to be without sin and are quick to cast stones, as he puts it in "You're No Different than Me" (*Bark at the Moon*, 1983; alluding here to Jn 8:7). There is suspicion of those who defend their own moral integrity by attacking others. To notice the speck in the eyes of another while ignoring the log in your own (Mt. 7:1–5) is, for Osbourne, far worse than honest acknowledgment of depravity, which he does in a number of places.[24]

Ozzy and theodicy

"Diggin' Me Down" (*Scream*, 2010) is an angry first-person address to the "Father" and "Mr. Jesus Christ." The song is a lament that expresses anger at all manner of calamities that are part of the human condition. "Why don't you save us?" the narrator asks. The song grapples with an enduring theological knot sometimes referred to as theodicy: if God is benevolent and all-powerful, why does evil exist? Why is God absent in the midst of suffering?[25]

Surprisingly, "Diggin' Me Down" is not just a religion-mocking rant that denies the existence of a deity. To do so would merely repeat an unimaginative, hackneyed idea. By addressing the Father and Jesus Christ directly, the songwriter cleverly heightens the dramatic force of the lyrics, an effective device for articulating the bewilderment and anger explored in the song. There is even an admission of struggling faith ("my faith is breaking") that recalls the language of the biblical laments.

> How long, O LORD? Will you forget me forever? How long will you hide your face from me? How long must I bear pain in my soul, and have sorrow in my heart all day long? (Ps. 13:1–2).

The closing words of the song are particularly striking as the singer couples weakening faith with awareness of his limited understanding. How will I recognize Jesus Christ when he comes? How will I distinguish truth from error? Will I know he is the Son of God as he claims? Is he an "obsolete façade"?

Osbourne's narrator concedes his doubts and questions in sharp contrast with many religious teachers who proceed as though mystery and ambiguity do not exist, and whose eschatologies morph into thinly veiled escapist fantasies. These, in effect, abandon real-world traumas and the questions they raise about God's goodness. Osbourne's lyrics, by contrast, are often constructive and world affirming in their own way, as in the anti-war stance of Osbourne's *Black Rain* (2007). This album decries the second Iraq conflict with a force reminiscent of Black Sabbath's anti-Vietnam anthem "War Pigs" (*Paranoid*, 1970). "Why are the children all marching/into the desert to die?"[26] We find similar sentiments in "Diggin' Me Down," where he laments a world suffering under slavery, genocide, and socio-economic inequity. He wants answers to these real-world atrocities, not the world-denying rescue of an elect few, which is a frequent theme in Christian eschatological speculations. The latter leaves little motivation to promote peace, help the downtrodden, or address environmental crises.

Sin is a recurring theme in Osbourne songs and biblical turns of phrase are often in view. The term ultimate sin (cf. album and song titles, 1986) recalls New Testament passages describing unpardonable behaviors (Mt. 12:30–32; Mk 3:28–30; Lk. 12:8–10; Heb. 6:4–8; 10:26–29). The original sin of "I Don't Want to Change the World" (*No More Tears*, 1991) is a familiar concept in Christian theology, rooted in the writings of St. Paul (see Rom. 5:12–21; 1 Cor. 15:22), and others (e.g., Ps. 51:5). Adam and Eve disobeyed, and consequently all their offspring inherit that corruption. This becomes part of a criticism used by the narrator's detractors. They call him sinner and speak to "all the people" about the "original sin" but he dismissively turns this back against them. They too are Adam and Eve's descendants so no less guilty: "I spoke to God this morning and he don't like you."[27]

We find this line of argument elsewhere. To criticize another always risks hypocrisy because there is no guiltless subject position. Those throwing stones at a woman caught in adultery walk away because they too are not blameless (Jn 7:53–8:11). The singer insists there is no pure land. Everyone's hands are dirty, or, as St. Paul puts it, all have sinned (Rom. 3:23). Osbourne attacks those who condemn others while forgetting their own culpability. For his part, he frequently acknowledges he is only one sinner among many, even if chief among them. At times, the first-person plural reminds us of our collective failures. In "The Almighty Dollar," money, greed, and consumption characterize the lives *we* lead.[28]

Ozzy the broken-crowned jester[29]

Religion in Ozzy Osbourne's music is not really about religion, or at least not entirely. As noted, there is no necessary connection between religious imagery and a songwriter's personal views. With reference to alleged connections between audience behaviors and religious practice, Robert Walser points out, "The vast majority of heavy metal fans don't worship Satan and don't commit suicide; yet many fans enjoy that fraction of heavy metal songs that deals with such things."[30] Instead, the distance between persona and personal belief found in the music of Osbourne and Black Sabbath suggests the overt religious content serves other purposes. Pete Ward finds their music operates "almost entirely at the level of representation." This use of religious imagery and language forms

> a part of the act rather than a part of the lived reality of the band or their audience. So the symbolic function of the occult in heavy metal operates in a way that is possibly more akin to the use of the occult by Shakespeare in a play such as *The Tempest*. In other words, the occult forms part of the artistic context in which audiences and artists are working symbolically with a range of issues and concerns.[31]

Satanic imagery is offensive to the mainstream and that is exactly why it attracts a certain audience—often the disenfranchised. It is taboo and a kind of transgression. If there is blatant resistance to organized religion, it is religion as a dubious form of authority viewed with suspicion. Insolence to one form of authority is insolence toward all of them. Most metal fans are not practicing Satanists, Robin Sylvan notes. They "are obviously drawn to Satanic imagery for other reasons." He argues these include "heavy metal's individualistic philosophy, its rebellion against normative authority, and its connection with the supernatural."[32]

Villains, fools, monsters. All such characters speak and act from the outside. They are at the margins in various senses of the word, and since they are on the fringes of ordered society, they represent threats to civility and safety. But we need them. We need art forms that put before us the ghastly, the horrendous, and the absurd. These protect against hubris and help us with self-definition (I am/We are not *that*). They question established values and traditions thus forcing us to consider why it is we believe and do what we believe and do. When art forces us to face opposing positions, it challenges us to think and articulate our own values and beliefs more carefully. This means greater self-awareness and deeper commitments to those values. Such contrary forces—in art, in religious discourses—expose weaknesses and flaws within us and within societies. Chaotic forces often suggest new ways of being, and ways of looking at the world previously forbidden or not considered at all. Here we find wisdom. God bless Ozzy Osbourne.

Part Two

Fans

5

Consecrating an *Extraordinary Being*: Fan Culture among Gilda's Followers in Argentina

Eloísa Martín

Gilda was an Argentine cumbia singer who became widely popular after she was killed in a car accident in 1996. In this chapter, I will show how a number of people who identify as Gilda fans contributed to making her into a star, an exceptional being.

Gilda's life was not unlike that of thousands of young women who struggle to succeed in the entertainment world, overcoming myriad obstacles to fulfill their dreams of glory and financial autonomy. But Gilda died before accomplishing her goals, and did not become famous until some years after her death. Most stars are already famous when they pass; however some stars do become even bigger celebrities after their death. Elvis and Princess Diana are two examples of this phenomenon, as is Selena, the Tex-Mex singer murdered by her manager who resonates as an archetype for some interpreters of the "Gilda phenomenon." Death rarely brings glory to stars, who may be remembered or even honored by their fans, though without ever reaching the status of myth. This chapter shows that Gilda's process of mythification cannot be explained without considering fans' agency over the last two decades.

Twenty years after her untimely demise, Gilda still has plenty of fans but, most importantly, she has become a popular icon portrayed in films, soap operas, books, and magazines in Argentina. The peak of her posthumous glory was Argentina's most recent presidential inauguration on December 10, 2015. After the ceremony, the new President Mauricio Macri joined VicePresident Gabriela Michetti on the main balcony of Casa Rosada to greet the crowd at Plaza de Mayo—a traditional moment of political consecration since the times of Peronism. The speakers set up around the square started booming with Gilda's hit "No me arrepiento de este amor" and President Macri began to dance, the presidential sash swaying to the beat. The song tells the story of a love against all odds that the singer is willing to fight for. As the crowd gathered in the square below sang along, VicePresident Michetti asked for a microphone and started an impromptu karaoke. The event was broadcast live on TV and shared thousands of times on social media.

During two years of fieldwork in Buenos Aires and my follow-up with fans via email and social media, I heard stories about the importance of Gilda's presence in the fans' lives. These people regularly visit her grave at the cemetery and have established a more enduring and faithful relationship with her. They consider themselves her caretakers, the guardians of her memory. My analysis is based on more than two straight years of ethnographic fieldwork among Gilda's fans, in different settings and with several fan clubs in the city of Buenos Aires and its suburbs. My work during this period also included in-depth individual and group interviews that proved particularly useful in two ways. First, the interviews helped me to avoid the standard answers that I observed fans delivering to the journalists who appeared at least twice a year, on Gilda's birthday and the anniversary of her death. Fans knew the typical questions journalists would ask and had developed the right timing for radio and TV interviews. They knew how to provide clever, succinct answers, to "give them what they are looking for," while incorporating the ideas and values associated with Gilda's "real" story and its true meaning. Their relationship with the media was fundamental to understanding the differences they established between the public discourse about Gilda and their intimate experiences, which had to be preserved from the potentially polluted and distortive space of the media. However, this conscious—and, I must insist, highly astute—management of their media presence illuminates the agency fans demonstrate with regards to defining and remembering Gilda.

Second, saving the interviews for the end of my fieldwork helped me ask better questions, avoiding what Matt Hills refers to as the "fallacy of internality"[1] that permeates most interview-based research. Hills argues that fans cannot be taken as an unproblematic source of meaning, and that it is essential to bear in mind that the accounts of one's own experience as a fan rarely can be constructed in terms of a discursively evidenced rationality when approaching fan narratives.[2] Subjective reasoning is never transparent and, as Hills noted, the reasons for fandom interrupt the flow of experience and produce a discursive kind of affection-free justification, because any conduct considered "normal" needs no explanation. In this sense, and in spite of the fact that most of the topics I raised during the interviews were already covered by my ethnographic fieldwork, the answers helped reveal the key elements that gave meaning to fans' trajectories.

This chapter aims to show how fans are inescapable protagonists in the consecration process of Gilda. Gilda's fans are aware of their mission of keeping her memory alive, and work in this sense. While reconstructing the meanings of her life and legacy, they contribute to Gilda's consecration. In this contribution, I will discuss how Gilda is transformed into an *extraordinary being* through the fan's performances and practices. Similarly to Latour's *"factish,"*[3] the concept of *extraordinary beings*[4] acknowledges the human origin of consecrated people, places, and times, pointing out the direct, active, and constitutive role of human agency and the possibly transitory nature of "extraordinariness." While Gilda could not have been a star at the time of her death, she becomes a star, a myth, an extraordinary being that—just like Evita—sang to the masses on the main balcony of Casa Rosada.

From Miriam to Gilda

Although the fans agree on most of her biographical data, it is difficult for two Gilda followers to agree on who Gilda was. Despite attempts to reify her figure, especially by the media, Gilda is an inherently polyphonic phenomenon: she is described as "the cumbia ambassador," "an angel," "a princess," "like a female Che Guevara," "my best friend," and so on. So who was the woman who became Gilda?

Miriam Alejandra Bianchi was born to a middle-class Buenos Aires family. When she was just a teenager, her father fell ill and then passed away; pressed for cash, her mother had to move the family to a housing complex on the outskirts of Buenos Aires. Gilda became a kindergarten teacher and married a small businessman at the age of eighteen. Together they had two children. In 1990, she responded to a newspaper ad for singers and began working in an uncommon genre for a middle-class woman: cumbia.

For a young, white, middle-class kindergarten teacher and mother of two, becoming a cumbia singer was a very unlikely career choice. Gilda was aware of the class prejudice and what her family would think. Apart from her mother and her godparents, her family believed she sang at restaurants on the side for a little extra money, and only found out the truth at her funeral. Tropical music, particularly cumbia, has been booming in Argentina since the 1980s. There are recording studios (that used to "own" the artists they recorded and represented),

TV programs, radio stations, magazines, and dance clubs. For almost forty years, hegemonic discourse has homogenized and stigmatized cumbia as grotesque, ludicrous, vulgar, banal, and low quality: it is widely viewed as cheesy music or music for *negros*.[5] In Argentina, *negro* does not necessarily depend on skin color or blood, but exudes negative connotations associated with class and morality. *Negro* is mainly a pejorative adjective applied to others, with the exception of cumbia villera fans, who adopt and reverse the stigmatizing terms by taking pride in being *negro*,[6] *villero* (a term used to refer to a resident of the villa, or slum) and *cumbiero*.

An agent thought her real name lacked pizazz and insisted she take the name Gilda before her solo debut. By the mid-1990s, Gilda was well-known but not nearly as famous as some other female cumbia singers. She had a contract with one of the two largest tropical music labels—a major achievement, considering that at that time, a different type of cumbia was popular, and the female singers had an entirely different look—and had appeared on several TV programs. Between 1992 and 1995, Gilda recorded four albums and had a few minor hits. While she had attracted a certain following, it was considerably less than the scores of fans she has today. On September 7, 1996, Gilda died in a car accident on her way to a show. Six other people died in the crash, including her mother and her daughter. A surprising crowd—surprising at least for the media and for Gilda's relatives—followed the funeral procession to Chacarita cemetery.

Since 1998, a number of TV specials and documentaries have been made about her life, along with dozens of books[7] including one for children[8] and countless magazine and newspaper articles. There were also several music compilations (both record label and bootleg versions) launched on the market soon after her death, and a posthumous album, *Entre el cielo y la tierra* (Between Heaven and Earth), was one of the top sellers in Argentina in 1998. That album won the Premio Gardel for the best tropical music album, the most important award of Argentina's music industry.

Fan clubs

A great number of fan clubs were founded before and after Gilda's death. Some of them dissolved as time passed, others split into smaller groups, and new groups were created through social media. Gilda's fan clubs are not legal entities, but all have a president who acts as the group's authorized spokesperson and assumes most of the management responsibilities, from handling money to organizing celebrations, trips to her sanctuary, votive offerings, and letters. The sanctuary was built by fans where the accident happened. It is a simple and small construction, by the road, where fans and devotees leave objects related to Gilda, and also votive offerings. Fans consider this is a very special place to "get in touch" with Gilda, and they organize trips all year round, and festivals each September 7.

The fan clubs in Buenos Aires meet each weekend at the cemetery to "be with Gilda," arrange the flowers people leave during the week, clean her vault, collect letters and offerings, and guide newcomers. However, they are also there to chat with friends, sharing snacks or drinking *mate*. They are also responsible for decorating the spot for Gilda's birthday and the anniversary of her death, publishing a free newsletter on September 7, and organizing trips to the shrine. Depending on the club, fans go to the cemetery every weekend, rain or shine; do volunteer work at a soup kitchen; collect magazine clippings, photos, and memorabilia in albums; spend hard-earned money to buy a new book or merchandising; ask for the day off from work to be with Gilda on the anniversary of her death; or use money that could be used to buy shoes for their children to rent a bus to travel to the shrine. Many fans cooked at Gilda's Little Hearts, a soup kitchen for children founded by the president of a Gilda fan club in one of the most dangerous slums in Argentina. Perhaps because they are organized around a deceased person, the primary activities of fan clubs dedicated to Gilda or Elvis Presley[9] are fundraising and goods donation. This is the case also for Star Trek fans, as shown by Jindra and McLaren,[10] where charities are performed according to the "philosophy" of the series. These gestures are viewed by the fans as a sacrifice, as a duty, as "what's expected," but they are also a way to express their love for Gilda.

Although "leisure" activities are part of what brought them together as friends with common interests, joining a fan club implies certain duties. Fans cannot shirk these duties because of other activities, responsibilities, and interests: that's why it is possible to find the fans at Gilda's grave on a rainy and cold Sunday, during an important soccer match or—at least for a few hours—on Mother's Day. Membership and regular participation in any of the Gilda fan clubs requires economizing one's time: even if one has family, school, or work obligations, it is important to set aside time for Gilda. This finding departs from many academic studies that present fandom as a manifestation arising from the fringes of society, never among "well-rounded" or "normal" individuals: fans are adolescents, single women, children, or the unemployed—people who have time to spare, time to waste.[11] Conversely, for Gilda's fans, joining a club because one has "nothing to do"—or even worse, quitting the club because a new job or a new love is taking up too much time—is heavily criticized.

Being a fan of Gilda is not limited to club meetings. Fandom can be observed inside fans' homes and on their bodies: besides wearing Gilda t-shirts and pins, fans decorate with images of Gilda, arranging posters and pictures on their walls, and displaying objects that relate, sometimes indirectly, to the singer. The use of religious objects in everyday life helps to establish and maintain relationships between extraordinary beings and fans. Fans buy, collect, and use these objects as a way to live their fandom and *connect* with Gilda, in continuous interaction with and through those objects. In Laura's[12] living room, for example, pictures of Gilda and other mementos (a mug, a clock, and a glass with her image) are combined with objects Laura purchased because she read that Gilda liked them: a cushion with the colors of Boca soccer club, Gilda's team, and a framed picture of crooner Ricardo Montaner, Gilda's favorite singer. Laura owns a t-shirt with Gilda's picture that she reserves for special occasions to keep from wearing it out. She wears a medallion with Gilda's face and, although she herself is a fan of the River Plate club, a beaded plastic bracelet in blue and yellow (the Boca team colors).

These practices cannot be reduced to mere consumption. The purchase, collection, and resignification of goods related to Gilda cannot be classified as either passive consumption or necessarily micro-resistance to the market, but instead take place in spaces that are constantly negotiated, in interaction with Gilda, where the dwelled-in world[13]—a world that includes space, relationships with others, and the fan's body—is demarcated and signified.

Gabriel marks his own personal space in the family house with pictures of Gilda from magazines and CDs on the walls of his bedroom, while Ariel displays photos of the singer in the family dining room: there is a large framed picture of the singer on one wall and another on the counter where a plastic rosary with beads in the Boca team colors hangs. In her analysis on the uses of Christians objects in everyday life, McDannell[14] states that these help establish and maintain relations with supernatural beings, family, and friends, creating a religious landscape that tells them and the world who they are. In this sense, the objects displayed in homes are not just decorations, or even an external reflection of intimate experiences; in regular interactions, these objects become a way to experience the sacred and sacralize Gilda. They make her, through these actions, an extraordinary being.

The fever for Gilda

I've got the fever for Gilda, I have all her stuff, the cassettes, the CDs ... And my room is full of posters, pictures ... If I see anything Gilda, I buy it. I have the t-shirt you saw me wearing the other day, this medallion [shows me a medallion with the singer's face around his neck], a key chain, my wallet and look ... [he rolls up his sleeves to reveal his shoulder, where a 12 cm tattoo reads "Gilda" in italics]. A friend did this one ... I traced her name from a CD cover. I want to tattoo her face here [on the chest, over his heart] but I have to go to a professional artist for that one, because [the drawing] is really complex ... (Rulo, age 21, informal conversation registered in fieldwork notes).

Rulo has "Gilda" tattooed on his shoulder, just as many fans of the Rolling Stones have tattoos of the group's tongue logo, AC/DC fans have the name of the band with the lightning bolt in the middle, and Maradona fans have all sorts of tattoos associated with the renowned soccer player. Like other fans, Rulo collects objects related to Gilda and participates in a Gilda fan club, working every day in a soup kitchen for children in one of the poorest slums in Buenos Aires. The "fever for Gilda" is one of the possible definitions of a fan. Different authors recognize that madness, passion, and excessive enthusiasm are all key elements within this "fever" of fandom.

As Doss[15] points out, the word "fan" has had negative overtones from the beginning. Fan comes from the Latin *fanaticus*, a noun referring to the believers of religious cults in the classical non-Roman world known for their exacerbated enthusiasm and excesses. Confusing excess with irrationality, several authors use this etymology to characterize fans in pathological and deviant terms,[16] describing fans as people with no life or people who want to escape from "reality."[17] Anticipating a critique of modern consumer society, other authors characterize fans as passive, the complement to the star within the star system, in works that totally disregard the active nature of any audience.[18] Even among authors who do recognize individual agency as a positive feature of being a fan, fandom is portrayed in terms of escapism or imaginative relief,[19] compensatory fantasy,[20] or personal liberation.[21] Fans are, for these authors, marginalized, sick, crazy, maladjusted losers. These are people living in fantasy worlds, who find alternative spaces to create status within their groups,[22] seeking their "identity" by mirroring an idol, and working out psychological issues in their fandom.[23]

Hills[24] states that the main problem of most of the approaches to fandom above is that they are loaded with a moral dualism in which popular culture is defined as "good" (i.e. rational, emotionally controlled, actively resisted) or "bad" (irrational, overly emotional, passive, conformist), further blurring the inherently ambiguous character of any fan practice. Fans appeal to notions of excess, disease, and madness to try to put into words what they experience as ineffable. But far from uncontrolled or insane, Gilda fan club members often display discipline and respect in actions that they associate directly with their fandom.

According to Bacon-Smith,[25] becoming a fan is a process that involves making a series of choices at different levels, each more specific than the last: first comes an interest, then a genre, then a subgenre, until finally, a specific product is chosen. Over the years, I have heard many stories about how Gilda's followers became fans, and how Gilda increasingly came to form part of their everyday lives. They recount how getting to know her and becoming a fan were intertwined, and how this process is related to other aspects of their personal life—problems at work, their love lives, family issues, personal difficulties, and so on. In many cases, Gilda came to play a very important role in their lives, as a source of comfort and strength, a friend and a confidant with whom they trusted their hopes and secrets.

Gabriel puts his hand over his heart and says, "She's in here, I've got her with me. I don't like going to the cemetery. For me, she's alive." He discovered Gilda on a mix tape he bought at the supermarket and then saw her on a television program. Later, he met the president of a Gilda fan club and was asked to join. He reiterates his fandom through daily work at the soup kitchen, where he serves food, helps clean up, or lends a hand wherever necessary. While Gabriel's experience fits within Bacon-Smith's processual model, Roberto's attachment to Gilda looks more like a break with a previous pattern of taste than a furthering of previous choices, and brings to mind the conversion of Paul the Apostle:

> I was into a different kind of music, some really messed up stuff ... that banging music, that shit ... I was crazy ... I was ruining my mind, I was a rebel ... So, my cousin says, "Listen, let me lend you this tape." "What's on it?" I said. "Cumbia. Gilda. Listen, I swear it's great ... " And it was the song "Fuiste" ... And I was sucked right in. And I grabbed all the other tapes I had, that heavy metal music I used to listen to, and I destroyed them ... I don't want to listen to any more music that's not in Spanish! And Gilda stuck and I started to like her and started buying her CDs ... And I started to collect other things. I saved my money and went shopping: I've got posters, everything I have in my house (Roberto, age 45, during group interview).

Even in the case of Roberto, who describes becoming a fan as a sort of conversion, an abrupt break and change in his life story, there is also a process of continuously making contact with people and things related to Gilda. Being a fan should be understood in processual terms, but is not always (or necessarily) linear or progressive, and largely depends on the fan's integration into a group whose common interest orbits around the singer.

Fandom can also originate in the emotional bond that forms when listening to Gilda's music. Fans describe that to get to know Gilda, listening to her music is critical. Once someone gets to know her, feeling affection for her just comes "naturally." Gilda's songs are also the most frequently cited reason for becoming a fan. For her followers, this attachment has nothing to do with personal taste; Roberto, in fact, used to like heavy metal before succumbing to Gilda's romantic cumbias. According to Semán and Vila, listeners use music "to establish themselves as social subjects, as significant for others, who in turn give them meaning in the social domain."[26] In addition, popular music is characterized by multiple and intense possibilities of interpellation, offering ways of being and behaving along with models for psychological and emotional satisfaction through sound, lyrics, and performances. For Gilda's fans, however, the explanation cannot be limited to musical interpellation and instead music mainly becomes important because *Gilda is in her songs*:

> I watched some videos where Gilda sends messages to people ... For me, Gilda's songs are all about things that happened to Gilda ... Because you feel them in your soul ... In one part of a video I saw, she says that you can't give up, you have to carry on ... that things will happen. That's the kind of things she conveyed to people ... (Mario, age 23, individual interview).

Gilda is present in her songs in several ways. First and foremost, this is because she wrote her own songs. Gilda's fans—and many others who enjoy her music—say they prefer her cumbia because of the lyrics. The fans emphasize the poetic value of the songs, because they were written by Gilda, who lived the situations they describe or was sensitive enough to appropriate the story of someone close to her and turn it into a song. In this regard, the fans do not value her creativity or her fertile imagination, but instead her ability to transmit her experience, as a parable or as advice, through song. Life experience is not merely the "inspiration" to write, and the story the songs tell interlace with the author, making Gilda the author into an ethical role model.

On the other hand, as an element of artistic performance, the song is valued because, compared with other female cumbia stars, Gilda "is the one who knew how to sing." Her thrilling voice makes the songs into something specific and different, conveying the message of the song and transmitting the same emotion every time someone hears her music. In this sense, beyond her recorded voice, Gilda is ultimately there every time one of her songs is played, an aural *manifestation* of Gilda.

Gilda, the only one

> She had something special ... You know what that's called? That is called having an angel. And not just anyone has an angel—it's very rare. So when someone who can't sing has an angel ... but you hear her singing, [you think] how can that be? It's ... This is something from above ... (Carlos, age 54).

Carlos is considered one of the most loyal members of the fan club, because he is a regular at the cemetery and zealous about all things related to Gilda. According to this fan, Gilda had and conveyed "an angel," a sort of appeal, an ability to attract the public, to stand out from the other singers, a gift that comes "from above."

Some researchers who study fandom opt to ask fans for the subjective or objective reasons they have chosen this actress, this singer, or that series as their object. Questions of this sort usually yield defensive or overly formal answers, because fans are often not entirely clear about why they chose a particular person to follow. Responses are composed *a posteriori* taking into account mainstream criteria of taste—the interviewer's or the public who they assume will read their answer. The difficulties to describe the singer's uniqueness are also related to the fact that fandom is a non-verbalized experience, "something else entirely." Stating that the feeling Gilda inspires "is impossible to explain" is already an explanation in itself, one that falls within the scope of the ineffable, of what can only be felt or lived in the flesh and the soul. It exceeds both, and by its very nature, it cannot be captured in words.

Charisma seems to be the attribute that gets the attention of fans and, according to Eco,[27] it is understood as a contemporary myth that represents the values of a society. If used as the sole explanation for fandom, however, this argument proves problematic, since some idols are precisely the contrary, offering a critique of both the status quo and the hegemonic order. Moreover, some idols are able to present themselves as having both dominant and subversive values, in the same way heroic figures do. These idols condense "at the same time an order and an anti-order, a need and a problem, an example of what is thinkable and a model of the impossible."[28] This is the case of both Elvis,[29] and Gilda, who presents the traditional image of the chaste woman and mother while also acting on her own desire and taking charge of her destiny. Fans, however, are unable to find the words to define the specific charisma they attribute to Gilda and can only liken it to having an "angel," and being exceptional.

> [Gilda] has something … You know when you're drawn to someone because they've got something … and it is not about how she's done up or her clothes … Because she wasn't like the others … The [other] girls showed off their asses and she didn't. Maybe that's what it was about her … [Gilda] wasn't like the others [female cumbia singers], she was normal. The others thought they were hot stuff because they were singers … but not Gilda. She was humble, like a regular person … Gilda was pretty skinny … she was pretty, but not seductive. Besides, the songs touched you … (Mario, fan club president).

Besides pointing out what differentiated Gilda from other contemporary singers, fans characterize her as a "regular," "humble" person who "approached people," and "a person like us, but extremely sensitive." The combination of all her unusual features—her voice, her sensitivity, her beauty, and her kindness—and the perceived proximity to the people in her audience are the key factors when defining her charisma.

The physical attractiveness of Gilda didn't require tight clothes or low-cut tops. As Claudio argued, "she didn't have to show off her body" because she had other qualities: she was "a good person" and "the only one who could sing," suggesting that the other female cumbia singers based their performances on pure seduction. This makes Gilda incomparable, unlike anyone else. Since it's impossible to compare her with any other cumbia singers, Gilda becomes part of a select group of singers whom fans consider outstanding; tango singer Carlos Gardel is the best example, since he is the only one who "sings better with each passing day."[30]

In different publications and videos, Gilda appears in the recording studio or at shows wearing clothes that were fashionable at the time, though she stands out from other singers. The female cumbia stars in the 1990s included Lia Crucet, nicknamed "the Tetamanti" because of her enormous bosom, and Gladys, "the Tucuman Bombshell." Both bleached their hair and girded their voluptuous curves in short, low-cut, colorful dresses. They defined the cumbia "look" for women and were mimicked by lesser-known singers. Gilda, in contrast, left her hair its natural brown and dressed more like the women who were dancing in the audience. Because she was naturally thin, she was not viewed as overtly sexual or seductive even when she donned a plunging neckline or a short miniskirt.

Analyzing the studio pictures and the images from CD inserts, it appears that her producers were betting on the singer's naïve and romantic image. For the cover of the album *Corazón Valiente* (Braveheart, 1995), Gilda is holding a bouquet, wearing a short lavender dress with a garland on her forehead.

During the Romanesque period, images of Catholic saints and virgins went through a process of "anthropomorphism" to make religious icons more relatable, attributing them with human feelings and desires.[31] Gilda took the opposite path with the art on *Corazón Valiente*, where the singer can be associated with beauty, purity, innocence, and desexualized sensuality, features that had never been seen before in the dominant aesthetics of the cumbia world. The image of Gilda in the lavender dress became her official image, replicated ad infinitum on prayer cards, medallions, statuettes, pictures, and other devotional items. Carozzi[32] referred to this as the restricted exhibition code: a series of gestures, phrases, and accessories that make a star into a recognizable character: Michael Jackson's white socks and glove, Elvis's pompadour, Evita's bun and raspy voice, and so on, are elements that allow others to identify them as characters while permitting them to perform with no potential for confusion.

Regardless of her musical talent or her beauty—which are both less important than the fact that she presents herself as simple, humble, and close to her public—what distinguishes Gilda is the fact that she performed without costumes or affect. Even on stage, a place that necessarily establishes a distance from the public, she "is just like anyone else," and "doesn't let it go to her head," reducing the natural distance of the stage by placing herself on the horizontal plane of *communitas*. This was, according to her fans, the secret to Gilda's charisma. In this regard, we should further consider the emphasis on everyday images of Gilda, on the fans' preference for pictures taken at home, where the singer is washing dishes, or wearing a simple cotton dress and no makeup, or holding a birthday cake. As Dyer[33] argues, the fact that the star is presented with an appearance and a personality, and as having more ordinary problems, does not mean she isn't special: the combination of the exceptional with the ordinary is precisely what sets her apart.

In this regard, what happens with Gilda has happened with other stars. Numerous scholars have recognized that authenticity is one of the qualities that fans value in an idol. Maradona, the Chicano singer Selena, Lady Diana, Madonna, and Bruce Springsteen[34] are considered "genuine" by their fans. For fans, "genuine" is used to refer to idols who are sincere, who wear their heart on their sleeve, who are loyal to their origins; there is, however, no concern for the "real" story or any "true" self. Thus, stars are both representations of people and "real" people: they are images produced, personalities built, as much as "characters" interpreting,[35] blurring, then, the distinction between the actor's authenticity and the character she is playing. Here it is necessary to emphasize the processual nature of being a star: the fan is necessary to the construction and performance of stardom. The idol and the fan depend on one another in order to exist, but not as a paradox that summarizes a universal desire to be recognized, not as illustrations of a relatively homogeneous process that justifies the "invisible hand" of the market through the production and consumption of cultural goods. Star and idol exist only in relation to the fan because the fans participate, because the fans actively produce the star—which is also a byproduct of fandom.

For Gilda's fans, like in Indian mythological films, the separation between actor and character is irrelevant. In these films, the actors and actresses playing gods spark fervor and devotion among the public, who would often remove their shoes and leave offerings in front of the screen; more affluent moviegoers even threw parties to worship them. What these films obscure, according to Das Gupta,[36] is the division between myth and fact, transforming the actor who represents a god into that god. As Srinivas[37] argued, this should not lead us to infer that audiences are so gullible as to believe that Indian gods and epic heroes are actually appearing on the screen. Following Latour,[38] it is only possible to understand how the line between fact and myth can be blurred if it becomes impossible to distinguish between reason and belief, between knowledge and illusion, and between construction and reality. Gilda is both real and artificial, and by analyzing her path to stardom, it is possible to observe how "construction and reality become *synonyms*."[39]

Following Latour,[40] then, Gilda is "neither wholly autonomous nor entirely built": the "illusion," as Gabriel described it, is something inherent to stars and their relationship to fans. And this illusion, both true and invented, is also produced by the fan's agency. Thus, fans' interest in "keeping Gilda's memory alive" and their concern for an adequate portrayal, spreading the word on who she "really" was and rectifying the mistakes published in the media, do not stem from strict adherence to the facts but from a desire to present the most reliable image of Gilda possible. Clearly, the need to emphasize a particular version denotes the presence of other narratives, parallel stories that remain in force. For fans, even though Miriam Bianchi may have performed sexual favors "to make it," among her many travesties, Gilda reached her destiny like in a fairy tale. To her fans, the "real" story is irrelevant, because it depends, in part, on them. This does not mean they refuse to acknowledge any negative characteristics

Gilda might have had; moral qualities are not the main fandom driver, if in fact they even enter into consideration. Gilda is not necessarily (or not always) a role model or someone fans want to identify with, either because she is an extraordinary being, or because her life is far from morally upright.

Thus, those who consider themselves the guardians of her memory are not concerned with an accurate biography. What is truly important for them is how they "met" her. The stories Gilda's fans recount are not Gilda's own stories and do not necessarily have the linear argument that characterizes hagiographies. Instead fans recount, in Carozzi's words,[41] "encounters that become memorable": the party when they first heard her music, the friendly gesture that made them feel loved, the night they dreamed about her, a song that gave relief at a difficult moment.

What they do know about Gilda's biography is based on what appeared in the press or on television. In their reading of her life, however, there are media filters and first-hand accounts obtained from family and friends who knew her when she was alive, or from their own experience or personal opinions on how Gilda would behave in certain circumstances. In this regard, it is not enough to acquire information about her life or know her songs by heart: fans have to *know her*. And *knowing her* involves accessing that special "something" that makes people feel attracted to her, inspiring love for her. It also involves letting Gilda into the fan's life, which means not just knowing her, but her *knowing them*.

Conclusions

Gilda's consecration as a star, a popular icon, and, ultimately, a myth of urban popular culture can only be understood if we look at the practices fans have developed over the last two decades. Even considering that most experiences are too intimate to share, *following* Gilda has become synonymous with accompanying her at the cemetery, cooking at a soup kitchen, talking to journalists time and again, visiting TV channels and festivals when one of her many impersonators perform, naming a daughter after her, organizing celebrations, and more recently, creating virtual groups and events through social media. But, most importantly, following Gilda twenty years after her death is a "mission": without the fans, they insist, Gilda would be left for dead. "To keep her memory alive," in mass media and social media; "to be with her" at the cemetery, but also in their homes; and "to help other people," like at the soup kitchen, are ways fans have found to follow her and to make her an extraordinary being.

Similarly to Latour's *factish*, the concept of *extraordinary beings* acknowledges the human origin of consecrated people, places, and times, pointing out the direct, active, and constitutive role of human agency and the possibly transitory nature of "extraordinariness." Gilda could not have been a star at the time of her death, just as after her death, she could not pass into oblivion. The process that took two decades, as Gilda went from an obscure corner of the tropical music market to the balcony of the Casa Rosada, would not have been possible without fans' agency.

6

God is in the House: Nick Cave, Religion, and Serbian Fandom

Sabina Hadžibulić

This chapter discusses Nick Cave fans' perception of his relation to religion.[1] Cave is one of the rock greats, with a decades-spanning career. Religion has always been a topic in all forms of his work. This chapter focuses on a group of Serbian fans, a group that is, due to their limited involvement in fan practices, not particularly visible, but certainly possesses extensive knowledge and intensive feelings for Cave's work. Because of the changeable position of religion in recent Serbian history, it seems relevant to discuss ways in which this group of fans interprets Cave's relation to religion, and what that means to them personally. Moreover, the way these fans relate Cave's religion to the religious situation in the society they live in is taken into consideration.

The goal of the chapter is to explore fans' views of Cave's relation to religion, with special emphasis on two particular matters. The first one refers to Cave's distinctive approach to religion. The second deals with criticism of established religion, particularly Christianity.[2] The analysis is based on data collected through Skype semi-structured interviews with Serbian diehard Cave fans.

After briefly introducing Cave's work and data on his presence in Serbia over the years, I will discuss his personal view of religion. The following section gives an insight into the position of religion in today's Serbian society. The main section of the chapter focuses on the analysis of fans' perception and interpretation of Cave's relation to religion.

The good son: Nick Cave

Nick Cave was born in 1957, and grew up in Victoria, Australia. In the beginning of the 1970s he first made himself heard as a singer and a song writer with the band The Boys Next Door, soon to become The Birthday Party. In the early 1980s, the band moved to London and made a breakthrough with its single "Release the Bats." Upon the band's demise in 1983, Cave formed his ongoing The Bad Seeds, with whom he has collaborated on sixteen studio albums over the last three decades. In 2006 Cave formed Grinderman as a side project to The Bad Seeds, and recorded two albums in the next three years. The band split up at the end of 2011, and Cave continued performing with The Bad Seeds. In addition to performances with the bands, Cave has, since the 1990s, performed live as a singer and piano player, his friend and fellow musician Warren Ellis on violin and accordion, and various performers on bass and drums.

Although best known for his musical work, Cave is a restless creator who successfully moves through genres and forms, from music and literature to screenwriting, acting, and even theatre.[3] A part of his diverse opus is "An Introduction to the Gospel according to Mark," which is his contribution to a 1998 Canongate Book pocket publication of The Gospel according to Mark. The lesson he gave for the BBC Radio 3 religion program in 1996 combined with the one he held at the Vienna Poetry Festival in 1998 is published as an audio recording, *The Secret Life of the Love Songs & The Flesh Made Word: Two Lectures by Nick Cave* in 2000.

Nick Cave performed in Serbia for the first time with The Bad Seeds in June 1990 in Belgrade, the capital of socialist Yugoslavia at that time.[4] Exactly eighteen years later, Cave and The Bad Seeds performed again in Belgrade, now Serbia's capital. In 2011 Grinderman's second album was promoted at the Exit music festival in Novi Sad.[5] The same festival hosted Cave with The Bad Seeds two years later. They performed in Belgrade again in 2017.

In November 2014, the film *20,000 Days on Earth* by Iain Forsyth and Jane Pollard about the life and work of Cave premiered in Belgrade. The film *One More Time with Feeling* by Andrew Dominik on Cave and The Bad Seeds' sixteenth studio album was presented in Serbian cinemas in May 2017. Moreover, both of Cave's novels as well as the collection of poetry, lyrics, and writings, *King Ink II*, have been translated and published in Serbia.

Oh my lord: Nick Cave on religion

The interaction with Christian theology and the Bible can be noticed throughout Cave's work—from lyrics, band names, and song titles to poetry, films, and talks. It dates from the early days with The Birthday Party and continues over the course of his versatile career. The list of his use of Christian imagery is extensive.[6] In an interview where he was accused of making a secular record with Grinderman, he explained: "God is in everything whether I'm mentioning him or not."[7]

Cave believes that he "deals with religion, love, violence, and sex at the same time as they are not separated from each other in any way, but are all part of the big stew."[8] To him, "writing comes as a form of protection, his way of making sense of the world."[9] In that regard, he once stated: "When I write, I feel spiritually elated. I become closer to God, and raise myself above a mediocre, flat, Earthly existence."[10] His relationship with God is generated through creative inspiration and, hence, is of an experiential kind. He admits:

> I'm a believer. I don't go to church. I don't belong to any particular religion, but I do believe in God … I've always had this faith, even if, at a certain time, I could not say it with the same conviction … For me, believing in God doesn't change life. It is neither an obstacle nor a relief. It has no influence on my behavior. Believing has nothing to do with morality, but with freedom and inspiration.[11]

Cave's words reveal that his relationship with God is not mediated by formal institutions and beliefs. It is rather a personal and direct relationship that keeps changing, and is connected to freedom and inspiration. He clearly distinguishes belief in God from belief in the relevance of organized religion. Moreover, Cave stated that he was "very interested in the Bible and the Christ story, but despised the Church."[12] As an eight-year-old boy he joined the choir at a local Anglican church and attended services for years. Nevertheless, he claims: "The God I heard preached about there seemed remote, alien, and uncertain."[13] Sometime later, he stated that he finds it hard to keep to any organized faith, though he likes the ritual. He explained: "A part of me likes that there is a community of people there, coming together with the same belief—that's a comforting thing. But, there is another part of me that wants to run a million miles away from that."[14] Cave has distanced himself from religious institutions. Christianity is deeply irritating to him. He believes that Christianity has misinterpreted the Bible, and that "the Church denies Christ his humanity, offering up a figure that we can perhaps 'praise' but never relate to."[15] In addition to that, Cave is very critical of "what religions are becoming and the more destructive they're becoming."[16] He believes that religion has gotten a really bad name, explaining:

> The concept of God in America is very different than it is in England. Because we see the horrendous outcome of religion as being an American thing, in which the name of God has been hijacked by a gang of psychopaths and bullies and homophobes, and the name of God has been used for their twisted agendas. So that you mention God, or belief in God, in England, it's almost associated with that kind of thinking.[17]

Cave's constant engagement with the Bible is a result of finding it an enormous source of inspiration. He referred to his work from the 1970s and 1980s as the Old Testament, and the 1990s and onwards as the New Testament.[18] He explains it further:

> The brutality of the Old Testament inspired me, the stories and grand gestures. I wrote that stuff up and it influenced the way I saw the world. What I'm trying to say is I didn't walk around in a rage thinking God is a hateful god. I was influenced by looking at the Bible, and it suited me in my life vision at the time to see things in that way.[19]

What came afterwards he describes as a state where he "started to feel a little kinder and warmer to the world, and at the same time started to read the New Testament."[20] He experienced a creative rebirth by connecting his creative visions to religious imagination through the figure of Christ. For him, "[Christ's] struggle is very much about the human struggle, and that's what I find so engrossing. There is no other story like it—not one that I respond to in the same way."[21]

And no more shall we part: Religion in Serbia

According to the last 2011 Census,[22] 91.2 percent of Serbian citizens declared themselves as religious. The vast majority (84.6 percent) is Orthodox and belongs to the autocephalous Serbian Orthodox Church.[23] Nevertheless, the situation has not always been the same. During the last century, Orthodoxy had gone from being a privileged official state religion before the Second World War to being a marginal and undesirable phenomenon over a fifty-year-long period of communist regime in socialist Yugoslavia. Finally, with the collapse of communism and disintegration of Yugoslavia in the last decade of the twentieth century, religion was revitalized and the Serbian Orthodox Church regained its credibility. It was at that time that Orthodoxy appeared as a significant factor in preserving the national identity of Serbs. The Serbian Orthodox Church became actively engaged in re-nationalization and homogenization, following a simple formula equating ethnic and confessional affiliation.

With the establishment of the first democratic government in 2000, the Serbian Orthodox Church and the state built a relationship characterized by higher and more frequent participation of the Serbian Orthodox Church in the state and political affairs. Changes are particularly visible in the public educational system as confessional religious education was (re)established in all Serbian schools in 2001, and the Orthodox Theological Faculty returned to the state-owned Belgrade University in 2010. Additionally, there is a strong demand from the Serbian Orthodox Church for the repossession of the property that was taken over as a part of the agrarian reform and the process of nationalization after the Second World War. Since 2001 Orthodox priests have been a part of the national army's mandatory staff. Orthodox religious celebrations stepped out of the private zone and became significant public events accepted and supported by the state and military authorities.[24]

Method and sample

My initial idea was to approach Serbian Nick Cave fans through Serbian fan media dedicated to Cave. I soon realized that those did not exist.[25] In my further quest, a music manager friend linked me with a friend of his, a longtime diehard Cave fan, who then proposed other respondents. I received similar help from two other friends. Eventually, the research sample became an example of a snowball sample formed from three different sources.

The informants are all highly educated professionals in their early forties, living in Belgrade. Four out of five are female. In terms of religious affiliation, three of them declare as believers but not church members, one is a church member, whereas one is agnostic. I talked with each of them via Skype on several occasions during April and May of 2016. This was preceded by e-mail introduction conversations at the beginning of the same year. All the interviews were conducted in Serbian, the informants' mother tongue, and later on translated into English by me, who also happens to be a Serbian Nick Cave fan. None of them is involved in any fan community, mostly because they feel no need to display their fandom publicly in such a way. However, they do listen to Cave's music, attend concerts, watch video clips and recorded concerts, as well as follow other forms of his work. In the analysis section below, names of the informants have been changed.

Straight to You: The analysis

In the remainder of this chapter I will look closely at the experiences of five Serbian Nick Cave fans. My primary focus is on the ways these fans understand and interpret Cave's personal approach to religion, as well as his criticism of established religion, particularly Christianity. I will refer to the responses according to their relevance for providing knowledge on topics in question.

Serbian fans on Cave's approach to religion

For most of the Serbian fans, the question of Cave's approach to religion seems enormously important to their understanding of his work. In connection with that, Ana, a fan with an almost three-decade-long fandom, argues:

> Religion is central to Nick Cave's work. If there were a frame that contained all the topics, and you saw those topics structured as concentric circles, then, the relation with God and religion would be the last circle, the biggest one that contained all the others. Even when he reflects on art, death, love … everything is contained in that last circle.

This comment suggests that fans associate religion in Cave's work with his unique way of interpreting the world. It is religion that provides him a lens through which he can better name and analyze important life issues to him such as art, love, and death. Therefore, it appears as a common denominator of all his creative expressions, which makes it particularly important for the comprehension of his work. A similar point is made by another fan, Mila, who believes that Cave's relation with religion dates from his early years and Christian upbringing: "When he was young he was afraid of God, he relocated the figure of God outside of himself." It changes as Cave becomes more mature as an artist: "Over time, he brings it closer. He is an artist, he keeps changing." However, it is in this relation that Mila recognizes the essence of his creation, and, consequently, acknowledges it as pivotal to his work: "Everything he does in life is in order to minimize the distance between God and himself. That's where his creation comes from."

For Ivana, a fan who closely followed Cave's career from the moment she attended his first concert in Belgrade, his approach to religion should not necessarily be comprehended as dominant or crucial. She finds Cave's artistic development to be complex, and hence interprets his connection to religion as just one of his many artistic expressions: "He had different phases in his artistic development. One can find a lot of things in his work … like, love for Marilyn

Monroe, or connection to Elvis Presley. I never found religion to be crucial to his work. It is just a part, but not a crucial one." In trying to explain what this distinctive approach means to her, she states:

> I think that Cave's fans, mostly my peers, grew up in times when religion did not matter. So, today, whenever someone tries to talk about it or even mentions religion it makes a sort of two-step-back attitude, it causes aversion. However, Cave talks about it in a subtle and special way ... he is not pushy, so that doesn't lead to aversion.

For many Serbian people who spent formative years in socialist Yugoslavia, religion still appears to be a delicate topic. Ivana's reasoning suggests that Nick Cave fans are, through their fandom, in a position to open up the door to this particular issue. Cave's unique way of presenting it through his artistic work results in generating an interest among his fans for consideration of religious matters which they were, to a great extent, unfamiliar with for a long time. This is elaborated further in Ivana's next comment, which draws on the experience of eleven Cave concert attendances:

> Cave is like a preacher man, he tells a story, he preaches at his concerts. He even has the same kind of voice and appearance ... He does not want to trick you, but to tell you so that you can see. He talks and gives an object lesson, so listeners have to question their deeds and thoughts. And it is very clear what he wants to say ... and you unconditionally believe in it!

This aforementioned belief is absolutely shared by three other fans that saw Cave's performances all over the world. One cannot ignore the impression that they all recognize a striking religious dimension in the way he presents his music on stage. Yet, at the same time, by having this stance, Cave additionally supports the way his fans interpret his entire work. They see him as a religious educator who takes on the role to directly transfer an important message through his lyrics. On one hand, their fandom brings them closer to religion and its issues, but, on the other, it distances them from the established way of understanding it. Ana particularly points this out:

> Cave thinks that God is wherever we look for him—in love, sex, but also drugs. He [Cave] is not running away from the dark side of man, and that's a very in-depth reflection on human nature—everything that exists, and we might say, was created by God, and should be acknowledged as human. We should not give advantage to one side, when one is nice and beautiful, and neglect the other when one is killing, making love, having deviant sexual intercourse. That's what I really appreciate about it, it is so different. Plus, he helps you think about it.

Ana greatly values Cave's approach to religion as she believes it offers a holistic view characterized by more mundane displays of human existence. She finds that approach to be closer to what the real world is all about. Her fandom, then, enables her to reflect on religious issues from a different angle which provides diverse knowledge. Thus, it helps her build her own view of the issues in question. Nevertheless, she is not sure if his approach is convenient for everyone, as she suspects it can offer wrong conclusions to young and unexperienced people: "He can help some young people to think about it [religion]. Although, he can also confuse them, as he deals with the dark side of human nature." It is as if, because of the peculiarity and complexity of Cave's approach to religion, she also addresses the fandom and finds it more suitable for mature and experienced fans.

The most striking example of Cave's approach to religion is found by Serbian fans in his vast body of love songs, which they highly appreciate. In that regard, Mila argues that the obvious connection between love and God in his love songs comes as logical since those two make a perfect entity: "I adore his love songs! Love and God are inseparable—one is in another and that's the essence!" Nina gives illustrative examples:

> There is a direct connection, starting from God being love—a Christian point of view. But, it is a special manifestation of it. Many of his songs are dedicated to some real or imaginary woman he was dating. And their presence is divine presence ... Those songs have different levels. Like, for example, "West Country Girl" is about his relationship with PJ Harvey, and those familiar with it can recognize her. On the other side, in many of his songs woman's presence is God or some divine messenger on Earth ... One of my favourite songs is "As I Sat Sadly by Her Side," where he is definitely in a dialogue with a woman, but I think that the woman is also an impersonation of some divine presence.

Significantly, Nina believes that Cave's starting point is Christianity, which is reinterpreted in his own way through the expression of deepest affection for women he is intimately attached to. That, further, provides him with a possibility to demonstrate different levels of that love. In some cases, his expression is based on a real life story. In others, it can be comprehended as a symbolic way to actualize his relation to God.

Serbian fans on Cave's criticism of established religion

Fans' views on Cave's criticism of established religion mostly stem from the way they experience his personality. For Nina, whose fandom dates from high school days, Cave is a creative person who keeps redefining himself through constant demonstration of independence. She explains it:

> It is as if he keeps resisting authorities. Like, "I refuse someone to tell me what to think and how to act." But, it is also a bit of rebellion. Well, Cave demonstrated typical behavior of an adolescent who does everything against his father, and he showed it on the first three or four albums—punk, madness, sex, drugs, and rock and roll in Berlin ... He doesn't want someone to determine in which way he should communicate with God, and what sort of relationship he should have. And he refuses rules, prohibitions, and dogma imposed by the church.

The previous line of arguments is largely supported by Teo, a fan keenly following Cave's work for more than two decades:

> Why would he agree with something imposed by some religious organization?! I mean, he has a head of his own; he is a talented thinker ... of course he cannot obey the church! The way he always lived is unique ... I don't see why it would make any difference in terms of religion. I am sure he is able to find his own way through religion.

Obviously, Cave's criticism of established religion is interpreted as expected or even logical among his fans. Cave is regarded as an independent intellectual who always finds a unique way to express himself regardless of the issue. He never obeys the rules, but follows his own personal cravings and goals. That is evident in both his life and career. Significantly, these comments show that fans are aware of and particularly emphasize the distinction between religion and church. They don't find it problematic that Cave is religious, but rather appreciate his aspiration to keep and fight for his personal view on religion which differs from the established one. Consequently, they accept Cave's criticism of established religion in a positive manner. In this respect, Nina argues:

> I think Cave has no songs that are politically engaged, not even in terms of church. He is not like Bob Dylan. He is more into personal dilemmas, doubts, but he still makes an impact on his listeners. Because, when you listen to him you think: "Hey, he is right, that's it! It's not only my dilemma, there is someone else feeling the same."

Similarly, Ivana, who declared as a believer but not a church member, says:

> One is able to see his relation towards the church in some of his songs. The best representative of this critique is "God is in the House." That's absolutely it! I completely agree with him. He talks about God-fearing people who sit in their houses with everything inside tidy and in perfect order as God is present ... God

is in the house. But, in fact, you see that they are not honest, but just scared and want God to leave the house. Well, that I find to be a real critique of the church.

Though they are aware that Cave's criticism is not always explicit, nor does it tend to generate some kind of activism among listeners, the fans take it seriously. They use the resources offered by their fandom—such as the lyrics about the criticism of established religion—to recognize the problems they seem to be concerned with. It is Cave's critical insight that provides a meaningful support to their personal speculations.

Serbian fans on the religious situation in Serbia

Accordingly, not only do Serbian Nick Cave fans identify themselves with him, but they also feel empowered by his critique. In connection to that, Ivana continues:

> There are so many reasons to criticize the church in Serbia. I stopped looking at religion through the church a long time ago, as wherever you turn around and look you see something stupid and ugly that has nothing to do with morals, especially not religious ones. And that keeps happening here! So, as far as I am concerned, Cave has my full support. At least, he will talk on my behalf. 'Cause, if one has a chance to express oneself and criticize, then that's totally OK. So, he is doing it for me, too.

In a similar manner, Teo, the only agnostic among my interviewees, claims:

> Cave has a very good attitude. He is someone who passed through so much, lived and worked on different continents, in big cosmopolitan areas, various cultural environments, and, hence, met many different religions and churches ... On the other hand, it is easy to reach people through music; it takes a few sentences and the message is direct ... I totally approve his critique due to the church's role in history ... It has been so manipulative towards people. If there would have been more of that kind of critique the church would perhaps be, so to say, more progressive nowadays.

Both Ivana and Teo are critical towards established religion themselves, and therefore supportive of Cave's attitude. Nevertheless, they feel limited in expressing their criticism. In that regard, Cave's critical view echoes even louder as they believe he is the one eligible to spread the message on their behalf. Ivana explicitly refers to the experience of living in Serbia as crucial for her understanding of established religion and her relation to the church. This argument happens to be of great importance for other fans, too. They easily connect to it when explaining the significance of Cave's criticism. Nina, a believer but not a church member, reflects on this matter:

> Nowadays, everyone is religious in Serbia as they were all communists once upon a time. They are not honest in what they do anymore … And much fewer people live in harmony with Christian principles and ideals now than in communism. Those are now people that steal, cheat, and even cheat on their wives … That's why I don't believe in church. That's not moral and I don't see they are showing what modesty and refraining from sin is by the way they live … During communism the church was separated from the state, and the state was not proscribing how to behave as a religious person. If you are one, then you know what to do, and that's it. And today, the church and the state's leadership have a totally different view on that, and they propagate something that cannot exist since Serbia is a state of all citizens, and not only Serbs … I think it would be brilliant to have someone in Serbia that deals with the church in a way Cave does; someone who reflects on things in the same way. It would make the society much healthier and wealthier.

In connection to that, the only church member among the interviewees, Mila, demonstrated a similar attitude, although in a more apologetic manner:

> It is inevitable to criticize the church. At least, this one that we have … I don't have contacts with other churches … I have a relative who is a priest. He has a very positive life attitude, and one can really look at him as a role model. He told me once, regarding the Serbian Orthodox Church, that "there is a rotten apple in every barrel." And I do believe that's how it is. If our society changes in the wrong direction, so the percentage of rotten apples is changing and growing. That reflects on the church, too. That's how it is with the state apparatus, church, health system, school, and family. We are all one organism. So, it is applicable to every segment of society.

Being in their early forties, the fans witnessed a prolonged post-socialist transformation that Serbian society has been passing through for two and a half decades now. Complex and comprehensive changes in society have had a significant impact on the position of religion, especially the Serbian Orthodox Church. In that regard, the fans make a clear distinction between Serbia during communism and now. Nina, just like Ivana, is very disappointed and critical of the current situation. Her bitter everyday experience based on the observation of church members' behavior, as well as following state and church politics, has had a direct influence on her negative view of established religion. She finds it hard to believe in church members' genuine faith as she experiences immorality in every social sphere. Moreover, she seems particularly upset about the absence of respect for diversity in today's Serbia. On the other hand, Mila, as a church member, generally has no doubts of the Serbian Orthodox Church itself. However, she is aware of the changes happening in all Serbian institutions and, hence, supports critique as an inevitable tool for reconsidering institutions' contribution to Serbian society.

Jesus of the moon: Conclusion

Nick Cave is an artist who continuously uses Christian imagery in different forms of his work throughout his career. Nevertheless, his religious beliefs are not related to institutional religion, but rather connected to a unique personal view on freedom and creative inspiration.

For Serbian diehard fans, his distinctive approach to religion is a strong statement of independence. Hence, many find it central to his whole work. Having this in mind, it is not hard to grasp the impact it has on them despite its unique nature. Cave appears as a kind of preacher man who, by spreading the critical word on the contemporary world, gives them a resource through which they open up important questions on religion in their own lives. Furthermore, it helps them contemplate significant religious changes in the Serbian society in which they live. Therefore, their acclaim for Cave's criticism is not hard to fathom. Through their fandom they recognize the immense need for continuous critique. At the same time, it supports their belief in its power for the benefit of all.

7

I'm Your Messiah and You're the Reason Why: Para-Religiosity in the Fandom around Prince

Carla Schriever

Within the fan culture of late pop icon Prince, religious narratives seem to involve diverse contradictions. While joining in faith and devotion for their fan object Prince, fans tended to be known for harsh criticism which even included practices of hate, coming close to what Jenkins calls "aca-fandom."[1] Even though the Prince fan community can be understood as long-term or even life-course fans, their worship practices vary from religious practices in other popular music fandoms, and I would like to examine these differences in this chapter.

Fandom and religion

Bickerdike turns to the theories of Matt Hills and Henry Jenkins to examine the relationship between fandom and religion as having been incited by "faith, personal taste and applicable societal norms differing from each individual."[2] In becoming a fan, diverse aspects of social norms and personal motivations and beliefs connect and eventually cling to an object featuring the needed characteristics the fan is aiming to fulfill. This fulfillment of needs tends to offer a religious understanding, even though the individual fan may refuse to believe this. However, fandom and fan practice, especially if understood in community terms, are abstract categories of collective practice, just like religion.[3] Similar practices such as gathering, the meaning of certain symbols, collective singing, certain dress practices, and the collection and sharing of associated goods resemble proceedings within different religious communities. In this dimension Hills perceives religion as offering a "template model for fandom practices" as both are "centered around acts of devotion."[4] In comparing fandom with religion

I would argue that fandom is not the simple replacement of religion but a para-religious and secular practice in a world centered around the fulfillment of individual needs.[5] According to Cavicchi's study on Springsteen fans,[6] fandom contains diverse parallels to religious practices, especially in the "development of a close attachment to an unobtainable Other, a kind of moral orientation, a daily life devoted to the inspiration and a community based on a shared assumption of devotion."[7] Bickerdike[8] continues this notion in perceiving the spiritual practices within fandom communities by focusing on an object which is designed in physical unreachability but nevertheless always available with a similar array of believers. She focuses on what I would like to call the "metaphysical" aspects of fandom being mediated by the work cooperation of the artist, which even transcends his or her physical existence, and the mediated narrative. I would divide this into the media-narrative which is a part of the fans' knowledge and what I would call personal-narrative featuring diverse emotional experiences the fan has had with the fan object over time, including physical encounters, face to face interactions, co-existence in the same space and time (e.g. concerts), individual emotional states concerning the artist's work and even dreams about or associated with their fan object. This mediated narrative combined with the importance of collective practice influences the fan's dimension of devotion. Rojek argues that, in contrast to religion, "celebrity culture is only a cluster of human relationships in which mutual passion typically operates without physical interaction."[9] Fandom seems to involve physical and metaphysical dimensions which seem to be different to dimensions and practices offered in religious communities. But they also share extensive features, such as a definition of canon and non-canon within community; both expressions of belief encourage massive amounts of community, both own special/sacred places of worship, and both change the devotees/fans' approach to life in general, which I will examine in the following research.

To examine the individual practices of fan worship I conducted an interview-based research with European Prince fans, which offered a closer look into personal practices of fan faith and community practices. First one has to understand that the fan culture around Prince features special characteristics which are influenced by the artist's antipathy against mainstream media discourse by the beginning of the 1990s. Most of the interviewed fans became fans during Prince's mainstream success "Purple Rain"[10] in the early 80s. Being in their adolescence, these new fans experienced an attraction because of the artist's anti-normative ideas, dressing practices, and behavior, which allowed a new understanding of normativity, especially because most of them grew up in middle-class environments: "He was so different from anyone I have ever seen, his shows were eye-opening" (Hannah, 46).[11] "There was no one who could just walk in a room, wearing high heels and still being the worst of all" (Mark, 51). To gain a better understanding of the different aspects of their fan/worship practices, the participants were interviewed via an online video-chat with open questions to allow them to explain their personal motivations and developments over time. Since most of them started their fandom in the 80s, Prince was at the height of his career. He often referred to religious topics which allude to some kind of self-construction as a messianic figure, a narrative that was later continued by a majority of the interviewees for an average course of thirty-five years. The selected interview participants are all from Europe, feature an analogous social background, and are part of Prince's most solid fan group since the beginning of his career, since he mainly focused on Europe within the last twenty years with concerts or releases. So the participants of my study had the possibility to experience physical and metaphysical dimensions of their fandom and to share wide knowledge of their fan culture canon and para-religious practices. This study derives from participant observation, since I have been part of the fandom for over ten years, which separates my own fandom practice from my participants because of the duration. In this case study I sought to explore the contradictory relationship many fans established to their fan object over the course of their fandom. Moreover I will focus on the physical and metaphysical dimension of fandom practice and on the sacredness of object-associated places and pilgrimage. In the end I will consider the fans' para-religious practices before and after his death in April 2016, and conclude the dimension of fan devotion transcending the life of the fan object.

Fandom, worship, and narrative

In the beginning of the 1980s, when "Purple Rain" was released, Prince was at the height of his success. He designed his stage persona to become an ambiguous figure, keeping his age, his gender, and his sexual orientation a mystery. Even though his shows used to be a mixture of sexually explicit lyrics, dance moves, and idioms, he always used to refer to God, even wearing a cross, depicting himself as a Christian. This combination of Christian motifs and sexual connotations irritated many potential recipients and invited a huge media hype around his persona. His fans, young adults in this time, soaked in his anti-normative ideas on how to combine religious practices and sexual fantasies in stage performances. His textual approaches to topics of sex and faith formed a different understanding of religious practices for many of his young fans: "Why hate your body, your desire? He taught me how to love my body, it is God-given" (Clare, 44). This revaluation offered a different ingress to the dimension of fandom practices: "For us he was the epitome of a new world, a spiritual leader" (Markus, 43). By ending concerts with songs like "The Love We Make," featuring a sexual connoted reading as well as religious motifs, was meant to reconcile the dimension of religious practices, obeying God. Following the idol's (Prince's) rules of love and peace and joining a movement designed for creating a more peaceful world: "Sacred is the prayer that asks 4 nothing, while seeking 2 give thanks 4 every breath we take, Blessed are we inside this prayer, 4 in the new world, we will be there."[12] Narratives in dreaming about a new joint world in which human beings would continue to strive for peace and togetherness built a major part of every concert experience. At the end of a 1989 concert in Dortmund, part of the LoveSexy tour, one can hear the crowd reciting the song's lyrics: "Love is God, God is love, girls and boys love God above."[13] The joint experience of religiously connoted songs and quotations led many fans to a new understanding of Christian terms. They felt affected by the combination of believing in a higher force while simultaneously believing in the prophet being Prince. When asked how this connection between religious terms and sexuality was received by his fans, many of them "see both as intertwined to understand the whole picture of life, things that are missing in religion" (Harry, 41). This combination showed its influence on the recipients by adding to their own ideas or even going beyond them to open up new dimensions: "Well, sex was created by God as the highest expression of love and God is Love so it really goes hand in hand, that's what I understand and the meaning I get" (Donnie, 48).

In addition, sexually connoted songs on albums, such as, for example, the famous "Darling Nikki"[14] which deals with a promiscuous woman dragging the male persona into sexual intercourse, to which he gladly consents, end with the sound of rain. Touré[15] argues that the sound of rain or water which is used at the end or directly after a song with sexual content, signifies an act of purification and thus a dedication to God and the admission of sins:

> To be honest, there is a paradox between both (religion/sexuality) where Prince is concerned. It seemed as if he had freedom within himself to behave in a very sexual way, and then to redeem his sin, he would have praise to God and declare his love for him. As an onlooker, this gave me a kind of comfort in that this

person I have chosen to follow so closely has license to be naughty because at the end of it all, he devotes himself to God. That made me less guilty as a consumer with the product I was buying into (Raymond, 55).

The different approaches to the combination of religion and sexuality formed a fan culture that became highly diverse concerning personal identities but also in the way of interpreting the artist's testimony. The religious dimension of fandom increased when the fandom narrative engaged with the para-religious depiction of the artist himself, reaching its peak by the mid-1990s when Prince changed his name into an unpronounceable symbol to regain his independence as an artist. The glyph merged ancient symbols for man and woman, creating a combination of female and male sign with a musical note. Mitch Monson, who designed the symbol logo, explained: "Like a human body, it's asymmetrical, imperfect. Lastly, the symbol also evokes a cross. It's impossible to know the depths of Prince's intentions, but the Love Symbol swiftly harmonizes ideas often in conflict—man vs. woman, sex vs. religion."[16] With the harmonization and the acceptance of everybody who was part of this one sign, it became the religious symbol for his fan community even after his death. The artist's self-depiction was read as being somehow messianic, a reason for many fans to take up the symbol and to use it in the course of their everyday fan practices, for example by wearing it as a necklace, or even having it scratched into their skin as tattoos. Wearing a Prince symbol defines a fan as belonging to the canon-knowing community and differentiates him or her from outsiders or regular fans. The knowledge they share also combines the respect for their para-religious leader and his wishes even when they contradict with fan's desires. Even though many fans continuously perceive him as their messiah or some form of spiritual leader since the beginning of their fandom, they experience a conflict between their own religion, for example Christianity, and understanding Prince as their messiah. This evokes two sides to Prince: Prince as the physical existence, the private person, and Prince as the stage persona, the owner of his artistic work and rights. For popular music fan cultures, using the artist's work for fan creativity seems a natural practice to show one's adoration, if given to the fan object or made available exclusively within the culture. Creating associated art work, covering songs, or writing fan fiction seems to belong to many different fan culture canons. Within the fan culture around Prince this has always been a controversial issue. The artist's approach was to give his fans less opportunity to buy merchandise, and at the same time forbidding them to create their own to honor him, posting videos on video channels like YouTube, filming at concerts, or even sharing pictures online. If fans tried to express their adoration in one of the enumerated forms, he used to sue them, a controversy that problematized the relationship between fans and the artist. In the last twenty years, this has greatly affected the fan community canon, because it divided fans into certain groups: those who respected his wishes and reduced their acts of devotion to fit his demand, and those who used to get into fights with him again and again:

> Once I was visiting Paisley Park, I met him there and we had a talk, he wanted to know how many bootlegs I owned and if I would give them back to him. I explained to him that I bought a lot and that I did it to express my love for him and that I will never let go of them. He turned away and I was escorted by his guards (Raymond, 55).

The quoted fan did not end his fandom at the doormat of Paisley Park, but continued like others who were sued on copyright issues and had to pay hundreds of dollars, a no-go for many fan communities. Respecting the artist and his rights is still one of the highest rules in fandom practice, but nevertheless getting into fights with him seemed to be equally important: "Now that he's gone, I will not post any more videos to YouTube—I don't see any sense to that anymore" (Frank, 47).

To tackle the sensitive area of his artistic rights seemed to be a way of getting in contact with their messiah, even in making him mad. It was a way to gain his attention which seemed to be worth the effort, money, and sometimes even pain. The results of the interviews show that this form of possible interaction and attention was ended by his death, and in this way doesn't need to be continued as the fan culture transformed into private space practice, which I will later on examine in more detail.

Even wearing the symbol, which he used to wear or use as stage decor, used to be a controversial topic in the fan-star interrelation. Even though for many fans the symbol was a highly para-religiously connoted sign, symbolizing their membership of the community and their devotion to Prince, fans had to turn to their own creative surroundings because of a lack of suitable manufactured jewelry by the artist himself. "I don't wear a cross, I wear a Prince symbol" (Martin, 45).

Fans used the symbol to identify each other and to situate themselves within the fandom hierarchy. Wearing the symbol means (even today) believing in the freedom of the artist's rights (even if there sometimes a contradictory issue), believing in the unity of the fan culture, while preferring the term fam, an acronym for family, over the term fan, which is considered as fanatic, and believing in the protection of the artist's property and his "love4oneanother" ethics, which have always been part of concerts and other gatherings. The religious dimension of the "Love4oneanother"[17] focus derives from the idea of Christian altruism; the topic was used by the artist to refer to the focus of his work in the late 1990s, in which he entitled a charity organization and a music video anthology with this name. For fans "Love4oneanother" has always been a part of their shared ethical canon, meaning to respect and to include the diversity of people gathering in the fandom around Prince. Even though this ethics always seemed to be in the foreground for many fans, it was perhaps suspended concerning concert experiences.

Fandom and metaphysical physicality

Many fans described their fandom as being majorly structured around live performances/concerts of the artist. Since the lack of mainstream media marketing led to unstructured tour schedules creating last-minute ticket sales and show notices, fans had to adapt to these practices to keep track of the artist's career. The metaphysical concert experience is understood as the most desirable artefact for fans in the culture; "collecting" these nonrecurring moments was of high importance for fans and for the fandom hierarchy. To situate oneself in the structure of fandom, the amount of concert experiences and the specifics of time, venue, duration, and set lists was important. Because of the short-term notice of concerts within the last fifteen years, fans had to organize their lives around fandom to participate regularly; this also included assigning concert participation a priority in one's personal life. "If he announced a concert for the next day, I called sick to work and left in the early morning hours right after I secured my tickets, everybody at home was informed. It was a life, always on call for him!" (Tim, 39).

Even family and job responsibilities had to step aside in order to focus exclusively on the participation opportunities of the fandom. In the context of my study I even talked to interviewees who told me that everyone at work knew about their priorities, and that they were allowed time off to attend concerts or even associated events. Since concerts were sold out within few minutes, fans did not have much time to reconsider their possibilities. "It just had to work—and it always did, somehow" (Maria, 41).

Being able to participate in concerts did not solely affect the fan interrelation, but was an expression of adoration for the artist. Since fans traveled for long distances (across Europe) to witness as many concerts as possible regardless of social responsibilities and even financial or health issues, I wanted to understand the effect these concerts had on them, as a single individual, in their interrelation with other fans and with the artist. Even though a front-row phenomenon seems to exist in most popular music fan cultures it appears to be gainful to revisit the motives behind the attraction of the first row, considering its physical and metaphysical dimension.

Prince had always constructed his persona in terms of a certain unreachability, giving few interviews, not signing autographs or interacting with fans. In their identification process with an idol, we know from Fritzsche's[18] study of popular music culture that fans tend to seek a certain proximity to their fan object. This seems to be the need to transgress the metaphysical relation and to create a physical reality of interrelation and coexistence. During the concert, the fan object, which only exists in the fan's mind in daily life experience, reveals itself as a physical human being. The experience of this physical coexistence adds to the connection between fan and fan object. In the moment in which the artist comes to the stage, the mediated narrative becomes a tangible materiality. In comparison with religious practices, the concert hall offers a space for community gatherings, in which people can sing and consume song narratives together. The mediated power of community is organized by the preacher, the God, the artist giving his teachings to the devotees, the fans: "Whenever I feel like I need answers in my life—I always return to what he taught me!" (Nadina, 41).

Another comparable element can be seen in the physical distance between the "holy" and the "devotee"; the stage can be understood as some form of altar for the mass. The holiness of the concert makes it appear unreachable. The fans are located on a lower level or on higher levels (seating) but with even more distance. Considering the standing places before the stage, this seems to symbolize the separation between the space of the "holy" and the space reserved for the "devotee." The space which is indicated between the stage/altar and the standing level/prayer benches separates the physical from the metaphysical. The fan object represents itself as unreachable and in this way it retains its metaphysical dimension. In the studied fan culture I witnessed situations in which the border was suspended and fans were welcomed on stage, but even at the same level fans stayed at a certain distance, which had not been discussed before accessing the stage. It was clear that physical contact was prohibited, so that fans who transgressed this border did not receive recognition in their community but were criticized or even expelled. The metaphysical element was also strengthened by the fans' wish to get as close a look at the stage border as possible, which was mostly described as aiming to "feel his energy" (Paul, 46); " experience his aura" (Tina, 44); or "to be showered with his light" (Mark, 51).

Expressions like these emphasize the metaphysical dimension of front-row experiences. The willingness to feel a certain metaphysical connection between the artist and the fan seemed to be the ambition for concert participation for many fans for a timeline lasting over decades. During the event, the metaphysical relation, the mediated narrative, the fan's unfulfilled wishes and fantasies cling together with the fact of physical coexistence, which evoke the possibility of a physical interaction. The dimension of this physicality also features metaphysical components that are charged with a para-religious significance, so that having the ability to transgress the border between physical and metaphysical by actual interpersonal contact involves a connection between the metaphysical longing and the actual encounter on this physical level. A simple touch of hands can be connoted as an act of blessing, which the fan/devotee receives from the metaphysical relation to the fan object: "When his hand touched mine—I felt like struck by lightning" (Mathis, 41).

Another dimension—Paisley Park

This interrelation of metaphysical and physical levels can also be examined by focusing on places of interaction from concert venues to associated places but especially when focusing on fans' relation to Paisley Park, Prince's studio complex built in 1988, and also his home during the last years. Deriving from the idea of metaphysical connotation I would like to focus on Paisley Park's physical connotations for the fans and its metaphysical relation, comparing the connotations of pre-death and post-death of the artist.

Considering fandom in connection with faith and religious practice raises the issue of a physical place for community gatherings. Since concert venues are highly temporary, another space is needed to express community, faith practices, and metaphysical focus. Paisley Park was built by Prince in Chanhassen, a suburban area of Minneapolis, in 1988, and designed by the architecture company BOTO Design from California. It contains two live music venues, rehearsal studios, archives, and private spaces. It has always been partly open to the public and for other musicians, using it as a recording studio, but it has also served as a space for small concerts, dance parties, and fan gatherings organized by Prince. Within the last years (2012–16) Paisley Park was intensively used for dance parties, which were organized and announced at short-term notice by the artist himself. In the early 2000s fans were invited for celebrations of different albums and projects, which were released at the time or have remained unreleased. In January 2016 he kicked off his "Spotlight, Piano and a Microphone"-tour in this venue, his home. Precisely four months after the concert he was found dead in the elevator.

Paisley Park has always given his stardom a stable, highly visible anchor in the physical world, and allowed fans to physically and metaphysically visit the idea of Paisley Park as it was described in the 1985 same-titled song "Paisley Park" which was featured on the record *Around the World in a Day*, his follow-up album after his mainstream success *Purple Rain*. With the phrases "There is a park that is known, 4 the face it attracts" and "the smile on their faces/it speaks of profound inner peace" shows that Paisley Park, in which these colorful people, the fans, share "a lifetime lease," opens up a religious dimension. The metaphysical dimension is understood in focusing on the lyrics, which say: "Admission is easy, just say you believe and come to this place in your heart. Paisley Park is in your heart."[19] Believing in the metaphysical narrative of an imaginary world in which everyone is accepted in their diverse individualities, the narrative of Paisley Park includes freedom of social rules and normativity: "Come 2 the park/And play with us/There aren't any rules/."[20] In Paisley Park, the idiom of believing in the transcendental place of Paisley Park affects the perception of Paisley Park even today. Fans that were able to visit the Park when Prince was still alive described the experience as life-changing: "There is no place like Paisley Park, you feel so welcomed and it's just like paradise" (Joan, 50).

The metaphor of Paisley Park comes to life in the tangible materiality of the building itself, containing all song, stardom, and fandom narratives. The materiality of Paisley Park structures the immaterial narratives and feelings combined in fandom practices. Even if never actually visited, the reality of Paisley Park as a building allows fans a place to go, a place to turn to, if they feel lost in the world. This way Paisley Park combines both dimensions, the church where the devotees come together to seek closure to the "holy" and to regain strength in commune singing and blessing (through performance), and the community center where groups of fans have the ability to practice their fandom together in an open space, which is seen as protected from other influences. "Being at Paisley Park was kind of being in a hide-out to me. I never wanted to return to normal life" (Claudia, 38).

Considering the notion of escapism, Paisley Park served as an immaterial and material anchor for the fans. Being in Paisley Park, being able to walk through the same entrance and to visit the same rooms gave fans the ability to become part of a narrative, fictional universe. Being a guest at Paisley Park also meant to follow the rules of the house, which for example excluded any kind of photography or recording. Taking photographs was normally prohibited, just as in a religious space. Fans were used to the rules, so they even corrected each other, if there was a case of violation of any rule. Comparing Hills's statements on Elvis and Graceland,[21] one could understand Paisley Park as follows: With Paisley Park "the significance of [in this case Prince]—something which would otherwise tend to be free-floating, and incidental to the process of signification—can be contained or 'anchored' in a visible, physical and public fashion."

That Paisley Park shares physical and metaphysical dimensions has also been discussed by Unsie Zuege, a journalist working for the *Chanhassen Villager*, a local paper in Prince's hometown. In a text published in April 2016, just before Prince's sudden death,[22] she explains how Paisley Park made it to the "Final Four" in the "Tournament of Fictional Places"—even though it was the only actual place on the list (featuring, for example, Hogwarts as well). In the end, Paisley Park won.[23]

In considering Paisley Park as a fictional place the journalists of the *Chanhassen Villager* draw their attention to the fact that Prince had written a song entitled "Paisley Park" in 1985 which constituted Paisley Park as an imaginary place above its physical existence.

Since after the death of Prince, Paisley Park in its imaginary components gained my attention, I decided to interview the journalist Unsie Zuege via email. She explained her understanding of Paisley Park as follows:

> My view is that Paisley Park is a state of mind, outlined so well in its song lyrics. A place where everyone belongs, and there is love and peace. And if that place could exist, we'd all choose to live there. And, yet, it does exist, and is now available to the public and to all his fans around the world. They can come to the physical Paisley Park, made of mortar and stone, so to speak, and visit it, and imagine how Prince saw his world. It is a magical, artful and spiritual space that Prince created to enhance his creative energy and focus on his work. No distractions. Just surrounded by everything he loved; the space was designed so that where ever Prince was in Paisley Park, when the muse hit him, he could plug in his guitar or electric piano in any room—any room in the building—and record whatever crossed his mind, anytime of night or day.[24]

Zuege's text shows that Paisley Park was understood as both the physical place, the building, and the metaphysical dimension mediated in the song lyrics but also in a lot of fan narratives and discourses. The importance of Paisley Park was that it was highly stable, and over the years it was a place to turn to for fans:

"Sometimes, I just wish I could hop on a plane, go to Paisley Park—and never return" (Barbara, 41).

That Prince died at Paisley Park serves as a form of consolation for many fans, which is also a reference to a song's narrative. In "Let's Go Crazy," one of Prince's most frequently performed songs, the lyrics are as follows: "Never let the elevator bring U down/Oh no/Punch a higher floor."[25] In fan culture, there seems to be a connection between the song's narrative and the physical happenings concerning the death of their idol. The "punching of a higher floor" seems to involve the notion that Paisley Park is seen as closer to a holy dimension than any other place within the culture. This narrative seems to be continued by the family's decision to put Prince's ashes on display in Paisley Park. The urn was custom-designed as a miniature model of the actual building, including details from both exterior and interior (e.g. a purple piano). The decision to put his urn on display became a highly controversial issue within the fan culture: "I feel glad that he's home" (Anna, 41); "Putting an urn on display is so tasteless, he was such a private person" (Tom, 48); "He is where he belongs and all of us have the chance to pay a visit" (Maria, 38).

Considering the connection with religious practices, it can be said that many churches and spiritual places of community contain the remains of their spiritual or religious leaders, which are also a place of remembrance. Knowing that Elvis has been buried close to Graceland allows fans to remain in "physical" contact with the descended. Having Prince buried in a miniature of his own house strengthens the significance of Paisley Park for the community. Paisley Park now functions as the epitome of a re-envisioned past coming to life. Death, especially under these circumstances, allows the re-telling of the para-religious narrative and reinforces the meaning of Paisley Park for the community. Fans are now able to book tours through Paisley Park, which makes fan pilgrimage easier to arrange than at any time previously. I would like to draw a parallel to Elvis and Graceland, in saying that Paisley Park "has had a significant and largely unacknowledged impact on the shape of his stardom and especially for his fan community, which echoes the importance of a real time space."[26]

Conclusion

In engaging with the idea of a para-religious structure in the fandom around Prince, one has to revisit the fact that many fans have been long-term fans for the course of over thirty years. Since fandom memberships have stayed very stable over the years, fans have been able to highly adapt to the artist's demands, ethics, and religious significations. They grew and they changed with him and developed a shared canon, so that now after his decease they express their responsibility for his legacy and the given respect for his property, terms in which they criticize the company running Paisley Park for caring less about his property after some fans climbed a piano during a tour. The dimension of criticism resembled the desecration of religious artefacts.

Even though Prince no longer is physically reachable, all interviewed fans addressed the topic of life guidance. Especially after his decease, many of the participants felt like he "transcended into another dimension" still giving advice and closure in times of emotional trouble. Focusing on the para-religious narrative, Prince fans seem to engage closely with the idea of the metaphysical. The metaphysical importance of particular places of coexistence with their fan objects (like concert venues, clubs, and also Paisley Park itself) will continue for years to come. Also these places will always carry a certain significance in the individual fan narrative. The relation to associated places and objects already is and will be highlighted the more that time passes. For the fan culture, their metaphysical relation to Prince who guided them through a diversity of life decisions, plans, and experiences, will stay intact, and for some this dimension will overlap with the other over the course of time, preserving an ideal figure constructed for their individual needs of worship. For some fans, after his decease the textual world of his songs appears even more linked to the mediated fan narratives, some combining it with the trope of self-fulfilling destiny in which song lyrics gain a tangible reality in the occurrences around April 21, 2016:

> He died in April, like in the words of "Sometimes it Snows in April" in which he is mourning his imaginary friend Tracy, which used to be the family name of his character in the movie *Under the Cherry Moon*.[27] In the night of his decease there was a full red (cherry) moon over his hometown and a rainbow the next day, just like it can be found on the cover of *Around the World in a Day*. I am sure that destiny fulfilled itself with him tweeting a few days before his death answering the health concerns of his fans with "Wait a few days before U waste any prayers" (Maria, 46).

Touching upon the connection of happenings and song narratives, I would like to end this article with a quote by another participant, summing up religiously connoted meanings and song narratives, reminiscing the words to the song "Let's Go Crazy": "I would like to believe he did not die in this elevator—he just punched a higher floor" (Paul, 46).

Part Three

Cultures

8

My Pravoslavnye: Russkii rok, Orthodoxy, and Nationalism in Post-Soviet Russia

David-Emil Wickström

While walking down the 6th Line of *Vasil'evskii Ostrov* in St. Petersburg in the early evening of January 1, 2016, I saw a woman making the sign of the cross before passing *Sobor vo imia Sviatogo apostola Andreia Pervozvannogo* (Saint Andrew's Cathedral).[1] Arriving at my friend Andrei's place a couple of minutes later I noticed a small icon with his name saint hanging next to his computer—even though he is a Buddhist. These icons are prevalent in Russia. As well as on the walls or in bookshelves at people's homes, they can also be seen on car dashboards and cash registers—even of those who belong to other religious denominations.

These are but two aspects of everyday public religiosity common in Russia which is not limited to one segment of society: it extends to prominent politicians like Vladimir Putin and Dmitri Medvedev who are often portrayed as participating in Russian-Orthodox Church services. Disregarding whether the post-Soviet reality is conceptualized in terms of a post-colonial situation,[2] nostalgia for the USSR/Imperial Russia,[3] or other theories it is arguable that one element that has grown stronger since the fall of the USSR is the role of the Russian-Orthodox Church fused to a religious-based nationalism. As Østbø argues: "The status of Orthodoxy and Russia's territorial orientation are two core issues of post-Soviet Russian nationalism. They are also the two crucial questions as regards the 'use' or interpretation of the idea of the Third Rome."[4]

This surge in publicly visible religiosity among both politicians and citizens since the collapse of the USSR is not absent from post-Soviet popular music. Still active Soviet rock musicians and songwriters like Iurii Shevchuk (DDT), Dmitriy Reviakin (Kalinov Most), Piotr Mamonov and Konstantin Kinchev (Alisa) are known for their Russian-Orthodox faith. Others like Boris Grebenshikov

(Akvarium) dabble with multiple religious influences—including Orthodoxy. As Gololobov demonstrates, this link between music and religion is not only limited to what is labelled *russkii rok* (Russian rock—as the music from the 1980s is referred to today and which includes the mentioned musicians), but also comprises the Siberian punk musicians Roman Neumoev (Instruktsiia po Vyzhyvaniiu), Egor Letov (Grazhdanskaia Oborona), and Oleg "Manager" Sudakov (Rodina).[5]

As Gilmour points out, expressions of religion and spirituality in popular songs function more on the connotative than denotative level—which also leaves a broader room for re-creation of religious material as well as interpretation.[6] While lyrics offer a prominent vehicle for analysis this also means that examining the broader social context surrounding the artists is an essential part in order to place the artists and their creative work within a socio-religious context. This chapter thus expands the focus beyond the artists' lyrics and charts some connections between music, religion, and politics. The aim is to explore how popular music intersects with religion, specifically Russian-Orthodoxy, in post-Soviet Russia. Questions raised here include how Russian-Orthodoxy has become so prevalent in post-Soviet Russia, the link between church and state as well as to nationalism, and the impact this has on popular music.

Almost three decades after the collapse of the USSR the Russian music scene has not only shown the enduring appeal of Soviet rock music, but also how artists like the above-mentioned have changed and adapted to both a new economic as well as socio-cultural reality. This chapter's first section focuses on one aspect of this new reality, the role of religion in the Russian Federation. By drawing on two examples (the group Leningrad and Pussy Riot) I chart how religion has intersected with popular music. This also provides the context for the second section which focuses on Alisa's lead singer and songwriter Konstantin Kinchev, né Panfilov (born 1958). After starting his career in Moscow he moved to Leningrad during the 1980s to join the vibrant music scene around the Leningrad Rock Club. Being one of the few musicians from the Soviet rock scene to survive (both economically as well as physically) the shift to a capitalist economy in post-Soviet Russia, Kinchev remains popular today. He not only plays for an audience consisting of the last Soviet generation born in the 1970s and early 1980s, but also for a younger crowd born after the collapse of the Soviet Union in medium to large venues including stadiums. At the same time his religious and nationalist shift has provided material for discussion and controversy. He thus provides a good case study to cast some light on one post-Soviet musical trajectory.

Caution must however be kept here, since, as Häger rightly points out, "it is not easy to claim that the artists and his or her work are part of a Christian 'symbolic universe' [especially] on the basis of a few examples from an artist's production."[7] The aspects discussed in this chapter represent only one facet of Kinchev and his group Alisa; many fans do not agree with Kinchev's religious turn even though they still listen to his music. Furthermore there is a difference between public religious display (which is similar to a popular music performance) and private faith. While public and private faith practice can be the same, this chapter can, due to lack of access, only interpret the public part. This is done by drawing on repeated fieldwork in Russia conducted since 2004 as well as articles and interviews.

A miracle of God—Religion in post-Soviet Russia

The church is, as Fagan writes, "the only pre-1917 national social institution to have survived the Soviet era."[8] Due to this legitimacy and centrality in pre-Soviet Russia she argues that "the Church is thus able to perform an essential sacralizing function for the ruling elite, and one which the Kremlin dare not let opponents usurp"[9]—as the next example demonstrates.

During a meeting with the confessional leaders of Russia's "traditional" religions on February 8, 2012, Patriarch Kirill told the participants that Russia left the economic crisis of the 1990s behind through a miracle of God with the active participation of the government.[10] The other religious leaders present, including Russia's Chief Rabbi Berel Lazar and the Grand Mufti Ravil Gainutdin, also spoke out in support of Putin.[11]

Seen in the light of Putin's 2012 election campaign this statement was made to point out the stability of Putin's policies throughout the 2000s as well as in the aftermath of the financial crisis. Such support has occurred repeatedly since the early 1990s and is not the first time Putin (as well as his predecessor Boris Yeltsin and Interim President Medvedev) has drawn on religious leaders to support his reelection campaign and policies.[12]

Besides expanding its reach through the construction and restoration of churches throughout Russia the Russian-Orthodox Church through its church officials and followers is also trying to expand its role within society—be it through organizing cultural events (as mentioned below), creating an orthodox wireless network,[13] or disrupting popular music concerts, festivals, exhibitions, and other public events.[14] This is not only the case within Russia, but also in the ("near") abroad. The actions include trying to regain parishes which have broken from the Russian-Orthodox Church following the revolution as well as using their influence (and priests) to lobby for legislation which is in the interests of the Kremlin.[15] These actions are not necessarily done directly, but indirectly through priests and other individuals drawing on Russian-Orthodoxy as an argumentational foundation, as the next example will show.

The band Leningrad, which since its inception has repeatedly provoked government and religious officials primarily due to its use of foul language, once again caused outrage through its clip "V Pitere—pit'" (In Piter, You Drink) released on YouTube, April 30, 2016.[16] The clip depicts a vodka-fueled evening in St. Petersburg with five (former) workers (among them a police officer) fed up with their jobs. Besides the then St. Petersburg Legislative Assembly deputy Evgenii Marchenko calling for an investigation due to the promotion of alcoholism and uncensored swearing, the St. Petersburg and Novosibirsk local chapter leaders of *Narodnyi Sobor* (National Union) used an upcoming Leningrad concert in Novosibirsk to call for a ban of the song.[17] The organization lobbies for a strong Russia while promoting traditional religious-moral values based on what they label Russian civilization. This is just one (recent) example of how individuals and organizations with religious ties try to exert their power within the general society.[18]

The church's involvement in social issues has been pushed more forcefully through Patriarch Kirill, the first appointed post-Soviet head of the Russian-Orthodox Church, and the results are also reflected in recent polls: A 2015 poll by the Russian Public Opinion Research Center (VTsIOM) concluded that 67 percent of Russian residents place feelings of believers above freedom of speech and expression.[19] Prosecutors have also been more active in persuing cases in which religious feelings have been hurt—including cultural events.[20]

A Pew Research Center survey pointed out that in 2015, religion was "very important" for 19 percent of the Russian population and 42 percent said it is "somewhat important."[21] These numbers have remained constant during the last fifteen years. As independent and state-friendly surveys have shown, in recent years the percentage of believers have, however, gone up compared with the final days of the USSR.[22] At the same time these polls also show a discrepancy between religious self-perception and religious practice, which raises the question whether the belief is based on an interpretation of the Bible and official church theology or on an popular reading of Russian-Orthodox theology. This includes practice (a low percentage of the population regularly go to religious services and take communion) as well as moral issues (about a third or less of the respondents opposed extramarital sex, abortion, and divorce) and superstition (in a 2016 poll 36 percent of all Russians said they believe in witchcraft/magic—*koldovstvo*).[23] As Furman and Kääriäinen stated in 2005, "the growth in religiosity practically does not influence Russian society's moral evolution. We can state a paradox phenomenon—the 'secularization' of morals running parallel with a growth of religiosity."[24]

At the same time the population is becoming more disillusioned with the church, as a report published by the SOVA Center for Information and Analysis concludes. This includes conflicts over church construction and art works as well as church believers' increasingly aggressive stance towards events that offend their beliefs (like those previously mentioned) which are in part fueled by the anti-secular rhetoric of high-ranking church members.[25] In addition, there have been numerous church scandals since the 1990s including rumors surrounding Patriarch Kirill's personal wealth.[26]

While the number of citizens claiming to be Russian-Orthodox believers has risen, this can in part be seen as an appropriation of an identity based on Russian history rather than a rise in religious practice. Fagan argues, "we can thus increasingly speak of two Orthodoxies in Russia: one oriented on church canons, the other on popular perception."[27] At the same time the stance of the government and church does not necessarily reflect the belief of its citizens (or even each other).

A Russian person is Orthodox in his/her soul—Russian history and Orthodoxy

On February 21, 2012, about two weeks after the above-mentioned meeting with Putin and the clergy, a group of performance activists staged a performance in the *Khram Khrista Spasitelia* (Cathedral of Christ the Savior).[28] By combining footage from that performance with footage from another performance at the *Bogoiavlenskii sobor v Elokhove* (Bogoiavlenskii Cathedral—recorded on February 19) and adding a (home) studio-recorded musical track (acoustics were too dry to have been recorded in a church), Pussy Riot uploaded their *Pank-moleben* (Punk Prayer)[29] "Bogoroditsa, Putina Progoni" (Mother of God, Drive Putin Out) to their Livejournal page and to YouTube on February 21, 2012.[30]

Besides the lyrics the performance itself touched on a (holy) nerve within the Russian-Orthodox Church: the band is seen performing (more precise trying to perform) in front of the *iconostasis* behind which the sanctuary lies. The icons embedded within the iconostasis are representations of the heavenly saints and thus a window between heaven and earth from which the heavenly beings can look down upon the earth. Thus, according to Russian-Orthodox theology, Pussy Riot performed in front of Christ and the Saints.[31]

Both locations also carry an important symbolic value. The *Khram Khrista Spasitelia* was first built in 1883, then blown up and converted into a open-air swimming pool by Stalin in 1931 and rebuilt between 1995 and 2000. It is *the* central Russian-Orthodox cathedral. Not only does it symbolize the post-Soviet Russian-Orthodox revival, but also the connection between church and state through its use by high-ranking politicians including Putin and Medvedev during high church holidays.[32] The *Bogoiavlenskii sobor v Elokhove* (completed in its current form, 1845) was the main church of the Moscow Patriarchate from 1938 until 1991—thus the "successor" of the destroyed *Khram Khrista Spasitelia*.

In other words, the performance was not only considered blasphemous for many believers, but it also taps into Russian and Soviet history. A criminal case was opened on February 26, 2012, resulting in the arrests of Mariia Aliokhina, Ekaterina Samutsevich, and Nadezhda Tolokonnikova. On August 17 of the same year they were sentenced to two years in prison for hooliganism motivated by religious hatred.[33]

Here a look at the historical role of the Russian-Orthodox Church and its links to Muscovy and the Russian Empire is warranted. After the baptism of Prince Vladimir in 988, Byzantine Christianity has been the religious foundation for the Kievan Rus', Muscovy as well as the Russian Empire. Following the fall of Constantinople in 1453 (and thus the end of the Roman Empire) the Moscow Patriarchate was founded in 1589. While the idea of Moscow as the Third Rome emerged in a text written around 1523–24 by a monk named Filofei, the myths surrounding Moscow as the Third Rome surged in the nineteenth and twentieth century.[34] This myth is "a key element in the 'reinvention'" of Russia in the post-Soviet context"[35] and figures prominently in the writings of post-Soviet ultranationalist Aleksandr Dugin.[36]

In order to bring the Russian-Orthodox liturgy closer to that of the other Orthodox churches, Patriarch Nikon proposed reforms in the seventeenth century. They included changing the spelling of "Jesus" as well as how the sign of the cross was made. This resulted in a split of the Russian-Orthodox Church following a council in 1666. While the Old Believers (as the group opposing the reforms were called) subsequently suffered a bloody persecution, this schism also opened for the western reforms introduced by Peter the Great in the eighteenth century.[37]

Orthodoxy (*Pravoslavie*) remained a central pillar in the official nationalism elaborated by Sergei Uvarov in 1833 and applied by Tsar Nicholas I to the Russian Empire.[38] Church and state were first separated in 1918 and this separation remained anchored in Article 14 of the Russian Federation's Constitution which became law in 1993:[39] "1. The Russian Federation is a secular state. No religion can be established as state or mandatory. 2. Religious organizations are separated from the state and equal before the law."[40]

The preamble to the 1997 law, "On the freedom of conscience and on religious associations," upholds each individual's freedom of conscience and religion as well as the equality before the law and the secularity of the state. The law, however, also "recognizes Orthodoxy's special role in Russia's history, in its establishment and development of spirituality and culture" before mentioning "Christianity, Islam, Buddhism, Judaism and other religions which have been an integral part of the historical heritage of the Russian people."[41] In other words, the law creates a tripartite ranking establishing the primacy of Russian-Orthodoxy followed by the "traditional" religions (Christianity, Islam, Buddhism and Judaism) and then the remaining beliefs.

While faith remains a complex issue in post-Soviet Russia it still plays a prominent role in ideas surrounding national identity and policy despite the constitution's clear separation of church and state. The primacy of Orthodoxy linked to the nation-state also reflects a common sentiment in Russia: In a 2005 survey 84 percent of the respondents agreed or mostly agreed with the statement "A Russian person, even if s/he is not baptised and s/he doesn't go to church, is Orthodox in his/her soul."[42] This not only provides one possible explanation to why even non-orthodox Russians have icons of their name saints but also reinforces the notion that the Russian nation is strongly intertwined with Orthodoxy—something this historical overview has demonstrated.

Of the same respondents in the mentioned survey, 73 percent agreed or mostly agreed with the statement "The government has to protect the Orthodox faith of the Russian people from its enemies."[43] This implicit fusion of religion and nationalism is a recurring theme in Kinchev's creative work. The next section picks up this theme by focusing on the intersection between popular music, specifically *russkii rok*, and religion using Kinchev as a case study.

Rock-n-Roll Krest—Russkii rok, Kinchev and religion

According to the journalist Denis Stupnikov, 2003 was the year the Russian-Orthodox Church started focusing on missionary activities for fans of *russkii rok*. With the blessing of high-ranking church officials the festival "*Rok k Nebu*" (Rock to Heaven) featuring Viacheslav Butusov (Nautilius Pompilius), Grebenshchikov, Shevchuk as well as Kinchev was hosted in St. Petersburg. In the same year Alisa's album *Seichas pozdnee, chem ty dumaesh'* (It is Later Now than You Think) was released, which Stupnikov claims is Kinchev's first album completely within the spirit of Orthodoxy.[44]

In addition to musical activities, a focus was also placed on the Russian-Orthodox meaning of *russkii rok* lyrics, with the site www.pravaya.ru starting to publish articles on Orthodox aspects of Russian rock music. This has also been the focus of Hegumen Sergii Rybko and Deacon Andrei Kuraev, who as church figures have written and spoken on the (lyrical) connection between *russkii rok* and Orthodoxy. They have also heavily lobbied for the use of rock music in missionary work including sermons at rock concerts. Rybko, who also runs a rock club in his parish in Moscow, regularly participates in rock festivals.[45] There he conducts missionary work—both in the audience as well as at times from the stage. In his eyes, rock provides a good way to reach out to the youth: "Rock asks a question, it is honest, it searches for truth and ridicules lies. When there were only lies around in my time, rock with its words, its music told the truth. Its protest: against evil and untruth, and, as is written in Scripture, 'the world lies in the Evil [One]'."[46]

This link between rock, lyrics, and ideology harks back to the USSR and the role lyrics had in legitimizing rock in opposition to *estrada*, the official Soviet popular music (and also as a way to compensate for inferior production capabilities and instruments). Poetically infused lyrics which makes the listener think were—and still are—considered central to *russkii rok*. Rybko touches on this in another interview: "In general, rock music brings people with the same mentalities together … Thinking people listen to rock. Rock music always carried some kind of its own ideology."[47] The lyrics' ideological (and for some, messianic) bent is also a reason many current musicians and listeners criticize *russkii rok*.[48]

That said, the subject matter of *russkii rok* is compatible with the teachings of the church. As Gololobov argues:

> Humanistic ideas and a focus on the moral aspects of life, central in Russian rock, do not really contradict Christian values. This is clearly acknowledged by the Russian Orthodox Church itself and, in particular, by the influential archdeacon Andrei Kuraev, who in his public speeches and numerous publications draws a clear link between the spiritual search of Russian rock music and the values of Orthodox Christianity.[49]

One musician Kuraev and Rybko refer to is Kinchev. While the previous music examples have been of musicians provoking the religious establishment, Kinchev has been drawn to the Russian-Orthodox faith since his baptism following a visit to Jerusalem in 1992.[50] In a statement from 2005 acknowledging Kinchev's faith, Kuraev said, "One phrase from Kinchev's lips weighs more than a hundred of my lectures."[51]

This is not only reflected in Kinchev's personal belief, but has also manifested itself in his creative work (discussed in the following section) as well as public appearances: Since 2001 Alisa does not play concerts during the Lent and Dormition fasts.[52] The news page on his website features annual announcements for the birth of Christ (with the music video to "Rozhdestvo"[53]—Christmas—embedded under the text) as well as his resurrection—including an icon of Christ.[54] Kinchev also wears a cross and an icon around his neck which are often seen in videos and live performances.

Due to the already mentioned missionary and religious activities, a meeting between the church and musicians was initiated by pravaya.ru's Mikhail Tiurenkov and (then) Metropolitan Kirill, at the time chairman of the Department for External Church Relations (DECR). Together with other prominent musicians including Shevchuk and Neumoev, Kinchev on April 6, 2006 was invited to discuss Russian popular music with Metropolitan Kirill, the DECR Vice-Chairman Archpriest Vsevolod Chaplin, Archpriest Maksim Kozlov, Rybko, Kuraev as well as other members of the Moscow Patriarchate and journalists.[55] In addition to the musicians pointing out the difference between their creative work (especially the lyrics' role in provoking thought in listeners) and other popular music, the topics included possibilities of Orthodox sermons at rock concerts and rock music's potential for missionary work. At the same time Metropolitan Kirill stressed that the Orthodox liturgy was not in need of modernization to make it more attractive—including not needing (electrically amplified) musical instruments (indirectly rebuking Rybko's calls for rock sermons). Instead he suggested youth meetings as a platform to discuss theological themes and where rock songs can be sung accompanied by guitars.[56] Here again the primacy of lyrics in carrying the meaning is stressed relegating the music to the back.

Kinchev's religious turn is a somewhat jarring gap to his fans, who are known as *Armiia Alisa* (Alisa's army) and who have a reputation of being right-wing nationalists. At the same time, as the following examples demonstrate, Kinchev's lyrics transport Christian values (albeit bluntly) embedded in a popularized, nationalist wrapping thus including his fans ideologically.

As stated above, Kinchev's creative work is an important outlet of his belief, and the mentioned song "Rozhdestvo" as well as "Pravoslavnye" (Orthodox believers) from his 2000 album *Solntsevorot* (Solstice) are just two examples where the song title alludes to his faith.[57] On a lyrical level religious imagery is a recurring theme with (banal) tropes such as cross (*krest*) and heaven (*nebo*) as well as images alluding to light and darkness often used.

Kinchev is publicly outspoken about his faith: In an interview he stated that the eponymous title track of the 2005 album *Izgoi*[58] (Social Outcast) is "about the Savior [*Spasitel'*]. The album 'Izgoi' is about all those, who made a conscious choice, trying to build their life in the image and likeness of the Savior."[59]

Another song featured on that album, "Rock'n'Roll Krest" (Rock'n'Roll Cross), provides an example of faith and redemption. The lyrics are straightforward: the protagonist is saved from a life of vice and finds redemption in the heavenly powers and the Rock'n'Roll Cross. The meaning is rendered intelligible for the listener through the mainly syllabically sung lyrics reinforced by the recitative-like verse. Paired with a straightforward up-tempo rock-beat, the guitar riff-based music sprinkled with keyboard pad sounds and effects is catchy. Once Kinchev turns to salvation in the refrain, a female choir (or synth-sounds sounding like female voices) singing ad-libs enter in the background. At the end of the second refrain, "Rock'n'Roll Cross" is chanted by a live audience before the guitar solo starts. The solo fades over to the verse—which slowly builds up in intensity, this time with the ad-lib choir in the background. Here the lyrics focus on the protagonist's proximity to the "face of Heavenly power" (*liki sily Nebes*) and culminates in "Behold—Again, the Rock'n'Roll Cross is flaming at the center of the light" (*Smotri—nas snova v tsentr lucha vpletaet Rock-n-Roll-Krest*) leading into the refrain. After the last refrain the audience is once again heard chanting "Rock'n'Roll Cross."

The official music video is based on a live concert recorded in Moscow on November 9, 2005, featuring the band members dressed in black playing in front of a cheering audience.[60] Kinchev is wearing biker gloves, a sleeveless shirt, and something that looks like a black kilt. His eyes are outlined with black makeup which is drawn on his face. His stage moves are in line with that of a performing artists within the rock/metal genre; however he has two specialties which distinguish his performance: While singing "Rock'n'Roll Cross" (e.g. 1:34)[61] he first does the sign of the horns (index and middle finger up while the thumb holds middle and ring finger down) when saying "Rock'n'Roll" before doing the sign of the cross when singing "cross" (index and middle finger up). He then does his "crucifixion" pose (1:42) where—slightly hunched forward—he spreads his arms out sideways (this pose can also be seen in the video to "Antikhrist" (Antichrist).[62] In addition, the video's opening (0:04) briefly displays a cross created through the light shining behind two half-closed doors.

The song can be summarized as a catchy hardrock tune drawing on stadium rock aesthetics. Since its release in 2005 it (as also other songs by Alisa) has been on rotation on *Nashe Radio* (Our Radio), a popular format radio station dedicated exclusively to Russian language rock music. Both the performance and the sound contain on the connotative level subtle hints to the song's faith message (ad-lib choir, gestures). The lyrics, on the other hand, almost function on the denotative level and promote a clear message of redemption through faith.

In an interview on March 31, 2011 organized by the Patriarch's center for youth work at the *Danilov* Monastery, Kinchev explained the different meanings of his hand signs—the sign of the horns (*koza*) is used for negative things while the sign similar to that of the cross (the ring finger held down by the thumb while the other fingers are up) for positive things.[63] This latter sign resembles that of the Old Believers with two fingers and coincidentally the sign in the video seems to be that of the Old Believers too.[64]

The above interview is also revealing in another aspect. During a concert on July 25, 2010 at the *Telebashnia* stadium in St. Petersburg, the band— including Kinchev—performed in t-shirts with the slogan *Pravoslavie ili smert'* (Russian-Orthodoxy or Death) and caused a minor scandal. The slogan is based on the Greek *Eleftheria i Thanatos* (Freedom or Death) which was a rallying cry during the Greek War of Independence in the 1820s and now the motto of Greece. Essentially a statement calling for violence against other faiths, the motto "Russian-Orthodoxy or Death" was added to the Federal list of extremist material on December 21, 2010.[65] In the interview Kinchev, however, pointed out that he did not mean that non-believers had to be killed. For him the phrase is a modification of a statement made by Feofan Zatvornik (1815–94), a former Bishop of Tambov: "I don't know how it is for others, but I can't be saved without Orthodoxy."[66] Thus in Kinchev's interpretation, life without Orthodoxy would be his death.[67]

Provocation, as this case clearly demonstrates, as well as provocative political statements have followed Kinchev throughout his career. As I have noted elsewhere, Kinchev's creative work over the past twenty years has also taken on a more nationalist tinge, which he among other aspects roots in his Russian-Orthodox faith.[68] One example is his song "Nebo Slavian" (Heaven of the Slavs)[69] which fuses a strong dose of nationalism with an ethno-religious foundation.

The lyrics' statement combined with the video's message is that the Orthodox Russian-speaking Slavs have repeatedly been invaded by non-Orthodox (Muslim) enemies but prevailed, defending their territory and their Orthodox faith. During the Alisa concert I attended on December 25, 2015 in St. Petersburg this seemed to be the most popular song judging by the audience's cheering and participation: It was also the only song that Kinchev had the audience sing the second refrain by themselves.[70]

His ethno-religious approach spans also to other believers within the Orthodox faith family. The same album includes the song "Nepokornye" (The Rebellious) in which he not only in the lyrics calls out to "my Serbian and Bulgarian brothers" (*Moi brat'ia Serby da Bolgary*) and brothers-in-faith (*edinoverets*) to fight against "the predatory breed/race inflamed by the terror of the caliphate" (*To terrorom Khalifata, Raspalialas' khishchnaia poroda*), but also musically: the melody is based on a minor scale with an augmented fourth (tritone). This creates a 1 1/2 tone step between the third and the fourth degree of the scale. On a connotative level this common musical trope refers to *Others* (in this case, Muslims) since it imitates and parodies scales used in South-East Europe (e.g. by Sinti and Roma as well as Jewish Klezmer musicians) as well as *maqams* from the Middle East (the scale resembles the tetrachord in *zirgüleli hicaz*). In the last line of each verse, which lyrically refers to Kinchev's (Orthodox) "brothers," the augmented fourth is resolved to a perfect fourth thus musically "normalizing" them.[71] Kinchev, who has Bulgarian roots, has pointed out that "Nepokornye" was composed as a reaction to the NATO intervention in Serbia in the 1990s. Under the slogan "Kosovo—Part of Serbia" (and thus clearly stating where they stood in the Kosovo-independence debate) Alisa performed the song at a concert in Belgrade in 2008.[72]

Another sovereign country within Kinchev's Orthodox faith family is Ukraine. Both the lyrics "Orange snot—intellectual dreams, in a foreboding of civil war" (*Oranzhevye sopli—ochkarikov sny, V predchuvstvii grazhdanskoi voiny*) as well as the video (Orange flags) to his 2008 song "Vlast'" (Power)[73] take a shot at the 2004/5 Orange Revolution in Ukraine which Kinchev did not support. Besides invoking biblical references with the biblical idol "Moloch," this song can on a connotative level be read as post-Soviet geopolitics and Russia trying to maintain its sphere of influence. His song "Naebali" (Fucked) from the 2016 album *Ekstsess* (Excess) also takes a shot at Ukraine and the current conflict there. During some concerts he has changed "*Ei, boitsy! Vas opiat' naebali!*" (Hey fighters, you've been fucked again) to "*Ei, khokhly*" (Hey Ukrainians) to make the lyrics more obvious.[74]

In an interview from 2014, Kinchev pointed out that Russia, Ukraine, and Belarus are one people/nation (*narod*).[75] His focus on Ukraine is also rooted in history and Prince Vladimir's conversion: Ukraine's capital Kiev is considered the cradle of Russian-Orthodoxy—something that Kinchev's statement from an interview in 2008 also alludes to: "I am for a great, holy Rus' with Kiev as the capital. The capital has to be here, and the country has to be called 'Rus.'"[76]

These examples should also be read as a popularized and more direct approach to the above-mentioned statement "The government has to protect the Orthodox faith of the Russian people from its enemies." While drawing on faith Kinchev at the same time builds a case for an ethno-religious state which has to be defended against foreigners and other faiths.

Not only does Kinchev touch on a geographical unity in public statements, he also called for the relationship between church and state to be strengthened. In a 2007 interview he said: "In general I see future Russia in a symphony of power: In all decisions the secular power is supposed to receive the clergy's blessing, the president has to walk hand in hand with the patriarch, then also the power will be strengthened. In general Putin currently occupies a good position."[77]

"Symphony" (*simfonia*) refers to the Byzantine ideal "in which church and state leaders work in tandem for the spiritual and temporal welfare of the people."[78] While this might be Kinchev's dream and despite the public displays of faith, there is, as Fagan demonstrates, no overarching common agenda between the church leadership and state. The church is symbolically instrumental in politics but the church strives (officially) to stay outside of party politics.[79] Fagan, however, also points out that a shift occurred with the transition to President Medvedev in 2008 and the election of Patriarch Kirill in 2009. Pressing for more influence than his predecessor and being more outspoken, Patriarch Kirill and the Patriarchate has under Medvedev "made substantial progress towards state patronage."[80] This is also reflected in the events discussed in this chapter's first section (Leningrad, Pussy Riot) which have occurred after Kirill became Patriarch and where both the legislative and the judiciary branch have become more active in protecting religious rights.

Conclusion

Konstantin Kinchev, who established a reputation of *enfant terrible* after he moved from Moscow to Leningrad, is a good example for the many disruptions and continuities that have marked the transition from socialism to capitalism in

Russia: Kinchev's image has shifted to that of a (more or less) established Russian-Orthodox rocker, and since 2010 he is an advisor to the Russian-Orthodox Church as a member of the *Patriarshii sovet po kul'ture* (the Patriarchal Council on Culture).[81]

He also pursues an outspoken religious and nationalist agenda which is supported by members of the Russian-Orthodox Church: While his lyrics and music primarily operate on a connotative level they at times are very close to a denotative level (e.g. "*Rock'n'Roll Krest*"). His provocations also figure so strongly because they often operate on the denotative level which then is softened by lifting it to a connotative level (e.g. *Pravoslavie ili smert'*). Kinchev's fans are open to this imagery. At concerts they bring paraphernalia with Russian-Orthodox symbols (the Orthodox cross, the writing "*My Pravoslavnye*"—we are Orthodox[82]) as well as nationalist symbols.

As the polls quoted in this chapter have shown (which coincide with my own observations), calling oneself Russian-Orthodox does not necessarily mean that the individuals are devout believers. Here Orthodoxy is one aspect of a post-Soviet national identity. This fusion of religion and nationalism is, however, not only symptomatic for Kinchev and his fans, but for a general post-Soviet revival of a nostalgic national identity linked to the primacy of Orthodoxy rooted geographically and historically in the *Kievan Rus'* and hence ethnicity and territory. Boym labels this revival *restorative nostalgia*, a search for a past based in national patriotic glory.[83] This nostalgia is also the foundation for organizations like the above-mentioned *Narodnyi Sobor*, and politicians as well as ultra-nationalists like the mentioned Dugin who root Russia's future in its Orthodox past. In her discussion of nostalgia in the 1990s and early 2000s Boym adds the still valid statement: "From a land of tomorrow [during perestroika], Russia has turned into a land of today dreaming of yesterday."[84]

The church has profited from this shift and taken on a stronger, more visible role in post-Soviet Russia. Since his election Patriarch Kirill has more aggressively pushed for church involvement despite the constitutional separation of church and state. On the other side, public support for the church's involvement is receding. According to a Levada-Center poll from 2016, 66 percent of all the respondents (up from 51 percent in 2005) do not think that the church should influence government decisions, thus the public support for *simfonia* seems to be dropping.[85] Whether this idea of yesterday remains the dream of tomorrow within the broader population today is still open.

"Can I Take My Dog with Me to Heaven?" Swedish Country Music and Religion

Thomas Bossius

In the lyrics and culture of US country music, expressions of a conservative, popular, and down-to-earth type of layman Christianity are common and quite central. It represents a kind of relation to Christianity and to being a believer rarely to be found in a country like Sweden. Sweden is often said to be the most secularized country in the world, and according to Svanberg and Westerlund there are good grounds for such a claim.[1] That said, it could also be stated that Swedish country music fans and musicians are in no way less secularized than the rest of the population. Because of the level of secularization in Sweden, open expressions and references to Christianity and being a Christian, as is usual in US country, are seldom found in the lyrics of the songs written by Swedes, or in the sleeve-notes of Swedish albums. Moreover, when Swedish artists select songs to record written by US songwriters, they commonly avoid songs with obvious expressions of a Christian faith. However, the lyrics of Swedish country music, just like those from the USA, mainly deal with the everyday struggles of ordinary women and men. The fact that they almost exclusively pinpoint themes like happiness and sorrow, lost and found love, life and death, loneliness and community, and children being born, growing up and leaving home, means that the basic existential questions of everyday life are a constant part of the negotiations taking place in the songs.

Swedish fans and musicians are also always close to US country music and culture. US country is the main interest for most Swedish country fans, and they regularly listen to and read about US artists, and occasionally meet some of them when they are touring Sweden. Furthermore a lot of the Swedish fans and musicians travel to Nashville and other parts of the USA where they get the opportunity to meet US fans and musicians. All together this means that they get a closeness and relation to Christianity in general, and to the white, Protestant Christianity of Southern USA in particular, in a way other Swedes do not.

Despite all these statements concerning the avoidance and distance to Christianity in Swedish country music, it should also be said that—maybe due to the just mentioned parallel closeness to US Christianity—there are quite a few exceptions to be found. Swedish secular country music artists do sometimes choose US lyrics with an obvious US Christian content, and Swedish songwriters do occasionally write lyrics with a more or less outspoken Christian content, which makes them a peculiar part of the secular popular culture of Sweden, and something that fans and writers have to position themselves in relation to.

The ambivalence of Swedish country musicians and fans concerning US Christianity is not isolated to religion, but mirrors a general ambivalent relation between them and the USA. The following quote from the Swedish country music fan magazine *Country News* gives a fairly good picture of the situation:

> If you have listened a lot to country music and are relatively familiar with the traditions, trends and features of this type of music, you have at the same time necessarily learned a lot about the continent that created this music. There is so much of the history, geography, culture and way of life of the U.S. woven into country music, in its lyrics and the lives and destinies of the artists. This knowledge has been gained whether you want it or not, but at the same time I think most of us with an interest in country music also have developed a real interest in the history and culture of the U.S. and a certain curiosity concerning what is going on in this huge nation, covering a whole continent, inhabited by over 200 million people, and stirring quite contradictory emotions in many of us. But this measure of positive emotions regarding the Northern parts of America must not for a moment be confused with any kind of sympathy for the politicians that at the moment hold the power in the White House. Or as BJÖRN AFZELIUS has expressed it: "You don't have to be a fascist just because you read Mickey Spillane or use steel guitar on your records."[2]

At the same time as it can be stated that Sweden is highly secularized, Sweden is in no way different from other Western countries concerning the parallel and concurrent processes of secularization and sacralization; and the so-called "re-enchantment of the world" described by Christopher Partridge and others is taking place also in Sweden.[3] Frisk and Åkerbäck, in a study on religion in contemporary Sweden, refer to a discussion by Partridge where he points out that the uses of religious symbols and images in popular culture don't necessarily have to be seen as part of secularization. Instead Partridge argues that they could be seen as part of a sacralization by its removal or blurring of the boundaries between the sacred and the profane, resulting in the sacred becoming a part of popular culture and as such more easily available and usable by common people.[4] At the same time as agreeing to this, Frisk and Åkerbäck point out the significance of secularization for the development and religious change in Sweden. In their material they can see the process pointed out by Partridge, concerning the boundaries between the sacred and the profane being blurred, but at the same time they also see the impact of secularization concerning the way contemporary popular religion is being designed and expressed:

> What we see from the material from Dalarna can clearly be interpreted as religious expressions, but this kind of religion is expressed in a secularized culture and has secularized features. The surrounding culture strongly affects how religion is expressed, and our culture is no exception.[5]

A central feature of the religious change that is taking place in Sweden is what Owe Wikström describes as a shift of interest away from the great holinesses towards smaller and more personal holinesses:

> More and more people seem to have lost faith in all covering belief systems and stories. Fewer and fewer people are going to church. Explanations referring to an extra-terrestrial world not considered likely are by most people. Instead people are creating their own private or "smaller holinesses." It is this kind of local or inner psychical worlds that function as counterweight against the all too trivial and plain sphere of everyday life. It can be the community of a family, the experience of music or poetry, the discovery of the symbols of your own dreams, or the quiet experience of nature.[6]

According to Wikström the modern individual is turning away from the great stories, the great religions, and the great otherworldly transcendences. This shift is connected to the general processes of individualization and privatization in modern society, and particularly to the shift from the great common religions towards individual or private invisible religions. Thomas Luckmann describes this process as a "profound change in the 'location' of religion in society."[7]

The lyrics of Swedish country music

As mentioned in the introduction to this chapter there is in the lyrics of US country an often outspoken and taken-for-granted everyday relation to Christianity. In the lyrics of certain songs or as part of the songs on the US albums, the singers express a relation to Christianity where God, Jesus, and a

Christian belief make up an integrated and quite "natural" part of everyday life, often together with things like drinking, cheating, cursing, moral looseness, leading a bad life—sometimes even including criminality and killing people—and where this and having a strong belief in Jesus and being Christian make up a whole. That kind of relation to Christianity is rarely found in Sweden. If Swedish artists refer to themselves as Christian it is most commonly done so as a statement in connection to the artist being a born-again Christian who supposedly doesn't drink, smoke, gamble, curse, cheat, commit adultery, commit crimes, or sing songs telling stories about doing all these things.

In a Swedish context, for popular music artists to promote themselves as Christian, and especially if they as a consequence of that choose to only sing songs with an obvious Christian content, in any genre of popular music, this almost exclusively means that your audience will be limited to listeners also identifying themselves as Christian. It will also mean that your records and concerts will be reviewed and mentioned only in various Christian media. When it comes to country music this differs slightly from other genres. When I did a study of the history of Christian popular music in Sweden, it was striking how invisible and non-existent the Christian artists were in the secular popular music press covering pop and rock music. I found no interviews and no reviews of either records or concerts.[8] When, some years later, I started my study of Swedish country music[9] it was therefore a big surprise to find in issue number 6, 1971, of the leading country fan magazine *Kountry Korral*, a Gospel column not devoted to sacred US country, but to Swedish Christian artists playing country music. In this regularly recurring column you could read interviews and reviews of Christian artists, some of which were even considered to belong to the best country acts of Sweden. Contemporary Christian Music (CCM) had its golden age in Sweden during the 1970s and 1980s, and sacred country was a central part of that; in some cases by artists mainly or exclusively playing country, and in some cases by artists using country as one part of a mix of rock, gospel, and country. A common feature was to mix songs by gospel acts like Andrae Crouch and Edwin Hawkins, Christian rock acts such as Larry Norman and Barry McGuire, and country/southern gospel acts like Oak Ridge Boys and Lawrence Reynolds.

These CCM and the country artists active in that field are of course interesting parts of Swedish popular and country music history as well as the present-day scene. In this chapter however I will not, apart from an occasional example, focus on these artists and their way of dealing with the basic existential questions. Instead my focus will be on the way artists, who do not first and foremost or openly promote themselves as being Christian, deal with these questions, and how they relate to and use Christianity—or other religions—as part of these negotiations.

As my examples I will focus on the lyrical content of some of the songs of three contemporary Swedish country acts, and also look at their relation to the existential dimensions as expressed in interviews and biographies. The chosen acts are three solo artists who mainly sing in Swedish: Hasse Andersson, Christina Lindberg, and Alf Robertson. All of them, except Alf Robertson who passed away in 2008, are active today (2018), and all of them are popular and respected artists in the Swedish country music culture, but also well known outside the frames of said culture.

Considering the lyrics of Swedish artists in general, an obvious observation that can be made is that it is easier and creates a lot less tension to sing lyrics with a US Christian or other Christian content if the song is written in English and sung with an US accent. At a country music festival or on a record, to sing an old hymn like "I'll Fly Away" in English can be done without people reacting or maybe even noting the Christian content of the song. It's just a good old song that parts of the audience recognize and can sing along with. Not least so since the motion picture *Oh, Brother, Where Art Thou?* (2000) made it part of contemporary popular culture, effectively blurring the line between the sacred and the profane. To sing it with the Swedish lyrics: "Jag reser hem till himlen, jag reser hem" (I'm going home to heaven, I'm going home), however, is a different thing better done in a chapel, a tent meeting, or on a record sold in gospel record stores. It would be harder for the audience to sing along to the well-known Swedish lyrics with their obvious Christian content, than to sing along to the English lyrics with the same content hidden in the fabrics of a foreign language. It's hard—but not impossible—in Swedish country to find songs with lyrics in Swedish carrying an outspoken Christian content or references to Christianity. It's still hard—but easier—to find that kind of content in songs written in English by Swedish or US songwriters.

In the next section of the chapter I will turn to the artists I've chosen and give examples of their way of dealing with the existential questions, and their relation to Christianity.

Hasse Andersson and the angel dog

Hasse Andersson's big breakthrough in 1982 came with the song that has provided the main title to this chapter.[10] The song was titled "Änglahund" (Angel dog) and told the story about a man who, after a show, asked the artist if he could answer the honest and serious question: "When our Lord puts out the flame of life, and it's time to leave this earth, can I take my dog with me to heaven? He's nice and he has been a real friend." The artist, who is the narrator in the song, answers: "I'm sure your dog will go to heaven when it dies." In the final verse of the song the artist contemplates his answer: "Who can really say if dogs that die have to stay on earth?," somehow implying that it's obvious that humans go to heaven.[11] This breakthrough for Andersson and his band led to a hectic life with extended tours and recording sessions during the eighties. Due to this pressure, Andersson on his way to a concert in 1984 collapsed in his car. In his biography Andersson says that he was 100 percent sure that he was going to die.[12] After recovering he wrote the song "Hej, Hasse, Hej" influenced by the collapse.[13] In this song Andersson makes references to the story in "Änglahund." In the song he is, after the collapse, approached by angels singing: "Hey, Hasse, hey, come and sing with us an angel song. Don't fight it, let what's happening happen. Your eyes will be shut by the sandman of your life, and soon you will know the answer to the question about your angel dog." The narrator in the song replies to the angels that he's not finished yet, and that he still has some things to do: "so I'll stay down here, but please keep a place for me, and tell everybody up there, that down here everything's okay." In both these songs there are clear but not obvious references to Christianity and a Christian belief. Phenomena like "heaven," "angels," and "our Lord" are all present in Christianity, but also in other religions and in popular belief and private religions not necessarily related to Christianity and a Christian belief.

The album that featured "Hej, Hasse, Hej"—*Tie bilder* (1985)—also contained two other songs dealing with death and heaven: "Den sista seglatsen" (The Last Voyage) dedicated to Andersson's recently deceased father, and "Frälsningssoldaten" (The Salvation Army Soldier). "Den sista seglatsen" is a metaphorical story about death. It tells a story about a lonely man setting sail for his last voyage. Standing upright and proud he sets sail over deep waters across the sea towards the horizon. Feeling the sea and the wind one last time he sails into the final night, "when the day of life has turned into dusk, and existence feels too narrow"; just like a star crossing the sky, he is crossing the sea on a last voyage. The song is full of symbols related to Christian and other religious perceptions of death and dying as a passage: crossing the river, crossing the sea, sailing to the other shore. But there are no references to anything like heaven or God, just symbols open to anyone's interpretation. Also in the liner notes of the album Andersson writes about the song and his father without making any such references:

To sail was a big and important part of his life. 72 years old he still sailed alone on his boat. In the summer of 1985 he became ill and was restricted to hospital for the first time in his life. He soon understood that his life was nearing its end, and once when I visited him he said: "I very much want to sail once more." Maybe he was thinking about one of his role models in sailing, Joshua Slocum, who was found dead in his boat, peacefully drifting across the sea. A worthy end for a true sailor. It didn't happen that way, but let's pretend.[14]

The song "Frälsningssoldaten" more clearly deals with Christianity while telling a story about a beloved soldier of the Salvation Army who every Saturday morning plays his clarinet together with his fellow soldiers: "When they sing about the Lord who lives up yonder" he forgets being old and stiff, and he says: "Listen now children when I play a song on my clarinet. Every tone is beautiful when I let it out. Even though I've been playing many songs I still miss the one that will be heard all the way up in heaven." The lyrics are based on experiences in Andersson's childhood and depict a warm picture of this man of God and his belief, but there are no actual references to a belief from the songwriter's side. Andersson in many of his lyrics paints warm and loving pictures of lots of different people, and the Salvation Army soldier is just one of them. It is obvious in the sleeve notes of the album that Andersson has a positive view of the Salvation Army. About the soldier depicted in the song he writes that he with his "positive and happy note" was "a wonderful representative for what the Salvation Army stands for."[15]

The overall picture of Andersson's lyrics is that he avoids being overtly religious (Christian) or political. While claiming not to be a political singer, he still has a strong social pathos in his lyrics, making a stand against inequalities and injustice, and for the poor, lonely and disabled. His lyrics, even when not referring to life and death as in the songs previously discussed, are almost exclusively dealing with the basic existential issues of the everyday life of common people and those who don't fit in. Even though commonly not using overtly Christian lyrics, Andersson in his biography calls himself a believer. His depiction of his faith puts him in relation to Christianity, but he describes himself as a believer in his own way:

> I'm a believer, but not very active. I don't go to church very often, but I like going there to be alone. I don't attend services very often. My God is not tied up, he's very generous and has humour. I can talk to him, and do so quite often. I have found my own way and my own religiosity, and it's not bound by a lot of rituals, but tremendously free. I feel very content with my belief, and I'm not worried. I have been sick and in a very bad state, but I have never been worried about

death. I know that when it's time, it's time, and I know someone is waiting for me over there. It feels incredibly good! I wish that everybody could feel that trust. I'm not the kind of person who has to tell everyone and try to save everyone, but I have found my thing.[16]

In line with his philosophy not to tell everyone about his faith, he, in his lyrics, as shown and previously stated, commonly doesn't use overtly Christian symbols. In 2004, however, gospel singer Cyndee Peters persuaded him to make a gospel album. The result was the album *Nära dig* (Close to You). Most of the songs on the album are hymns and spirituals sang in Swedish or English, but there are also three original songs, of which two have lyrics written by Andersson's wife, songwriter Monica Forsberg, and one by Andersson himself. The lyrics of one of Forsberg's songs "Jag tittar i mitt fönster" (I look through my window) are quite typical for Andersson, dealing with the insignificance of humanity and the individual in relation to nature and the universe. The other two original songs however express an obvious Christian faith. In the song "Det finns ett träd" (There is a Tree), the lyrics of Monica Forsberg are directed towards the children with an appeal to them to "Let love guide your steps, hold on strong to God's hand, walk along his way." The song "Käre Fader" (Dear Father) written by Andersson is a prayer to God to protect our world, to teach us to listen to His words, and to show us the way to go. In the biography Andersson says that he plays these songs in the four to five church concerts he gives every year.[17]

Alf Robertson, his country and our world

Singer-songwriter Alf Robertson in his biography expresses a way of being a believer that is very similar to what his good friend Hasse Andersson does: "Alf says that he's a serious believer—'I have always kept a certain eye in that direction'—without being a member of any certain congregation."[18] He lost his faith for some time when his parents died and he himself got ill: "I terminated the acquaintance with God behind our house in Skåne where we lived. But faith has come back. I usually go through what's happened during the day and ask for forgiveness before I go to bed."[19] The author of Robertson's biography Börje Lundberg continues: "Now it's 2008 and he gladly goes into a church or a chapel to sit down for a while."[20] In the biography it is said that Robertson sometimes prays to God for help, but that he hates religious hypocrisy, and that religious excesses scare him. In his performances later in life he always said something about "our Lord and the Heavenly Kingdom," but he was careful not to "write it on people's noses": "To become an agitator can be damned dangerous, both concerning politics and religion" he states.[21] With this in mind, Robertson on his albums expresses both political and religious standpoints. On the title songs of the albums *Mitt land* (My Country, 1980), and *Vår värld* (Our World, 1983) he talks about his love both for his country and our world, but also about all the injustice and prejudice that makes life hard for ordinary people. On the song "Mitt land" he recites the lyrics accompanied by the Swedish national anthem, and on "Vår värld" he in the same way recites the lyrics now accompanied by the European anthem: the music of "Ode to Joy" from Beethoven's ninth symphony. These themes are followed up also on the next album *Tellus* (1984) where the title song deals with the way humanity drives our world towards disaster. This almost pretentious song is followed by the up-tempo country song "Från religion till renat" (From Religion to Renat),[22] which starts with the narrator waking up with a terrible hangover not knowing where he was or what he did last night. This song is also about the trials and tribulations of the common man, in relation to the injustices of those who are in power and threats like nuclear power, war, and famine. The song is an adaption to Swedish conditions of the Tom T. Hall song "Everything from Jesus to Jack Daniels," and the refrain goes: "I have tried everything from religion to Renat, but I didn't get any wiser because of that. I have tried everything from religion to Renat, the only thing they both did was to get me on my knees. [...] Personally I have lost faith in almost everything and everybody, so now I live day by day and here's my report for today: I have tried everything from religion to Renat etc."[23]

In the Robertson biography, Lundberg refers to "Vår värld" as "leaning towards religion."[24] This leaning receives an ambivalent reception among fans and reviewers. When the album *Vår värld* was reviewed in *Country News*, the reviewer Thomas Buskhagen was ambivalent about the religious parts of the content. He liked the song "Balladen om Birger Bergman" (The Ballad of Birger Bergman) which "makes moderate fun of certain religious phenomena,";[25] when it comes to the title song he says that Robertson's recitation is bordering on the banal, but that he manages to keep it on the right side. His biggest problem is with the overtly Christian song "När du går över floden" (When You Cross the River) written by one of Sweden's, at that time, most famous CCM artists, Pentecostal singer-songwriter Pelle Karlsson. Buskhagen writes: "this and some other songs give the album a religious touch that somehow doesn't fit in on Robertson."[26] *Country News*, like the rest of Swedish country culture, is no outspoken opponent of Christianity and sacred country. They do not prefer it, but they are not opposing it, and they do not deny its existence or refuse to deal with it, like, for example, the rock magazines do when it comes to Christian rock music. Robertson himself doesn't make any secret of his beliefs, but at the same time he doesn't live or preach like a born-again Christian, and his lyrical themes are most commonly addressing other issues. At the same time as being a believer, Robertson takes pride in being a heavy drinker, smoker, and womanizer. When commenting on his furrowed face he said: "That's how you look after 1 400 bags of Whisky, one million cigarettes, two heart attacks and three marriages."[27] So, although being aware of Robertson's beliefs, his fans expected something else from him than downright CCM lyrics. When he occasionally recorded that kind of song, the fans had problems deciding what attitude to take in relation to them.

It's interesting to compare the review of Robertson's album with the review of the new self-titled album by the well-respected Pentecostal country-act Curt & Roland in the same issue of *Country News*. The reviewer Ole Romin is positive first of all because of the album being a good quality country album, as expected from Curt & Roland. About the Christian content Romin writes:

> I have through the years had problems getting excited by gospel music, and it hasn't been so much because of the music as the lyrical content. In gospel music, the lyrical motives are limited, you can't vary indefinitely, and because of that it's easy to get stuck in a labyrinth of repetitions when you make gospel lyrics. But there's no rule without exceptions and to me Curt & Roland have always been one of those. They are exceptionally good musicians and singers, and at the bottom of it all there is country music giving color and flavor to their music.[28]

As can be seen, it is not the Christian message per se that the writers are opposed to. When it is presented by artists defined by themselves and others as Christian artists, and not too simplified and single-minded, they can accept it. But when it comes from an artist like Robertson a too obvious Pentecostal message just doesn't fit into his sphere of authenticity.

Andersson and Robertson revisited

As can be seen in the examples given, the great holiness in the shape of a personal and individualized relation to Christianity is present in the music and lives of Hasse Andersson and Alf Robertson. Both of them in their biographies express a personal faith and describe themselves as believers. Even though confessing a relation to the church and God in a way that puts them inside the frames of Christianity, they are both careful to distance themselves from dogmatic and regulated religion, and none of them are seen as, or are promoting themselves as, Christian artists. Especially Robertson strongly opposes what he considers to be religious hypocrisy and excessive expressions of religion. What they both picture in their stories about their religion is a free, personal, and individual belief in a great holiness, with an emphasis not on life yonder but a strong connection to the trials and tribulations of the everyday here on earth. Their faith offers a sense of security and reliance, but doesn't lead to any actual restrictions or regulations in their respective everyday life. Both of them are artists with a strong social pathos taking an obvious stand for those not in power. If anything is holy for them it is their love for the common woman and man, with a special place in their hearts for those on the outskirts and bottom of society.

In both cases their religion is close to what Luckmann describes as invisible private religions. Even though showing an obvious affinity to Christianity, none of them actually abides by the rules and regulations of that religion; instead they have their own personal adaption of it, which is clearly stated by Andersson saying: "I have found my own religiosity, and it's not bound to a lot of rituals, but tremendously free."[29] Also they both declare that their faith is not something that they want or need to talk about, especially not in order to convert someone. As said before, Frisk and Åkerbäck point out that contemporary popular religion in Sweden is influenced by secularization.[30] In the cases of Andersson and Robertson we see good examples of Christianity being a heavy influence on contemporary popular religion, but also of Christianity being influenced by secularization and carrying secularized features. Andersson and Robertson show no signs of being influenced by any new spiritual movements or religions other than Christianity. Instead their spiritual and religious thinking, their private invisible and individual religions, are based on a Christian belief, a religion they've been exposed to since childhood.

Christina Lindberg and the last delightful years

Just like Hasse Andersson with "Änglahund," Christina Lindberg had her breakthrough with a song dealing with ageing and death. Together with the Swedish dance band Lasse Stefanz she recorded the song "De sista ljuva åren" (The Last Delightful Years, 1988), which became a major hit breaking all records on the Swedish top ten chart Svensktoppen.[31] The lyrics of the song are about an ageing couple wishing for their last years together to be the best they had: "So let the last delightful years, be the best years of our lives, the happiness we're feeling, let it stay till the end of days. And when I reach the day when my heart stops beating, then you shall think about the moments that were the most beautiful in our life." In an article in the newspaper *Helsingborgs Dagblad* the writer analyzes why this song became such a big hit and so tremendously popular:

> When Christina Lindberg sings about the last years of life, millions are listening. The Svensktopp-poetry in a musical framing is a folk poem that delivers dreams and offers safety. When Christina Lindberg and Olle Jönsson, the singer of Lasse Stefanz orchestra, formulate these feelings, they have touched something essential for the Swedish people.[32]

The lyrics of "De sista ljuva åren" make no reference to any great holiness, but are all focused on life here on earth and the dimensions of here and now. When the first one of the couple dies the narrator urges the one that remains to think about all the good times they've had together. Nothing is said about the other one to do the same from the other side, or about waiting to be re-united on the other side. Time and the relentless passing of time are mentioned, but this is also restricted to life on earth: "Your cheek is marked by time, not as lean as it used to be. Your hair has a touch of grey, marked by the passing of time. But even though we have changed something still remains that time can't touch, it's the feelings that we share."

When bringing up the subject of believing in her biography, Lindberg says she "believes in good energies," and she continues: "My father was a believer, but I don't believe in a 'man in the sky'. I'm still a seeker and absolutely believe that there is something, unclear what. But I don't believe in Hell, if it exists it's here on earth. We create our own demons."[33] She also expresses an openness and sensitivity to the spiritual side of life.[34] She, in her own words, has always had a sixth sense and an ability to get in contact with the other side, and she tells stories about meeting her deceased grandfather and father. This kind of spirituality isn't openly expressed in her songs, but there is, in the lyrics written by herself and her songwriters, a sense of spirituality touching both greater and smaller holinesses. One example of this is the song "En ängel följer i ditt spår" (An Angel is Following Your Track) with the refrain: "An angel is following your track, a guiding light on the road you walk on your travel here on this earth. In sorrow and deceit the angel stands fast, she follows every step you take. In the shadow of her wings you find peace."[35] Another example is the song "En hälsning till morgonen" (A Greeting to the Morning) with the refrain: "And I turned to the winds, floated like an eagle, with morning dew on my wings. I felt like never before. And I turned towards the sea and settled by the shore of hours, looked out over the surf and danced the waltz of the waves."[36] Unlike Andersson and Robertson, Lindberg is obviously influenced by new spiritual currents and movements. As said before, angels are a common feature in many religions, including Judaism, Christianity, and Islam. But apart from being connected to these and other great and traditional religions, angels in their own respect are also part of what Frisk and Åkerbäck refer to as "popular religion."[37] Looking at how the angel in "En ängel följer i ditt spår" is presented, and with Lindberg's view on religion in mind, it feels more likely to be interpreted as an expression of contemporary popular religion rather than as an expression of a belief in any of the great religions. The other example "En hälsning till morgonen" is not obviously to be interpreted as spiritual in any way, but it shares certain streaks and symbols with spiritual movements like Neo-Shamanism and New Age and their way of looking at and relating to nature and the surrounding world.

Most of all, Lindberg's lyrics in general touch upon the subjects of lost and found love, and of found love as a homecoming. A common theme in her lyrics is about traveling long and lonely roads, and about being a seeker and a stranger. This theme is most probably a consequence of Lindberg belonging to a family of travelers, a minority group that also in Sweden has historically been subject to racism, prejudice, and marginalization. In her biography Lindberg says that: "When I was a child my father said: 'You shall be proud to be a traveler, but don't tell anyone about it!'"[38] She says that she has never experienced it herself, but that travelers have been despised and very badly treated: "Many of the travelers were forced to live at the bottom of society. Outcasts of society, they have been forced to travel and stick together in order not to starve to death … No one wanted to have anything to do with them, far less hire them. That's the way it was for my father's family."[39] Until the publication of her biography she kept her father's request not to tell about her heritage. Even though Lindberg hasn't herself experienced discrimination and marginalization because of her roots, she still expresses a feeling of being different and an outsider. During her upbringing her family kept moving and Lindberg talks about this in quite a positive but ambivalent way: "One day in May that special feeling comes again, a kind of restlessness in the soul … If you are nine years old it means a travel towards new adventures, you never know, it can be really good. I can't be more than outside and I've always been that…".[40]

For the individual living in late modern society these lived experiences of marginalization and alienation are not something distant and incomprehensible, but something that many of the inhabitants in contemporary western societies as a result of the process of cultural modernization can relate to and recognize in themselves on a psychological level. According to Thomas Ziehe, the basic trait of the process of cultural modernization is that the traditional and common patterns of interpretation are decomposed and individualized.[41] This means that modern individuals are disconnected from common interpretations and have to become seekers in order to find their own interpretations and create their own systems of belief. As a result of this, individuals in late modernity not only become seekers, but also travelers and outsiders in their own diversifying environment. In popular music cultures from the 1960s onward, travelers, nomads, and drifters of different kinds have been a central theme, symbolizing feelings of alienation and disconnectedness from contemporary society. In relation to this Lindberg's experiences and feelings fit well into the lives of, and are readily understood by, the consumers of contemporary popular culture.

Conclusion

As can be seen in the examples given, all these three artists in one way or another express a relation to a great holiness. In the cases of Hasse Andersson and Alf Robertson it comes in the shape of personal and individualized beliefs in connection to Christianity. Christina Lindberg is the only one of the three clearly stating not to believe in "a man in the sky," which must be seen as a mark of distance to Christianity. Still, her belief in good energies and a spiritual dimension also put her in relation to a great holiness, albeit not being connected to any defined religion or great story.

At the same time as relating to more or less specified greater holinesses they are all careful to put themselves outside the frames of organized religion. Furthermore none of them in their careers or main lyrical themes place religion and their beliefs up front. Instead they keep them more or less hidden, and their respective beliefs are all best described as invisible private religions.

Maybe more important than the great holinesses in all their lives is their relation to and emphasis on the smaller holinesses. The sanctity of family, friends, common people, the community between groups of people and between countries, the sanctity of nature and planet earth, are all much more common themes in their lyrics, as well as in their biographies, than expressions of a belief in the greater holinesses.

10

Punk and Religion in Indonesia

Jim Donaghey

In "the West" the vast majority of punk's engagements with religion are antagonistic and oppositional. This perspective is generally taken for granted, and was certainly one I shared as I began research into the punk scenes of Indonesia. Being the world's most populous "Muslim country," religion was always going to be a central theme in the interviews there, but through my assumed prism of punk anti-theism the questions were to be focused around the regular harassment of punks by "Shariah police" and Islamic fundamentalist gangsters, rather than how often interviewees went to mosque or their relationship with Allah. I expected that Indonesian punks would be as fiercely opposed to religion as their comrades elsewhere in the world— if not even more so in the face of religiously motivated repression. During the course of the interviews it rapidly became apparent that this assumption was skewed by my own experience of punk and my Western positioning in a neo-colonial context, and was in need of urgent redress. Contrary to my assumptions, *most* of the interviewees replied that they were Muslim (though there were several instances of atheism/anti-religiousness, particularly among anarchist punk collectives). The relationship between punk and religion in Indonesia seriously challenges hitherto "stable" definitions as developed in the Western context.

Interviews and participant observation were carried out in September/October 2012 and January 2015 across Sumatra, West Java, and Greater Jakarta. Grounded theory informs the research method,[1] with an emphasis on giving voice[2] to respondents and allowing analyses to develop from interviewee testimony rather than my own preconceptions (as far as this is possible). Owing to the sensitive

---

An earlier version of this chapter was published as Jim Donaghey "'Shariah don't like it … ?' Punk and Religion in Indonesia," *Punk & Post Punk* 4, no. 1 (2015): 29–52.

nature of the material, all interviewees have been given pseudonyms, and were offered a veto over any quoted content that is attributed to them.

Banks's *Hardcore Guide to Christianity* zine specifically mentions Islam in the list of "system[s] of control and obedience" that are incompatible with punk.[3] The interviewee responses from Indonesian punks seriously problematize this assertion—though they don't dispute it entirely. As will be discussed further, many of the respondents were punk and Muslim, but held these two spheres as separate. One purported example of a synthesis between Islam and punk is Taqwacore,[4] but the significance of this engagement is seriously overstated. *The Taqwacores* began life as a work of fiction by Michael Knight, and half-a-dozen or so bands subsequently took the "Taqwacore" mantle from fiction to reality, resulting in these bands getting together with Knight to tour in the US and Pakistan for a documentary film.[5] However, as Imran Malik of a "Taqwacore band" called the Kominas says, "it was fabricated and forced by someone who was trying to sell a narrative, a sexy narrative. Since then, a lot of those bands have either ceased to exist, or said they're not Taqwacore after all."[6] I mentioned Taqwacore to a number of interviewees in Indonesia, and though some of them had heard of individuals who attempted to synthesize punk and Islam in this way, none of them knew any of these people personally and did not know of *any* Taqwacore bands. In fact, the relationship between Islam and punk in Indonesia is far more interesting than the bodged synthesis that Taqwacore represents.[7]

Religion in Indonesia

The 2010 Population Census[8] in Indonesia reported that, of a population of nearly 240 million, 87.18 percent were Muslim, 6.96 percent Christian (i.e. Protestant), 2.91 percent Catholic, 1.69 percent Hindu, 0.72 percent Buddhist, 0.50 percent Confucian, with 0.51 percent identified as "Others."[9] The massive dominance of Islam (mostly Sunni) is immediately apparent, but so too is the small number of recognized religions—just the six listed above. In fact, the Indonesian state recognizes *only* these religions, which makes it essentially unlawful to practice any religion other than these, or to be atheist. Religion is present in every aspect of the state's functions, to the extent that each person's religion is stated on the Indonesian National ID Card. Religion is enshrined in the "*Pancasila*" founding principles of the Indonesian state, the first statement of which is "Belief in the one and only God" (*Ketuhanan Yang Maha Esa*).[10] This has repressive consequences for unrecognized religions and atheists. For example, Alex Aan was imprisoned for two and half years in 2012 for posting "God doesn't exist"[11] on a social media website and "stating that he was a member of the Minang atheist Facebook group."[12] He was charged with blasphemy and encouraging others to embrace atheism,[13] and initially faced a jail sentence of up to eleven years. He was also fined 100 million Rupiah (£5071.24), beaten by inmates while awaiting trial in prison in Padang, "rejected by his community and endured public calls for his beheading."[14] According to Andreas Harsono, one of Aan's lawyers, there has been a noticeable shift in public and state attitudes to religion in Indonesia in recent years: "The situation is getting crazy ... We used to discuss these issues. Now there is no discussion. The discourse today is 'This is un-Islamic and immoral.'"[15] Indeed, groups of violent Islamic fundamentalists, such as the FPI (*Front Pembela Islam* or Islamic Defenders Front),[16] have been increasingly influential. In 2012 a sold-out Lady Gaga concert in Jakarta was cancelled after the FPI issued threats to Lady Gaga and her fans. After the concert was cancelled Salim Alatas, an FPI leader, said "[t]his is a victory for Indonesian Muslims ... Thanks to God for protecting us from a kind of devil."[17] In 2013 another group of Islamic fundamentalists, Hizbut Tahrir, staged protests against the Miss World beauty pageant, with the Indonesian Ulema Council declaring a fatwa against the event, and the FPI pledging to disrupt the pageant if it went ahead,[18] forcing the organizers to move the event from Jakarta to the island of Bali (which is predominantly Hindu, and largely tourist oriented). The FPI was "initially subsidised by the military and police as part of a street-level militia,"[19] and still functions with a degree of legal impunity since "law enforcement officers ... in most cases [do] nothing to protect the victims."[20]

In an even more explicit example of the repressive combination of religion and state, Aceh province has since 2001 (with an expansion of powers in 2009) enforced aspects of Shariah law with a dedicated "civil" police force.[21] Punishments include public caning.[22] "Civil offences" include: tattoos, gambling, sale and consumption of alcohol, men wearing shorts, "illicit relations" between men and women, "homosexual conduct," as well as sexist prohibitions on women being seen in public without hijab, a ban on unaccompanied women leaving their homes after sunset, and most recently a ban on female passengers straddling motorbikes.[23] But state-enforced religious repression is not limited to traditionally conservative areas like Aceh. In April 2015 a ban was introduced on the sale of alcohol by small shops, affecting all of Indonesia (though with some concessions for Bali's tourist areas), while at the same time Islamic political parties "proposed a total ban on drinking."[24] The Human Rights Watch NGO recently highlighted the continuing practice of forcing female police recruits to undergo "virginity tests"[25] across Indonesia. And as Andre Vltchek points out, religious interference into the state has popular support, even among young people. He writes that "[a] 2008 survey[26] conducted by the SETARA Institute for Democracy and Peace in Bekasi, Depok and Tangerang showed that 56 percent of the young people in Greater Jakarta supported the Sharia-based laws."[27] The influence of religion in Indonesia extends beyond the functions of the state into all areas of society and culture. A major factor in this is that the only affordable educational institutions for most people are the madrassas (Islamic schools, often funded by fundamentalist Saudi Arabian Wahhabists), but, as Vltchek argues, "it comes at the price of religious indoctrination."[28] Vltchek also points out that "[f]or many Indonesians, mosques are the only available places of social and public gathering."[29] Religion is deeply engrained into the social fabric of Indonesian life, as well as being enforced by law, and promoted by vigilante fundamentalists such as the FPI. Unsurprisingly, this impacts upon punk in Indonesia too.

Religious repression of punk in Indonesia

Punks in Indonesia have been at the sharp end of state/religious oppression in recent years, and indeed, the globally reported events of December 2011 in Banda Aceh were the catalyst for my own research there.[30] As discussed above, Aceh enforces Shariah law,[31] and the civil police in Banda Aceh considered a punk gig being held there to be an offence, despite official permissions having been obtained. Sixty-four punks were abducted at gunpoint and taken to an official facility where they were beaten, their clothes burnt, piercings removed, men had their heads shaved while women were given "respectable haircuts," before being forced to bathe in a stagnant pond which functioned as a "cleansing pool." They were eventually released after a ten-day "Qur'an bootcamp," and were awarded certificates for good behavior. Many of the abductees had come from distant cities across Sumatra, or even as far away as Jakarta, and had no way of informing their families or workplaces about what was happening to them. At no point were they arrested or charged with a criminal offence. This action actually had a precedent in Aceh in the form of *razia jibab* (hijab raids) which "involved vigilante-type actions by groups of youths who captured and lectured uncovered women. Very often, the crowds abused the women they caught; in the worst instances they cut the hair of those accused of being sex-workers, and of transsexuals." And "[f]rom 2001, the ordinary police began to carry out *razia jibab* of their own, lecturing uncovered women and providing them with free [hijab] as part of the 'educative' approach."[32] International human rights organizations were critical of the abduction of the punks, but the Banda Aceh authorities were bullishly proud of their actions. The photos that emerged of the abduction were not taken by intrepid human rights journalists; they were taken *and published* by the authorities themselves. According to Ian Wilson, Deputy Governor Illiza Sa'aduddin Djamal insisted that "the raid was necessary and would be repeated as punk constituted a 'new social disease,' a manifestation of degenerative foreign culture that was polluting Acehnese youth … in conflict with the Islamic and cultural traditions of Aceh and Indonesia, and hence must be 'eliminated.'"[33] Inspector General Hasan, the Banda Aceh police chief, echoed the sense of religious duty behind the abduction: "We're not torturing anyone … We're not violating human rights. We're just trying to put them back on the right moral path."[34] Susanto and Ridwan, interviewees from Medan, were subjected to the ten-day internment. They said the authorities "do not understand about our lifestyle, our music … They do not want to accept us … they do not accept that there are punks in Aceh."[35]

Just a few months after this incident, reports emerged of two punks being caned in Banda Aceh after being apprehended by the Shariah police on suspicion of pre-marital sex. Matt Brown of ABC Radio Australia was present at the public caning and noted: "what caught my eye wasn't the public humiliation or corporal punishment, it was the fact the pair were dubbed 'punks' by the official in charge."[36] Being punk is *officially* recognized as transgressive. An interviewee in Banda Aceh, Teuku, added that the governor and deputy governor also had political motivations for targeting punks. It was, said Teuku, "just a tactic or a trick of the governor or the deputy to attract the society,"[37] ahead of elections happening early in 2012—*and they were both re-elected*. The authorities' perception of punk as a "social disease" is also widely held by the people of Banda Aceh. After explaining the purpose of my visit to some Acehnese university students I was told that I could "help these young criminal punks back to a good life."[38] Handoko, an interviewee from Tangerang, had also been among those abducted. He said "Aceh's society were shocked by this kind of way of life, even though punks in Aceh didn't make something to worry them. They just look on us as a social disease on a religious city."[39] The influence of religion is not limited to the state, but extends across society, so that religiously motivated repression of punks is actually a vote-winner for the authorities in Banda Aceh.

However, as Wilson notes, "harassment of punk has not been an isolated occurrence, or one confined to Aceh, with anti-punk raids being commonplace in cities throughout the country."[40] Several interviewees discussed instances where the FPI had attacked punks. Zaqi, who was interviewed in Bandung but formerly lived in the more religious city of Yogyakarta, recalled "caliphists" "sweeping ... [to find] who have the mohawk, and cut the mohawk [with a machete] ... They cut the mohawk because of religion."[41] Farid Budi Fahri, senior FPI member and "purported Islamic music 'expert'" said in 2011 that "the underground community" had launched a "war" against Islam. According to the *Jakarta Post*, he "went on to speculate that the underground music community ... has been subverted by the Zionist movement to spread ideas that would contradict Islam." He said "[t]he conspiracy is within the music, the lyrics which carry messages and the ideology which would create a lifestyle and counter culture." He also discussed the FPI's efforts "to approach punk communities ... so that they can return to the true Islamic teachings," and said that the FPI would "expand its anti-underground initiatives."[42] In July 2012, a group of around thirty FPI members raided the Prapatan Rebel distro[43] in Bandung, tearing down and confiscating banners featuring pentagrams, which the distro used as its logo. Soirin Ahmad Abdullah, Chairperson of the Advisory Board of the FPI, defended the action as spontaneous, and said it was justified since the pentagram is "the Jewish label."[44] This points to the anti-Western sentiment that also informs religious repression of punk. Interviewee Gilang noted, "the religion is in all places in Indonesia like ... fanatic[al] ... They refuse everything about west[ern] culture."[45] And Mr. Hostage identified "punk [as] a Western culture, which is something new in here in Indonesia."[46] In a post-colonial context, the rejection of a punk as an element of "Western culture" is potentially very powerful (although Indonesian punk has its own indigenous expressions). However, many of the cultural attachments to Islam in Indonesia are influenced by the Middle East, so are no more indigenous than punk—though as interviewee Nadya noted, this is not necessarily recognized: "They think that all things Arab is [a] Muslim thing ... They've never been in Arab [countries] ... Indonesians misunderstand that ... Here, if you speak Arab[ic] ... people would say 'amen' because they would think [it] is a prayer or bless[ing]."[47] Despite the huge raft of recent concessions, religious political elements do not get a totally free hand in Indonesian legislation—there have even been limited attempts to curb the power of the FPI (ironically, in the form of "anti-anarchy" laws, discussed below). While fundamentalist Islam remains extremely influential, increasingly so in fact, Indonesia is officially a secular state and there are elements of Indonesian society that seek to protect that separation (even if it exists only nominally in practice).

Whatever the subtleties around clerical influence, religion is the predominant justification for state repression of punk in Indonesia. Wilson writes that the "recent upsurge in anti-punk raids and attendant criminalisation of punk identity is a familiar government reaction to the adoption of oppositional identities by ... street kids and poor urban youth."[48] In May 2012, Wilson joined a number of "senior" Jakarta punks, to meet with "state officials ... to discuss the anti-punk raids. The meeting confirmed government's *deeply entrenched misunderstandings* of what punk is and stands for."[49] Dominic Berger's impression is "that punks are at most seen as recalcitrant youths ... not something that is 'political' or a threat to the state."[50] Indeed, while there exists a definite taboo against leftist politics in Indonesia,[51] punk's primary political companion, anarchism, is fundamentally misunderstood by the state. Berger, who researches aspects of Indonesian state repression, informed me that Indonesian police have "very little to no knowledge about anarchism as a political concept."[52] The extent of their misunderstanding of anarchism was indicated in March 2011 with the creation of a new "anti-anarchy" police division[53] to quell "religious-based mob attacks"[54] and rioting by groups such as the FPI. As has already been made clear, the FPI are conservative Islamic fundamentalist zealots not libertarian communists. Mr. Hostage, an interviewee, said that "the religious communities in Bandung didn't have special problems with the anarchists or the atheists. They had problems with how punks dressed and tattooing and [that they] pierced their body." So, in their preoccupation with the outwardly visible contraventions of Islamic doctrine, the authorities misunderstand punk. They fail to grasp punk's connections with anti-statist,[55] anti-capitalist, and anti-religious politics—which might make more sensible grounds for repression after all. For them punk is a social disease, an offence to Islam, and they repress it *in specifically religious terms*.

Muslim *and* punk ...

As stated, repression of punk in Indonesia is largely[56] religiously motivated, so it might be expected that Indonesian punks would be especially hostile to religion as a result. While some punks are openly atheist and anti-clerical (usually those associated with anarchist politics), the majority of punks interviewed in Indonesia described themselves as Muslim, and many attended mosque regularly. Interviewee Nadya, from Bandung, said "[punk] guys here, they go to the mosque for the Friday prayer and then they pray five times a day. Like it's normal for some people, it's just like [a] choice." Surprisingly, attending mosque does not appear to create any special difficulty for punks. Gilbert said that "nowadays it is possible to pray in the mosque wearing punks' attributes."[57] Septian, who plays in a popular street-punk band in Jakarta, attends mosque in his punk attire. He said that people at the mosque are inquisitive but friendly: "they want to know what is this, or they want to touch [my spiky hair]."[58] The street punks in Banda Aceh, where religious oppression has perhaps been most fierce, said simply: "if we're punk, and we pray, what's wrong with that?"[59] This attitude was echoed by Teuku in Banda Aceh. He possessed several recent issues of *MaximumRockNRoll* zine, which generally espouses anarchist politics,[60] and on the walls of his room hung posters with anarchist imagery and radical slogans,[61] but alongside these hung a large portrait of Ayatollah Khomeini. I perceived this as something of a contradiction, but when I asked Teuku about it he replied that his uncle had been a big fan of the Ayatollah,[62] without further qualification, and without seeming to acknowledge my perplexity. Teuku responded to this particular point after reading a draft version of this chapter, saying:

> Well, it's kinda tough to renounce your religion here, people grow up with a staunch religious upbringing most of the time. *I'm culturally … very Muslim*, I still do pray … five times a day, fasting during Ramadan. I do it for fun and I just succumb to these social pressures, but it's not as hard as it may seem. Religion is a big deal here, religion is very mainstream, perceived as natural and those [who] don't believe in one are very much like social pariahs.[63]

This emphasis on being *culturally* Muslim is key, as will be discussed below, but for many of the interviewees in Indonesia, punk rubbed alongside religiousness, and was accepted as normal. However, this is not to say that the adoption of the label "Muslim" is unproblematic for Indonesian punks, and indeed, many interviewees offered substantial qualification. Some interviewees made an effort to distinguish their religiousness from the actions of the FPI and other fundamentalist mobs. Hengki and Yandi, from Medan, said that groups such as the FPI "use a religion as a shield. But religion isn't like that. Islam isn't like that. It's just them using the politics … They were just using the situation, because they actually want cash, money … They use religion to make themselves look stronger."[64] Dimas in Jakarta shared this perspective: "[The FPI] act brutal, they do not consider about the religion … The religion is not teaching brutality, but they do the brutality behind religion's name. But actually, they work for the government y'know, they're actually just a seal for their power. That's it."[65] Similarly, Vltchek notes that "whenever religious cadres commit a crime, it is almost always labelled as 'thuggery', or something that is 'hiding behind religion.'"[66] Vltchek argues that this is because "it is illegal to criticise religion in

Indonesia."⁶⁷ This prohibition must have inevitably influenced the interviewees' responses, but their main motivation, it seemed, was to defend their version of religious belief from the fundamentalism which has increasingly come to occupy Islam in Indonesia. This can be seen in the song lyrics of "They are Not a Moslem" by Disabled: "You call it religion. Your movement is a crime ... Is it call religion? Fuck! This is a bullshit. Is it call Islamic? Fuck! This is a crime."⁶⁸ The CD inlay notes that the song is about the FPI, criticizing their violent conduct and their successful campaign to ban Lady Gaga from performing in Indonesia on the grounds that she is a devil-worshipper:

> Islamic Defenders Front is more suitable to be replaced with Islamic Destroyers Front ... Are they too Islam or too stupid? Do they deserve the name of Islam? Rioting and destruction in the name of religion. In order not to be dragged into the legal system, they act in the name of religion. This is not Islam.⁶⁹

So while Disabled speak out against the actions of the FPI and their ilk, they are not critical of Islam as such, rather seeking to rescue Islam from associations with fundamentalism.

Less qualified expressions of religiousness can be identified in a survey of some releases by Indonesian punk bands in the last few years.⁷⁰ For example, Injakmati include explicitly religious sentiments in the thanks section of their *Rotten Conspiracy* 7". Three of the four band members thank "god," one of whom thanks no one else. One band member thanks "Allah SWT"⁷¹ but ends his list of thanks with "Viva anarchy & revolution!"⁷² echoing the dualism observed in Teuku's posters. Similarly, GunXRose thank "Alloh SWT, and Rasululloh SWT."⁷³ Unlike the other bands mentioned, religion also extends into the lyrics of GunXRose, in the song "Lenyapkan Zionis" which translates as "Eliminate the Zionists."⁷⁴ In this context, accompanied as it is by thanks to the Islamic godhead and prophet, the anti-Zionism takes on a religious/sectarian dimension strongly reminiscent of the FPI's obsession with "Zionist conspiracies." While this was the only encountered example of religion making a direct influence on the music of punk bands in Indonesia, the propensity for bands to thank god/Allah or Mohammed illustrates that many punks are actively *and publicly* religious. Interestingly, the *Kill Me With Your Lips* tape by Street Voices includes "thanks" to "everyone who support us, *who pray with us ... who drunk with us*."⁷⁵ Here the public display of religiousness sits alongside a public contravention of Islamic doctrine, in the form of consuming alcohol—so even where punk and religion appear together this is not necessarily in a form that fulfills expected Islamic orthodoxies, and offers no easy synthesis.

... but not Muslim-punk

Interviewees were very conscious of the potential dissonance between Islam and punk, and typically explained this in four ways: as something personal (so not open to further interrogation); as an unsynthesized dualism; as an expression of cultural religiosity; or as a result of severe social pressure to conform.

Mr. Hostage offered an analysis of the presence of religion in Indonesian punk:

> Because of the limitation of technology over here ... they didn't have any idea that religion is like the opposite of punk. So, y'know they're still doing their conservative belief while doing their punk thing ... So it's like finally they know punk perspective, a common punk perspective, about religion, but yet they still continue to do what they believe in because of their *personal reason*, y'know.

Mr. Hostage's emphasis on "personal reason" was a commonly repeated theme. For example, Putri in Bandung said "like the prayers and everything, that's just individual."[76] Agus and Yohanes in Jakarta said religion "comes down to [the] individual, [it's] personal."[77] Dimas, perhaps expressing discomfort about my questioning on the subject, said that the issue should not be others' concern: "it's not their business about my religion." Total Anarchy,[78] a thrash-punk band from Bandung, said religion is "a matter of something inside our heart ... not to be ... socialised ... Somebody could be what they want, or even if someone doesn't have religion ... it's OK for us. What's important is we're not bothering each other."[79] As Eka pointed out, even broaching the subject of religion in conversation is likely to cause offence in Indonesia: "so many friends ... they feel offended when you talk about this."[80] This perhaps explains the "it's personal" response—interviewees found the questioning offensive and wished to close down this avenue of interrogation. However, several interviewees also expressed a personal religiosity as distinct from belonging to religious institutions. The street punks in Banda Aceh said "[y]es we are [Muslim] ... Sometimes, there many spots [missed prayers], but that's individual, it is really private, our relationship with One above ... Having or not having religion, to me, is everyone's right." And the street punks in Tangerang said that even though they are criticized for having tattoos, "it's not for human beings to judge, the Mighty One is, right?"[81] This personal interpretation of religion was repeatedly expressed in interviews with Indonesian punks, particularly in reference to religious repression of punk. By emphasizing a personal religiousness, the actions of religious institutions are presented as separate, much in the same way as other interviewees were at pains to distinguish their religiousness from that of the FPI.

A clear separation was held between religion and punk on the part of most of the interviewees. Septian in Jakarta said "some punks here still believe in religion ... just for their self. They believe, but [it] is separated. This is punks [gestures left]. This is religion [gestures right]. You cannot put it in [together]. But they are still doing punk Indonesian y'know?" Total Anarchy said "we can separate when we need to play music, and when to talk about religion ... It's unrelated ... that's why *we never put them together*." The Banda Aceh street punks said, "to me, there's no connection between punk and religion." So, these interviewees are punk and they are Muslim, but they are not Muslim-punks or punk-Muslims. Despite being religious they still consider religion incompatible with punk, holding them as distinct parts of their lives, and even as separate parts of themselves. As discussed above, this dualism is not viewed as problematic by most Indonesian punks—despite recognizing a contradiction, they feel no compulsion towards a resolving synthesis.

Putri discussed the cultural significance of religion, saying that even though "most of us usually have our own opinions about religion ... we still celebrate the religion ... Most of us still respect our parents, and go home, and stay ... with them [during religious festivals], 'cause there's feast and celebration, that kinda thing." Taufan, also from Bandung, agreed: "Yeh it's like, when we grow up we just adopt the religion from our parents, it's already like automatic."[82] Mr. Hostage made a similar point: "Religion over here is like almost a culture, so it's like, you've been taught this religion from childhood and all that." Several of the interviewees described themselves as atheists (though they asked for direct attribution of expressions of atheism to be removed from the article), but traditions still hold huge social and cultural significance for them, even as these occasions are emptied of their "religious" aspect.[83] As Demerath notes, cultural religious affiliation "is less one of present conviction or commitment than of continuity with generations past and contrast with rival groups and identities."[84] A Muslim identity can be carried without any deep commitment to the religion—indeed, as discussed above, the state constantly emphasizes religion in its functions, not least by stating each person's religion on the National Identity Card, so there is little space for any identity that does not fit around one of the six recognized religions.

But this does not adequately explain why *so many* punks describe themselves as Muslim, and does even less to explain why punks are actively religious, *despite* acknowledging that punk is essentially in opposition to religion. Religious pressure, both social and state, are a further reason given by Indonesian punks for their continued religious affiliations. As Eka describes:

> If you don't have religion ... [society is] gonna feel that, "aw, you're evil, you're immoral" ... You['re] gonna deal with so many like moral punishments, social punishments from your surroundings if you talk about religion or you're against religion, or you criticize religion.
>
> So, if you say you don't live in a religion, or you say that you have sympathy for communism or communist ideas, you're gonna deal with the same shit, like really, even you don't need cops to come to you, the people themselves will ... [They] can do anything, whatever they want to you.
>
> Violence, like really even direct violence, starting from verbal to non-verbal violence and terror.

There was also a perception that punks who were not religious would eventually "go back" to Islam. Eka said:

> I see lots of my old punk friends ... maybe late 30s, and they start to get married, work in a normal way, live a normal life, and they always marry with the girl with the hijab.
>
> Most of them think that their life when [they were] still in the street, when they was still punk, it was a mistake. It's part of the wrong path that they took before, now they want to go back to the right path, that's why they start to go back to pray again.
>
> They consciously say "I don't want to marry like punk girl, because they're the same as me, like filthy" and they think that if they went back to religion, their sins will be clear again.

This points to the sexist attitudes that are held by many punks in Indonesia (largely informed by religious/patriarchal norms), but also illustrates the pervasive influence of religion—even people who escape religious expectations in their youth succumb as they get older. Religious repression is a substantively different force in Indonesia than in "Western" contexts, with the effect that the relationship between punk and religion is also *substantively* different.

Anarchist anti-theist punks

Most of the punks interviewed in Indonesia described themselves as Muslim. However, a significant minority of interviewees described themselves as atheist or "not religious." This obviously constitutes an act of considerable bravery in Indonesia, quite distinct from professions of anti-theism in many other parts of the world. Interviewees expressing an anti-religious position did so through an anarchist framing, and as discussed elsewhere,[85] punk politics is generally informed by anarchism. For punks informed by anarchist politics, religion and the church are parts of the state's oppressive apparatus, and serve to justify domination and submission.

Some of these people were not affiliated to any particular group, such as one interviewee who said "I don't believe in religion, and so too their gods," but many of them were involved in organized anarchist groups, for example the Bandung Pyrate Punx collective and InstitutA in Depok. InstitutA is an anarcha-feminist info-shop which grew out of the Jakarta punk scene. Despite being located in one of the most religiously fundamentalist parts of the Greater Jakarta Area, they have openly anti-theist literature in their library, LGBTQ stickers in their windows, and a large mural which criticizes Islam on an outside wall.[86] An activist there, who was formerly involved in the Jakarta punk scene, described religion as a "creation of men to create conflict, to control people, to oppress people, to take benefit of other people in the sake of [an] afterlife," pointing to an explicitly anarchist atheism. The InstitutA group also screen-print patches featuring gay and feminist slogans and imagery which they sew onto bags and t-shirts to sell under the moniker "Needle 'n' Bitch." Promoting homosexuality is illegal in Indonesia since it contravenes Islamic law, and even making basic feminist statements presents a challenge to Islam, so this kind of propaganda takes on a huge significance. Even within the punk scene their activities are viewed by some as "something 'too much' and not really necessary."[87]

Bandung Pyrate Punx put on gigs and festivals and produce merchandise for bands, as well as recording and releasing CDs and tapes. Their activities are based around their shared housing project "Pirata House," which itself goes against religious custom since unrelated people of different sexes sleep under the same roof. The poster for their eighth annual "Libertad Fest" in 2015 bore the slogan "8th years of no lords!" echoing the anarchist "no gods, no masters" catechism. The island on which the festival was held also had its Indonesian flag replaced with the anarchist red-and-black flag for the duration. Bands associated with Bandung Pyrate Punx, such as Krass Kepala and KontraSosial, also use anti-religious lyrics and imagery. For example, Krass Kepala's "Arogansi Agama" ("Religious Arrogance") has the lyrics "stop religious arrogance that legalises violence against social activities,"[88] or KontraSosial's "Religi Konsumsi" ("Religious Consumption") in which they sing "[p]rophet ad victim, wearing a Nike brand turban, our ad victims, religious propaganda."[89] They critique religion and capitalist consumerism as mutually reinforcing phenomena, and in the explanatory note provided in the CD inlay they write, "[l]adies and gents, we introduce to you the CONSUMERISM RELIGION!!! Shopping is worship that guarantees you get to heaven."[90] Zudas Krust, from Jakarta, pick up on Krass Kepala's attack on "arrogant" religion in "Perang Agama" ("Religious War") with the lyrics: "[h]igh dose of arrogance, killing and intimidating, establishing their heaven. Never care about how much blood they spill. Religion war in the name of God."[91] Also on the *A Loyal Slave to the Apocalyptic Order* tape is "God System Slavery" with the lyrics: "No good deeds goes unpunished. Religion … religion … religion … for so long!!!"[92] Zudas Krust echo KontraSosial's critique of consumerism and religion in "Percepat Kiamat!" ("Hasten the Apocalypse!") with the line "[w]ishing rewards from the idols [sic] tower, to be fast of the doomsday, God damn with heaven, if reward just shopping."[93] The cover of the tape on which this song appears, *Here Lies Your Gods*, features skulls in a mass grave, declaring a Nietzschean "God is dead," while also implicating religion in mass murder and genocide. "You Call It Moral" also appears on this tape, with the lyrics: "[i]t's 'in the name of God' written on your forehead. Slashing and bashing, your moral fuelled with hate."[94] Duct Tape Surgery, also from Jakarta, sing "Listen to what they're saying. Religion. Tell me what to believe in. Point of no return. I've lived for no reason," on the song "Fate."[95] The artwork for KontraSosial's *Endless War* CD contains further anti-religious messages: the disc itself is circled with the words "No Gods x No Masters x No Slavery x No Oppressions x" which points to the anarchist underpinning of their anti-theism; and also features a Madonna and child with their faces replaced by skulls, a revolver in the Madonna's hand, and rows of missiles forming angel wings behind her, conflating religious iconography with violence, war, and death. Of course, the détourned Madonna and child is based on Christian iconography, with aesthetic similarity to punk bands in "the West." And indeed, the expressions of anti-religiousness are largely comparable to those encountered, for example, in the UK and Poland in rhetoric and aesthetic, and particularly in terms of their anarchist underpinning.[96] The anarchist framework provides salient terms of reference to express this anti-theism in a context where the opportunity to do so is extremely limited. In Indonesia, to speak out against religion is to risk your freedom and your life, so the individuals, bands, and collectives that do so have much more at stake, and are making a much bigger statement—and as a result is something that only a small number of people are willing to do openly.

Conclusion

The influence of religion in Indonesia is substantively different to "the West." Religion infiltrates into the state and is at the root of organized terror campaigns, the affordable schools are madrassas, pressures from society and family are intense, and atheism is unlawful. As such, religion wields huge power in Indonesia and it does not allow its influence to be escaped easily. The examples of openly anti-religious punk discussed above are exceptional. *They are also illegal.* In "the West" punk opposes religion, even if religion is far less concerned with punk. In Indonesia the "opposition" flows predominantly in the other direction, with religious groups actively repressing punks, while punks seek to maintain affiliation to a religious identity or culture. Any sense of an expected or "ordinary" relationship between punk and religion completely breaks down. Punk culture is an international entity, with significant commonalities traversing scenes across the globe, but these scenes are also heavily localized and develop in tension with co-existing local cultures. As such, Indonesian punk has a very distinct character—interviewees repeatedly expressed the idea of a "punk Indonesia." As described, the relationship with religion here is one of Indonesian punk's most distinctive characteristics. The impact of an aggressively enforced religious culture results in a locally distinct relationship between punk and Islam which *does not map onto Western punk contexts*. Of course, it is naïve to expect such a mapping, but this also speaks to any investigation into "exotic" or "other" punk scenes, and serves as poignant warning to maintain vigilance against the re-expression of neo-colonial attitudes from the privileged "Western" punk perspective.

11

Dylan Goes to Church: The Use of Bob Dylan's Music in Protestant Churches

Andreas Häger

The 13th century cathedral is crowded and the Sunday evening service is just about to start. Three musicians, with guitar, piano and percussions, are lined up just in front of the gilded altarpiece and behind the central altar, which holds the communion chalice and paten. The guitarist strikes a chord and starts singing. The song is Bob Dylan's "Shelter From The Storm."

This description is based on my field notes from the "Forever Young" mass in the cathedral of Västerås, Sweden, in October 2016. The topic of this chapter is the use of Bob Dylan's music in church and more specifically in rock masses or "Dylan masses." Before entering a discussion on this topic, I will briefly introduce the phenomenon of the rock mass, as well as present some thoughts on Dylan's relation to religion and how it is perceived.

A popular music mass or rock mass is a communion service set to popular music—the style is not necessarily always strictly rock, but it is a popular and modern style in contrast to the typical church idiom. It is not merely a matter of bringing an electric guitar to church, or using a rock or pop song as postlude, but giving rock music a central role in the service. In a Nordic Lutheran context, this type of mass has been used regularly since the mid-1990s, as part of a general process of change in the ways the divine service is celebrated. Examples of Dylan masses from the Lutheran majority churches of Scandinavia as well as from an American Protestant context are included in the chapter.

There are different ways to use rock music in a rock mass, depending on the degree of change in comparison with a traditional mass. Firstly, there are masses, such as the Finnish 'Metal mass,' which follows a traditional order, using existing hymns and liturgical music, but with a rock accompaniment.[1] Secondly, there are masses with new lyrics and new music written especially for a mass.[2]

The Dylan masses discussed in this chapter fall into a third category, masses taking existing popular music, not written as church music or with an explicit religious intention, and using it in church. These masses usually focus on one artist or group, rather than taking songs from different artists. An example that has been used internationally is the so-called "U2charist."[3] In the Göteborg diocese in the Church of Sweden, masses with music by international artists, for example Emmylou Harris, Pink Floyd, and Bob Dylan, as well as by various Swedish artists, have been used.[4] One American congregation that has used Dylan's music also has organized masses with music by many other artists, including Joni Mitchell, Pearl Jam, and Stevie Wonder.[5]

Bob Dylan is one of the major artists of the rock era. He has released over forty studio albums, is still touring regularly past the age of seventy-five, and has been the subject of scores of books. One topic in the books and fan discussions on Dylan is his relation to religion. This discussion relates to several aspects of Dylan's work and life: his recurrent use of biblical references in his lyrics, his occasional covering of traditional gospel songs, and not least that, being born Jewish, he went through a conversion to Evangelical Christianity at the end of the 1970s. He released two albums with gospel songs, *Slow Train Coming* (1979) and *Saved* (1980). The following album *Shot of Love* (1981), includes some songs that can be described as gospel songs, and some songs in other idioms. During the beginning of this period, Dylan exclusively played gospel songs during his concerts, and also gave long speeches not least on eschatological matters.[6]

A regular issue in discussions on Dylan and religion is whether Christianity still plays a part in his life. He has been interpreted from a Christian perspective[7] and from a Jewish one.[8] The issue of Dylan's own religious views is kept alive not least by Dylan's own evasive comments in interviews.[9] I view the Dylan masses, and also the media discourses around them, as part of the discussion on Dylan's relation to religion and particularly as attempts to interpret this artist and his work from a Christian perspective.

Material and research questions

The material for this chapter consists of three different Dylan masses. These are the "Saving Grace" mass, which I attended in Göteborg, Sweden, on April 28, 2006; the "Forever Young" mass, which I attended in Västerås, Sweden, on October 23, 2016; and the Dylan mass in Richmond, Virginia, USA, which has been used in the St. James Episcopalian church on five occasions, once a year since March 2013, and which are all available in full on YouTube (in the text I refer to this mass as the "Richmond mass").[10] There are also video clips from the Saving Grace mass online.[11] The Dylan mass in Richmond takes place on Sunday morning, while the two Swedish masses have been evening events. I have additional material from eight other Dylan masses, also from Scandinavia and North America. Some of this additional material is used in the second part of the analysis, on Dylan as liturgy.

There are program leaflets to all the masses, listing the order of the elements of the masses, the songs used, as well as words of prayers and other liturgical elements. Some also include information on Dylan and on the ideas behind the mass. The program leaflets are intended as guidelines for those who attend the mass, but can also be published online as help for others who want to organize a similar mass.

In addition to the material from the masses, I have some media material, with newspaper reports on the masses, web forum discussions, and web material from organizers. I have interviewed as well as had email correspondence with some of the organizers of all three masses.

The Richmond mass is organized within a particular congregation, first and foremost by the church musicians of the congregation. The Saving Grace mass was organized by a group of musicians and ministers, in cooperation with a local congregation, the student chaplains at the university, and the diocese. The Forever Young mass was organized by a freelance musician who offers congregations the opportunity to have either concerts or masses with Dylan's music.

The task of the chapter is to discuss how the Dylan masses contribute to the construction of Bob Dylan's relation to religion. Bringing his music—and not just his gospel music—into church is a way of creating a close relation between Bob Dylan and institutional Christianity. But Dylan's music, and the drums and electrified instruments used to perform it in church, are part of rock music. I want to look at how these two cultural spheres meet and how they are negotiated into a unified—or not so unified—event. What is done in the services, and in the discourses around them, to turn Dylan into church music or liturgy? And in what sense is the music still rock music, even though performed in a church? How is the event framed as a church service and as a concert?

On the other hand, it is necessary to question a taken-for-granted dichotomy between rock and religion. This difference between two distinct cultural spheres that is a premise for this chapter (and for the whole book) is a cultural construct. There is of course nothing inherent in the electric guitar and in the organ respectively, saying that one belongs in church more than the other—it is the result of tradition, of habit, and habits change, which these Dylan masses are examples of.

In the chapter, I will first analyse media discourses on the Dylan masses, which tackle the issue of why Dylan's music is being used in church services. In the further analysis of the actual masses I first look at which songs are used, and how they are integrated into the mass. In the final section of the analysis, the focus is on how the masses are accomplished and realized through nonverbal practices.

Why Dylan in church?

Using Bob Dylan's music, or any other popular music, in church, is of course an exception to the norm of hymns and liturgy, and as such needs to be legitimated, explained, and motivated, to the attending congregation, to the church, and to the general public. This legitimation takes place in different contexts, in the media, in discussion forums, and in communication from the organizing parishes, not least in the actual services. The legitimacy of performing Dylan's music in church is also explicitly questioned by some.

The primary grounds for legitimation of bringing Dylan's music into church are the lyrics and the message they are perceived to convey. But Dylan's own person, his character, and his personal beliefs, are also used as reasons for using his music in church. Other reasons are providing variation in the church services or simply liking the music and being a fan.

Most of the sermons in Dylan masses touch on Dylan in some way—from making his Christian conversion the main topic, as in the sermon in Saving Grace, to using phrases from his lyrics. The sermon in the Richmond mass in 2014 serves as an example of quite explicit religious legitimation of Dylan in church:

> I have always found something about his scripture soaked lyrics that stirs me with fierce authenticity. Those lyrics have shown me Christ, which is the aim of all worship and music ... I think it is really, really cool [laughs] that the work of this poet, who frequently calls us to a life of discipleship in his songs, has found a place in our worship life here.[12]

On the website of Thomas Cervin, the Swedish musician behind the Forever Young mass, the above question is stated explicitly: "Why Dylan in church?"— and the answer[13] is:

Dylan's lyrics are colored by language and images reflecting his path through life: Commitment to peace and justice. Search for love. The happiness of love and the pain of separation. The yearning for spirituality. Salvation and faith. The reflections of a mature man. Etc.[14]

Cervin's focus on Dylan's lyrics is also reflected in the fact that many of the songs used in the Forever Young mass were done in the lead singer's own translations to Swedish. In the short introductory speech at the Forever Young mass, the priest states that Dylan is a poet who has touched people all over the world because he writes about what is important to people—and goes on to say that what is important to people is therefore important to the church, and to God. These comments, both on the website and in the words of the service, emphasize an existential aspect of the lyrics.

The choir director in St James's in Richmond, Virginia Whitmire, who initiated and organizes the Dylan masses at this church, wrote in an email to me:

> The idea is to look at lyrics through a spiritual and Biblical lens, not necessarily as originally intended by the artist … provocative, ageless lyrics which could be interpreted several ways, depending upon the listener … There was also the added advantage of Dylan's Christian songs.[15]

It is clear that the lyrics are the reason for using Dylan, but the lyrics are not described as proclaiming an unequivocal religious message, but rather that they can be interpreted from such a perspective. And the "Christian songs" are not the main reason for using Dylan, but a bonus.

Valle Erling, band leader in the Saving Grace mass, explains:

> Because he comes from a Jewish tradition, he uses these religious images, the Jewish images from the Bible … he is a story teller, stories mean a lot in the Christian tradition … when Dylan tells stories, everyone can participate in the interpretation, and interpretations are as important as the text, that's why I think he is very suitable for church.[16]

The Saving Grace mass focuses on Dylan's gospel music and the period when he was an outspoken Evangelical Christian. In the introductory words to that mass, one of the organizers says:

> Dylan has often had to defend his choices, and the answer he almost always gave is "It's honest, it's honest." Honesty is a common theme in Dylan's life and work. This was also the case at the end of the 1970s, when his career took an unexpected turn. Passionate, committed and honest, he sings of a newly found conviction and just as before, he stands firm in spite of a massive protest. It is perhaps above all Dylan's passion that has inspired us to do this service tonight.

In this context, the reason for using Dylan's work in church is not his lyrics but rather Dylan himself, and his honesty and conviction. On the one hand, it seems paradoxical that a service with his gospel songs deemphasizes the lyrics—about believing in the face of hostility and scorn, about the second coming of Christ, and about "pressing on to the higher calling of my Lord." On the other hand, the person that is emphasized is the newly born again Dylan, and the qualities mentioned are those of a committed Christian.

In the church leaflet for the first Dylan mass in Richmond it is stated:

> Dylan wrote, "the more you live a certain way, the less it feels like freedom," and life certainly validates those words—routines shackle us. This is the motivation behind the Dylan Mass—a new vocabulary in the sanctuary, both musically and lyrically, for the age old truths for which we hunger.

This introduction to the Dylan mass emphasizes the need for variation in church services. It seems a quote from Dylan gives the ambition to break the shackles of routine a greater legitimacy. The statement that the music of Dylan also proclaims "the age old truths" works as a counterbalance to the notion of change.

Meeting Valle Erling to interview him on Saving Grace, he almost immediately gives a long quote from a Dylan song, clearly establishing himself as a fan. The above quoted priest in the Richmond mass tells the congregation that she likes Dylan. Having a positive attitude towards Dylan and his music is a prerequisite for organizing a Dylan mass, and many organizers and musicians are fans. In my correspondence with Thomas Cervin he tells me that he has always been a Dylan fan and his band members wanted to play Dylan covers on the occasion of Dylan's seventieth birthday in 2011. "Besides, I look like him and sing and play the guitar and the harmonica. The church suddenly asked for my services and already 2011 I had a lot of freelance gigs in church. It felt natural." The reference to the similar looks is relevant as it brings up a certain kind of fandom practice, impersonation, to which I will return below.

As previously stated, the Richmond Dylan masses are available on YouTube (as are other masses from the same congregation). The first of these masses, from March 2013, has had over 100,000 views and over a hundred comments on YouTube (while the others only have a few hundred views).[17] Of the comments, some are positive—"Have watched this several times and wish I could have attended the service in person"[18]—and some are quite negative—"I regret clicking on this video. The female 'priest,' the music, and everything offend me equally." Some emphasized the need for variation in church services: "I think this is an amazing idea! From time to time the Church should experience different ways to worship." None of the positive comments mention the quality of Dylan's work specifically; instead the legitimacy of the Dylan mass is based either on the competence of the performance or on the possibility of variation.

Not everyone appreciates variation; one comment simply asks "why are they playing guitars in church?" Among the negative comments, none actually criticized Dylan's music; on the contrary, there are several writers who state that they like Dylan, for example: "Oh good Lord. Look, I love Bob Dylan. But there is a TIME and a PLACE for it. This isn't it. This is sacrilege, no matter how well-meaning it is."

A different line of criticism comes up in the post: "this screams Church Growth 101 just like all the other Episco-fads"—dismissing the service as an inauthentic attempt to lure more people to church, and also dismissing the Episcopalians as being prone to such attempts. This comment brings up one possible reason for holding a Dylan mass that was not mentioned explicitly by any of my informants: that it may attract more people to church—although Erling notes with satisfaction that the Dylan masses he has been involved in always have drawn good crowds.

The legitimations of the Dylan masses point out that Dylan belongs in church because his lyrics are seen to convey a Christian message and in part because he went through a conversion experience in the 1970s. Playing Dylan in church because one is a fan emphasizes that the Dylan masses are still part of rock culture.

Dylan as liturgy

The designation of these masses as "Dylan masses" is due to the fact that they use songs by Bob Dylan as the main music of the service. Some masses include some other liturgical songs, but in all the masses, Dylan's music is central. The choice of which songs to use is central to the shaping of the mass, but of even greater importance is how the songs are integrated into the mass, how they are shaped into liturgy.

Saving Grace focuses on two albums from Dylan's gospel period. In Richmond, the song selection stretches from "Blowing in the Wind" from 1962 to two songs from 1989. In the five Dylan masses in Richmond, eight to ten songs are used in each mass, and two to four of these are from the gospel period.[19] Forever Young uses songs from 1962 to 1997, and includes no songs from the gospel albums. In the larger material I have collected, including eleven Dylan masses from

Scandinavia and North America, all masses except for Saving Grace include a majority of non-gospel material. Three of these masses include no gospel songs at all. The Dylan masses are not a matter of bringing Dylan's gospel material into church, but using songs from a large selection of Dylan's work, and not least some of his most popular songs from the 1960s.

The use of these songs is legitimated, as previously stated, through a discussion on the value of their lyrics. In the services, the use is legitimated through the integration of the songs into the mass, making them a part of the liturgy. This is done through various practices. The songs are placed in the mass to serve certain functions of the mass elements, which can be signaled by the designation of liturgical labels to the songs. Dylan's lyrics are used in prayers in various ways. Some alterations to Dylan's lyrics are used to make them fit better in the mass. Traditional liturgy can also be set to Dylan's music.

In a previous study on the use of Dylan's music in church services,[20] the adaption of Dylan to the mass and to liturgy is discussed in terms of translation of Dylan's lyrics to Norwegian. The argument is that translations intended for use in church tend to emphasize Christian elements in the lyrics, to a greater extent than translations done in a secular context. Dylan is appropriated by the church through these translations.

The choir director of St. James's in Richmond tells me:

> The Lectionary and liturgical season determine the songs we do. There is always a theme, a thread running through the readings in an Episcopal service and I search for lyrics that echo or illuminate this theme. Some songs have become fixed. We always begin the service with "The times they are a'changing" and end with "Blowing in the wind." These serve to open people's hearts and minds as they sing words that they sang so many years ago as idealistic young people who thought they would change the world. These songs serve as a reminder of our better selves and our responsibility to strive to be better. And the younger generations know these songs, as well. The other thing that determines the placement of songs is what is taking place in the service. I place songs that are well-loved but not necessarily pertinent to the message of the day in the prelude. I place quieter, more reflective and meditative songs during communion.[21]

In the Richmond mass, as many as four songs are played as "prelude" before the official start time of the service. During communion, there are two songs.

The songs that vary mostly between the different Dylan masses in Richmond, the ones related to the readings, are played before and after the sermon. A clear connection between reading and song comes in a service when the Epistle was from Romans 8, including the 9th verse: "If you declare with your mouth, 'Jesus is Lord,' and believe in your heart that God raised him from the dead, you will be saved," which was followed by the song "I Believe in You." A reading from Ephesians 5:8 " For you were once darkness, but now you are light in the Lord. Live as children of light" is followed by "I shall be released," with the line "I see my light come shining."

In the program leaflets for Dylan masses, songs are not always listed merely by name; sometimes they are given additional descriptions, such as "Prelude," "Confession," or "Blessing." These headings communicate the intentions behind the choice and order of songs, and tie songs to their function in the mass and thus to a Christian framework of interpretation. An example of this comes from another mass than the previously mentioned, the Dylan Eucharist at United Methodist in Geneva, Illinois, where "Blowin' in the Wind" is called "Invocation of the Holy Spirit" and "Ring Them Bells" serves as "Prayer of the People," and so on.

In the program leaflets for the Richmond mass, some songs have an accompanying Bible verse. The song "Watching the River Flow" is in the leaflet preceded by Revelation 22:1, which starts: "Then the angel showed me the river of the water of life, as clear as crystal, flowing from the throne of God and of the Lamb." I interpret the river in the song lyrics as a metaphor for life passing by, while the narrator rather would do something different and be somewhere else: "Wish I was back in the city."[22] The Bible verse may work as a lead into another interpretation, seeing the river as "the water of life," a metaphor for salvation. "Knocking on Heaven's Door," where the narrator declares that he no longer wants his guns, is in the leaflet accompanied with a famous passage from Isaiah 2:4: "They will beat their swords into plowshares and their spears into pruning hooks," thus emphasizing a pacifist interpretation of Dylan's song.

Thomas Cervin describes his selection of songs in the Forever Young mass:

> I follow the order of the mass to underline the message Welcome—confession—credo—kyrie—Love meeting—Prayer—Community and celebration. I choose between around 20 songs—very few from his specifically "Christian" period, however. The liturgical year also matters. Ring them bells at the end of the church year. Shelter from the storm during autumn etc. I only take songs that have spoken to me and that I like.[23]

The elements listed by Cervin are by themselves a reinterpretation of traditional mass, and the only elements with original names are placed in a different order. The Forever Young mass I attended at least partly followed this pattern. It started with "Shelter from the storm," with every verse ending with the words "come in she said, I'll give you shelter from the storm," welcoming the attendees. "Knocking on heaven's door" serves as a confession, and "I shall be released," is the declaration of forgiveness. These two songs are however also followed by a read confession and forgiveness.

The use of Dylan's lyrics in prayers can consist of quotes or near quotes employed as whole prayers, or quotes incorporated in existing prayers or liturgical text. In the Saving Grace mass, words from Dylan's "Forever Young" are used as Benediction at the end of the service. The song is written as a wish for a happy and successful life, allegedly for Dylan's son. In the same service, in the Prayer of deliverance, the parts in Swedish are read by the congregation and the minister responds three times, with the three different choruses from "What Can I Do For You" which the band has just performed.

In the Richmond mass, the Great Litany from The Book of Common Prayer is adapted to include a line from the chorus of "When You Gonna Wake Up," including the title of the song but changing the pronoun to "we."[24] A verse from the song "Saving Grace" is used in the Benediction. Regarding this use of lyrics in the liturgy, the choir director from St James's tells me that "the intention was to show show the similarities between Dylan's lyrics and scripture and to tie the music and the spoken word together." The Doxology, beginning with "Praise God from whom all blessings flow" is sung to the (slightly modified) tune of "The Times They are a-Changin'."

In the program of the mass from the United Methodist Church in Geneva, Illinois, the listing of songs are accompanied by short texts, some of which are formulated as prayers, apparently to be read silently by the individual attendee in his/her seat. "Blowin' In The Wind" is in the program accompanied by the following prayer: "Come Holy Spirit, enliven our worship. Be the answer and the wind that brings the grace and love of God." "The Times They are a-Changin'" has the following prayer attached to it: "We understand, O God that you are always in motion and in mission. As the times, traditions and ways community change, help us to make your presence known in a world of change." These creative paraphrases incorporate Dylan's lyrics into a central Christian practice, prayer.

At the end of the Forever Young mass, the lead singer makes a different kind of connection between Dylan and liturgy:

> For the first time in the service Cervin gives an introduction to a song, saying: "A divine service is a celebration, and he who leads us in celebrating this night when we are dancing beneath the stars is Mr. Tambourine Man."[25]

That a mass is a celebration ties closely to a traditional Christian understanding, as exemplified by the word "celebrant" as a term for the officiating priest. However, it is a most untraditional interpretation that Mr. Tambourine man is the leader of this celebration.[26] The introduction is, albeit slightly awkward, a way of connecting the mass to rock music by way of a famous character in Dylan's universe.

The following song in the same mass, "Blowin' in the Wind" is introduced as "his big breakthrough" and "the one you learned in school." Here (just as in the quote from the choir director in Richmond) the popularity of the song is explicitly referred to as a reason for playing it.

Regarding the selection of songs, it must be emphasized that all Dylan masses I have come across, with the exception of Saving Grace, are mostly based on Dylan's non-gospel material. This is a way of stating that Dylan's work in general, and not only the songs from the two or three gospel albums, is "scripture soaked" and proclaims "the age old truths." There are examples of religious language in some of the songs, and it is possible that names of saints, significant terms as "heaven," or even archaic language such as "ye," signal connections to Christianity. The connections to Christianity are reinforced by the various ways in which the songs are integrated into the liturgy. But it is also clear that the song selection is influenced by rock culture, as the general popularity of the songs impacts the choice.

Doing a Dylan mass

When rock music is performed live before an audience, the event usually would be understood as a concert. I have attended several rock masses (other than Dylan masses), where the welcoming words mention that the event is not a concert, but a divine service. In our interview, Erling several times talks of Saving Grace as a "concert." In the Norwegian study referred to above, the term "concert service" is used to describe a Dylan mass.[27] As these examples show, an important aspect of doing a rock mass is how the activity is framed as a service or as a concert. Seeing a rock mass as a concert or a service respectively are competing but also complementing frames of interpretation.

Already the name "Dylan mass" or "Dylan Eucharist" frames the event as a divine service. Another aspect that contributes to this interpretation of events is the fact that it takes place in a church building, which is the case for all the Dylan masses in the material and most of the rock masses in general I have attended or seen images from. The celebration of communion is something these masses have in common with other masses, as is the use of a liturgical order—although to a varying degree, with the mass in Richmond being more directly based on a regular liturgy than the Swedish masses I have observed. The Swedish masses still include a number of prayers, including a communion prayer and a general intercession. Some of the liturgical interactivity is preserved, concerning standing up at certain points, and shaking hands with people in your pew during the part known as Pax or Peace. The officiating priests always wear some form of liturgical clothing.

Most Dylan masses I have come across, either live or in the form of a written program, include a sermon—as do all other rock masses I have attended. The Forever Young mass is one exception. The priest states in his words of welcome that Dylan's lyrics will go uncommented during the mass and that they let the lyrics speak. There were no readings from the Bible in this mass, while the Richmond mass always includes two Bible readings.

As hymns and organs are the norm for a church service, one way in which the Dylan masses are framed as concerts is the use of rock music and—to some extent—rock bands. In the Saving Grace mass, the music is performed by a band of eight people, with drums, bass, keyboards, guitars, and wind instruments, and four backing singers. In Richmond, there is an even bigger band, including a church music group called "The guitar ensemble," and the services may feature as many as eight guitarists at a time. They also use drums, bass, and keyboards, and a choir always sings backing vocals. As mentioned above, the Forever Young mass is played by only three musicians, using guitar, piano, and percussion. In all these masses, harmonica is also occasionally played.

One major difference between the Richmond mass and the two other masses in the material is that the musicians and singers in Richmond stand in the gallery in the back of the church, while the performers in the Swedish masses are standing in front of the high altar, facing the audience/congregation. Even though the Dylan mass at St. James's in Richmond is mostly carried out by musical amateurs, they are in the church announcements described as "artists," which verbally frames the event as part of rock culture.

There are various elements of rock culture and rock performance present in these masses. A musical practice used both in Richmond and in Saving Grace is counting in the songs; in Richmond this is often done by a clearly audible "one two three four" from one of the musicians. This is of course a practical matter, but it still is an element brought into church from rock performance. Not all songs are counted in audibly; some are started by a single musician on piano or guitar.

The musicians and singers move to the music. In the Forever Young mass and in Richmond they sway to the beat of the music, and at the end of the former make a few dance moves. In Saving Grace, which has more of a rock setting and rock feel, especially the guitar players move in ways that are iconic for rock guitarists, standing with legs apart, moving the whole body to the beat of the music. The backing singers in Saving Grace use choreographed dance moves in some of the songs.

Another example of an element from rock concerts in the Saving Grace mass is its use of lighting. As far as it is possible to tell from the videos, the Dylan masses in Richmond use the regular lighting of the church, fairly bright, and the same throughout the church. In the Forever Young mass, the cathedral is darker than usual, with regular lighting in front of the high altar, where the musicians are performing. In Saving Grace, the church is dark and the area in front of the high altar is lit with spots, as in a rock concert.

A concert is a collective event, with the audience taking part in many ways, by singing along, cheering, clapping, and dancing. In Saving Grace, there is applause after every song, and also cheering. In the Forever Young mass, the priest informs us in his welcoming words that the musicians have asked us not to clap between the songs but rather to save the applause until the end of the event. In Richmond, no particular instructions are given but there is no clapping between songs. The priest thanks the musicians during announcements, and once during a sermon, and this is always followed by applause. There are also applause and some cheering at the end of the mass.

Singing together is of course a central aspect of a regular church service, even more so than at a rock concert. In the Dylan masses, the one most similar to a regular service, the mass in Richmond, is the one containing the greatest amount of singing along. But there it happens only in two or three songs, and after explicit instructions, given in the leaflet.[28] The instructions make the congregational singing part of the liturgy for the mass rather than the participation of a concert audience. They include for example the choruses of "The Times They are a-Changin'," "Blowin' in the Wind" as well as of "Knockin' on Heaven's Door."

In the Forever Young mass, the lead singer invites us to sing along at the end, for the chorus of "Mr. Tambourine Man" and the first verse of "Blowing in the Wind" (which is the only verse sung in English). In the Saving Grace mass, there was no audible singing in the pews, but the level of volume was much higher than in the Forever Young mass—it was more like a concert also in that respect.

When the Forever Young mass has ended, the audience applauds and the musicians take a bow. Thanking for applause by bowing is a practice not only from rock culture but from theater and music performances in general. In Saving Grace, the band and the backing vocalists take bows between songs. In Richmond, where the musicians are on the gallery and not in full view from the pews, this practice is not present.

Encores are a concert practice that takes place in the two Swedish masses.

> After bowing, the lead singer in the Forever Young mass briefly looks at the priest who nods, and the lead singer says "We'll do an encore," and the band starts playing "Quinn the Eskimo (The Mighty Quinn)."[29]

The brief exchange with the priest is a concrete instance of actual negotiation with a representative of the concert, the lead singer, and a representative of the church service, the priest. It is clear that the priest has the final word, but also that the concert frame wins out and the encore, with ensuing applause, is performed. In the Saving Grace mass, a repeat of a song played earlier in the mass was performed as an encore.

Rock culture also includes practices regarding how musicians, and fans, are dressed. Black is a common color for rock clothing, and a recurrent visual feature of rock masses is the contrast between musicians dressed in black and clergy in white. In the Saving Grace mass, the band are dressed mostly in black, while the backing singers are in all white. In Forever Young, two of the three band members are wearing black. In Richmond, the musicians are wearing a more varied style of dress, perhaps their regular church clothes.

One requirement regarding clothing that still is valid in church is that men should not wear anything on their head (with the exception of some clergy). In rock culture, however, different types of headgear are common. In the Richmond mass, several of the musicians wear different kinds of hats. In the Swedish masses, none do so, perhaps because they are more visually exposed to the audience, as they play in the front of the church.[30]

Rock masses based on existing popular music almost exclusively center on the music of one single artist or group, rather than for example take thematically relevant songs from different artists. This brings the rock mass closer to a concert format, as rock concerts typically consist of an artist or group performing some of their most popular songs. The Saving Grace mass takes this one step further by using songs from a certain period in an artist's career, songs which during this period were performed at the same concerts.[31]

Covering other artists often, especially on an amateur level, involves trying to sound as similar to this artist as possible, in musical arrangements, in style of singing, and in gender—almost all vocalists are male. As mentioned above, Thomas Cervin, the singer in the Forever Young mass, told me that one reason for doing Dylan's music was that he looks like Dylan. In the Dylan masses I have studied here, it is clear that there are attempts to sing like Dylan, both when it comes to the use of voice and in phrasing. I asked Erling if he sees himself as a Dylan "impersonator" or imitator, and he agreed that he is to a certain extent.

In a critical online discussion on the Richmond mass, one comment refers, rather sarcastically, to the musicians as "Elvis, oops, I mean, Bob Dylan impersonators."[32] In a Swedish fan forum discussion on the Saving Grace mass, a fan who had attended the mass notes that the singers' voices were "very suitable" to these songs.[33] Compared to other songs performed by the same band on other occasions, Erling as lead vocalist uses a much more nasal tone in singing Dylan's songs, and he himself also states that he sings Dylan differently, calling it "stepping into his world."

The band setting in the Saving Grace mass, with two keyboard players as well as the inclusion of female (and three out of four black) backing singers, indicate an attempt to duplicate Dylan's own band during the first gospel tours of 1979–80.[34] There was even an attempt from the organizers to engage Dylan's original backing singers for the mass. The arrangements of the songs are very similar to Dylan's gospel tour. The close similarities between Dylan's version of "In the Garden" from 1980[35] and the Saving Grace version[36] of the song may serve as an example: starting with organ and piano, with the female backing vocalists and later bass, drums, and guitar coming in on the same beats in both versions. But not all songs have identical arrangements.

The central element of a mass is the communion. This is the most contemplative part of a mass and the one least dependent on verbal content. As quoted above, in the Richmond mass, "reflective and meditative songs" are used during communion. In the other masses, the communion songs are also more quiet and slow. On the other hand, this may be the part of the mass where the contrast to more traditional music—during communion perhaps, a choir singing or quiet organ improvisation—is the most evident.

The Dylan mass in Richmond is on Sunday morning and attracts a regular church crowd. The attendance at communion, as evident from the videos, is high. The Swedish masses, taking place in the evening and to a greater degree catering to a general public, have lower communion participation. In order for the musicians to take part in the communion, they have to take turns to play or the music stops for a while. In Richmond, it is possible to observe how at least some of the musicians leave the gallery to go down for communion. In the Forever Young mass, the priests had already cleared away the communion elements as one of the musicians approached to take part in communion (this musician also participated in other elements of the liturgy, such as prayers). In Saving Grace, the musicians had no opportunity to take part in the communion, as they were playing throughout.

In Richmond, one of the musicians can be seen walking to communion with his hat in his hand; when he is back on the balcony playing, the hat is on again. I think this tiny gesture of removing the hat and putting it back on is a good example of how this participant in the Dylan mass alternates between two frames of interpretation: when he plays, he is a rock musician behaving as in any other rock concert; when he goes off "stage" and down to communion, he participates in a divine service and acts accordingly.

Conclusions

This chapter has dealt with different aspects of Dylan masses: why Dylan's music is played in church; how the songs are integrated into the mass; and how the service is realized.

I have looked at how the masses are motivated and legitimated by the organizers, but also how they are questioned and criticized. The main motivation given by the organizers is that Dylan's lyrics have a message suitable for church. Another motivation is that it is good to have variation in the church services. Liking the music and being a fan is also an important reason for wanting to play it in church. Playing rock music in church is always an attempt to attract people to church.[37]

Dylan has written and recorded a number of gospel songs, but the masses studied here and the Dylan masses I have come across, often use his non-gospel material. An important aspect of this chapter is the study of how the songs are integrated into the liturgy, through giving them a liturgical label, or by using song lyrics in other parts of the liturgy, such as prayers.

A rock mass is an event that is a mix between a rock concert and a divine service. In the last part of the chapter, I discuss which elements in the Dylan masses emphasize their belonging to the category of church service, and which elements frame them as parts of rock culture. There are many non-verbal aspects of a rock concert that are brought into the Dylan masses, such as applause, moving to the music, clothing, lighting, and so on.

The research issue in the chapter was to look at how the Dylan masses contribute to constructing a relation between Bob Dylan and religion. The answers to why Dylan is played in church are explicitly part of such a discussion, for example by stating that his lyrics proclaim a Christian message. The choice of songs and the integration of the songs into the liturgy are mechanisms for incorporating Dylan's music into a Christian sphere. But in the actual "doing" of the masses, in how the music is performed, and in other actions of the participants in a Dylan mass, the event is still to a significant extent framed as part of rock culture, and as a concert. Rock music is a cultural form that is prevalent and distinct, and therefore resistant to easy appropriation.

12

Theater in Search of a Storyline: The DJ as "Technoshaman" in the Digital Age of EDM

Melanie Takahashi

The term "disk jockey" (DJ) was first coined in the 1930s and since that time, the DJ's role, equipment, venues, sources of music, salary, popularity, and audience have evolved dramatically. Previously an unmemorable radio announcer and song selector, the DJ's status has risen to such heights that some music genres assign the DJ a god-like status. This ascension in prominence is no more apparent than in the electronic dance music scene referred to as EDM. The DJ is no longer tucked away in the corner of the club, but today's EDM DJ is front and center stage where the focus is on him,[1] and the journey he promises to deliver.

The first scholarly publication that linked the DJ as a spiritual guide first appeared in 1999 in an article by Scott Hutson who referred to the DJ as a "technoshaman."[2] Referencing the rave scene,[3] Hutson argued that under the direction of the DJ, raves were more than hedonistic escapist events void of meaning, but rather provided a sense of community, personal transformation, and spiritual healing among its participants.[4] In 2003, using Hutson's work as a platform, a colleague and I further elaborated the link between spirituality and raves in survey research among participants in central Canada.[5] From this fieldwork, several central themes of the rave experience emerged: connectedness, embodiment, altered states of consciousness, spirituality, personal transformation, utopian models of society, and neotribalism. We concluded that the rave phenomenon could potentially develop into a new religious or revitalization movement, although at that time it was too early to tell.

Almost two decades later, the DJ who was once the center of the underground subculture rave, has risen to become a superstar and emblem of what is now referred to as the global movement EDM. While EDM events share many of the characteristics of raves,[6] the worldwide popularity of electronic music has propelled what started as an underground movement, into the mainstream. While there are still pockets of underground events being created, developed, and maintained, many now associate EDM with Vegas clubs, top forty hits, touring international DJs, circuit parties,[7] and outdoor music festivals. The global value of EDM is estimated to be a $6.9 billion industry with EDM being the fourth most popular genre of music to be streamed in the United States in 2014.[8]

Having begun my research on the "god-like" status of the DJ in 1999, I have had the opportunity to witness the evolution of rave culture and its music over time. I have argued elsewhere that the DJ's craft has evolved into an art form, with the DJ an expert in the science of sound manipulation in eliciting altered states of consciousness (ASCs).[9] Referring to the work of ethnomusicologist Gilbert Rouget and his cross-cultural analysis of music and trance, this earlier research revealed that similar to the musicians in possession trance, the DJ uses specific techniques to induce the ASCs that will take the dancers on an emotional, physical, psychological, and spiritual journey.[10] When I first began my research, raves were just beginning to enter the world of mainstream consciousness. Rave culture was largely unknown and the DJ was still an obscure figure. Media coverage sensationalized drug use, and harm reduction strategies became the focus of most research. Almost two decades later, the landscape has dramatically changed: the raves, the glow-sticks, the turntables, and the ethos PLUR (Peace Love Unity Respect)[11] have ceased while electronica and the cult of the DJ have continued to thrive. Today, the DJ is operating in a completely different culture; we are now living in a gadget-driven digital age and the rapid rise of this technology has had a major impact on how we exchange, receive, and process information including music. Today's EDM goers are tech savvy and come wired with brains suited to multitask but with a higher propensity for distraction, and need for immediate gratification. With the turntable being replaced by the laptop, DJs have been forced to adapt not only to this new group of listeners, but also embrace a completely different "instrument."

Expounding from my earlier groundwork, and informed by more recent fieldwork in the San Francisco Bay Area, this chapter will examine the impact of digital technology and the DJ's shift to mainstream status in the post-rave setting. Are EDM events still comparable to their earlier rave counterparts in sharing characteristics with possession trance? Controversies surrounding technology, authenticity, and creativity will be reviewed to ascertain if the DJ can still be considered an artist, in light of the turntable's demise. I argue that digital technology has expanded and refined the musical inducers for trance to such a level that EDM's hallmark production technique of the "build-up" and the "drop" parallels the "crisis" and the "fall" in spirit possession. At the same time, the mainstream status of EDM, the new audience it attracts, and the dominance of digital technology have in some cases shifted the performance style, experience, and connection the dancers have with the DJ. The impact of these developments on performance value, experience, and the resulting states of consciousness will be the focus of this chapter. Finally, the hermeneutic model, the "cycle of meaning," will serve to answer the lingering question as to why there have never been documented incidents of spirit possession at rave and EDM events.

From analog to digital: The human component?

During the time of raves, the DJ was a relatively elusive figure positioned at the top of the hierarchy because of his mass accumulation of subcultural capital, in tandem with his responsibility in defining and shaping it. Seen as a measure of taste and authenticity, youth subcultures like rave were reputed to embody the antithesis of mainstream capitalist values. It was the access to new sounds that had yet to be marketed to the mainstream that rendered the DJ a "guarantor of subcultural authenticity" assigning him the status of an "exclusive owner with discerning taste."[12] Coinciding with the success of EDM, the lowered cost of equipment and the easy access to music files have stripped the DJ's exclusive ownership of subcultural capital. Digital technology has allowed anyone with a computer or smartphone to have instant access to it. A DJ can remix or produce a new track and have it be instantly accessed via social media networks, podcasts, and music-sharing apps with the click of a button. The culture has also changed with the millennial generation such that the DJ is now playing to "a social and mobile media savvy crowd that celebrates exposure of the self."[13] In contrast, today's success is measured on cultural capital in the number of video hits, hashtags, likes, tweets, pins, and followers on Instagram, YouTube, Facebook, Snapchat, Twitter, and Pinterest.

In an industry where the DJ was once at the top of an elite hierarchy, digitization has resulted in a democratizing effect over access to cultural capital, making former barriers penetrable. A high school student can easily set up a sophisticated and professional workstation and recording studio for under $1,500. Digital files are also much less expensive than vinyl, allowing equal access to an extensive music collection. Amateur DJs can learn their skills from YouTube videos, online DJ courses, instructional books, and college classes are all readily available, with many of these online resources being free. This democratization at the level of access to new sounds, skills, equipment, production, and distribution, has created a breeding ground of talented DJs subsequently making the competition for gigs and residencies that much more competitive.[14] Many of the aficionados of underground EDM scenes lump touring DJs with mainstream commercialized events that are overpriced, predictable, clichéd, and tend to attract a crowd that aren't necessarily there for the music. These DJs are often accused of "selling out" and caving to the masses. There is a feeling that the source of authenticity is in the local scenes which tend to be less commercialized, more innovative and underground: all factors that cultivate a good vibe,[15] and one that is reminiscent of the raves.

The retirement of Panasonic's Technics 1200 turntables in 2010, marked what many considered to be a technological crisis in EDM and DJ culture; part of the DJ's reverence was founded on his mastery of the turntable, a symbol also emblematic for rave and EDM culture.[16] For some, the death of vinyl was more than a technological blow, but it also questioned the very identity of the DJ; what is a DJ without the disc and how can a DJ spin[17] without a record? The ability to seamlessly segue from one track to the other—referred to as beatmatching—was a measure of the DJ's virtuosity on the turntable. It brought a human component to the technology as listening skills and a sense of rhythm were essential and the possibility of "trainwrecking"[18] added an element of risk.[19] With the shift to digital and the controversial "sync button," a DJ can now bypass months of training and have perfectly synchronized beats and mixed songs with the push of a button.[20] With this technology, DJs are able to prerecord their sets in advance and simulate playing live since it is difficult to ascertain what the DJ is doing behind a computer screen. When CDs, MP3s, and laptops first entered the scene, the DJs that used them were initially frowned upon and considered "cheaters" for depending on technology that replaced a keenly developed ear.

Irrespective of the politics, proponents of digital technology view this medium "not as the 'death of vinyl' but rather as a liberation from the physical limitations of the natural world."[21] Removing the emphasis away from beatmatching allows room to focus on other creative elements of performance. The freeing up of the hands enables multitasking, and, among the DJs who have embraced this technology and the new production techniques it affords, has made the boundaries between sound and its effects on the body and consciousness limitless. Ultimately, whether one wants to be a technician or an artist is a matter of choice. A DJ can choose to be lazy and get away with it, or a DJ can be an artist and embrace all that this technology offers creatively. As one DJ remarked: "Creativity is not dependent on type of medium; it is our choice to use this creative energy of inspiration in our application of mixing music, no matter what form we keep our archive in."[22] While some DJs continue to use the turntable, these vinyl purists are rapidly becoming a thing of the past as most turntables[23] have been phased out of clubs in favor of digital.[24]

Musical drivers: The "crisis" and the "fall" vs. the "build-up" and the "drop"

There have been noted similarities between possession trance ritual, and the rave context.[25] Possession trance is rooted in a cultural context and in particular a ritual one; this is what distinguishes it from possession illness, an uncontrolled and generally unwelcomed possession experience requiring some kind of spiritual or medical intervention.[26] In his exhaustive cross-cultural comparison of the relationship between music and trance, ethnomusicologist Gilbert Rouget claims that music is fundamental in triggering, maintaining, and socializing trance in the ritual arena.[27] He distinguishes two distinct types of ritual trance: possession and shamanic. One of the key differences between the two is the individual's relationship to the music; the shaman is always the musician responsible for his own entry into trance thus allowing him to communicate with spirits without losing his identity. Initiates in possession ritual have what Rouget calls a double submission: they must surrender control to the music becoming empty repositories, to which they will then succumb to the will of the gods and become completely transformed.[28] It is through music and dance that the spirits are summoned, and it is through dance that they make their presence known. A ritualized process, initiates will often go through several preparatory rites of passage where they learn the music associated with the gods, and the dance steps to appease, flatter, and invite them into their bodies. The ceremonies themselves are long lasting and are commonly structured so that they begin slowly and gradually intensify as the evening proceeds, with the onset of possession being the ultimate climax of the event. Participation is never isolated but experienced in groups with a wide repertoire of gods, accompanying music, and dance steps associated with each. Many dancers submit to the possession at different points in the ritual and thus the process of building the intensity, leading it to climax, and then resolving it, continues to cycle throughout.

Although Rouget emphasizes the learned aspects of socializing trance, he does acknowledge the inherent power of music and observes shared musical elements that are prevalent cross-culturally in trance ritual. The interruption of the music's flow or "rhythmic breaks" being the principal provocation of trance, suggests that the rhythm and not the melodies are what control the entry into an altered state of consciousness.[29] Instrumentalists will employ tension-building techniques such as altering the rhythm through changes in time signature, syncopation, and polyrhythm, combined with increases in tempo (*accelerando*), increases in volume (*crescendo*), and silence.[30] Referring to possession trance among the Palo Monte of Cuba, Murphy provides a thorough description of the crisis and the fall:

> The music seems to be coming from inside as if by their movement they were liberating the sound from within themselves. One woman in particular is carried away by this energy, and others begin to channel theirs toward her. The dancing circle clears for her alone, and the drums focus directly on her. Her eyes are closed, and she is whirling and whirling. She bumps up against the human ring that encloses her and gently rebounds back to the circle's centre. The call and response between soloist and congregation has become tighter and more intense … Then, with a sharp slap from the iya, she falls to the ground. The drums are silent, and the room echoes.[31]

The physical collapse of the dancer and loss of consciousness, referred to as the "fall," is the resolution and conclusion of the crisis. Once the participant regains consciousness, the spirit has vacated the body and the self has been restored. Also noted by Rouget is the power of sound vibration to elicit a visceral reaction. He refers to the vibration as something palpable where the notion of bathing in the music is more than a metaphor, allowing the sound to be perceived directly through the skin.[32] It is the application of these procedures that musicians use to set the tone of the ritual, the pace of the dance, and the climax and resolution of the journey undertaken.

The nuanced aspect of accomplished DJing in EDM is centered on the manipulation and control of energy referred to as "the vibe." The vibe is the general atmosphere and energy created by the music and the participants. Without music and the DJ there is no vibe, and experienced DJs intuitively learn how to build and control the energy in a room through what insiders refer to as "crowd skills." One of the ways this is achieved is through the "build-up" and the "drop," a technique that mirrors the theme of the crisis and the fall in possession trance. Like possession trance, disruptions in the music's flow through tension and release is the essence of the celebrated build-up and drop sequence that is so emblematic of EDM. These production techniques are used by DJs to build tension and energy to a climactic point where the anticipated wait for the drop (being the bass) is the only resolution. These are considered the peak moments of the event where chills, an increase in heart rate, the feeling of an adrenaline rush, intense emotional reactions, and the feeling of connectedness have been reported. Just like trance ritual, the continued cycling of build-up and drop occur throughout the night. The centrality of this process in EDM culture is reflected in the common insider phrase "peaking the floor." The build-up effectively stretches the listener to a point where the drop is the only thing that can emotionally satisfy. During this kind of anticipation, the brain activates the dopamine reward system, resulting in a state that many describe as euphoria.[33] Resembling Rouget's observation of the music transcending the auditory to include perception through the skin, the EDM dancers often report chills during the build-up and drop sequences. In a study examining the relationship between music listening and the chills response, it was found that over 80 percent of chills occurred at the highest moments of pleasure, thus supporting the hypothesis that chills are not random but correspond with peak pleasure responses.[34]

Thus, while Rouget, in reference to possession trance, emphasizes the learned aspects of the dance steps, the music, and the spirits being invoked, I argue that the build-up and the drop to some extent socialize EDM dancers to anticipate what's coming next. While possession trance is not the expected or desired outcome, a certain level of socialization is apparent since dance moves during these points in the night tend to be coordinated and many participants describe the moment of the drop as a shared experience that brings unity and connectedness to the floor. Combined with MDMA, also known as Ecstasy, these responses are only magnified. There is a level of consistency that expedites this learning process as EDM tracks have been shown to be formulaic and repetitive. Most tracks comprise of two build-ups and drops, with the second being more intense than the first.[35] A skilled DJ will not only know when to place these moments within a track, but at the macro level will also construct a set whose structure gradually builds tension to a pinnacle that is then gradually resolved as the night progresses.

I have argued elsewhere that like possession, DJs use similar rhythmic techniques to disrupt the flow of music acting as catalysts for trance.[36] In addition to the aforementioned rhythmic and sound procedures outlined by Rouget, technology has intensified these experiences by perfecting the rhythmic and sound triggers, as well as introducing other tension-building elements that go beyond an acoustic instrument's, and in some cases even a turntable's, capabilities. Increases in pitch, volume, and tempo, along with lasers, pyrotechnics, and fractal imagery are timed with the music to maximize the effects of the build-up to result in a bigger drop. In addition to these preexisting methods used by DJs, the digital format has not only honed the efficacy of these techniques through automation, but has also enabled new procedures for building tension and intensifying the drop. In general, digital technology has narrowed the margin for human error; automation enables a seamless transition between tracks that have varying BMPs thus widening the range of tracks that can be mixed together. There are many tension-building options such as adding in a white noise sweep, the drum-roll effect, using silence right before the drop, or using synth risers in taking a single note and holding it for the build-up section while increasing volume, pitch, and tempo. Automation of volume can also foster tension by keeping the build-up a few decibels lower than the drop, thus giving the drop that much more power and impact on the floor.[37] The possibilities are endless and continue to grow.

Empowerment, catharsis, transformation, and dissociation

In ritual possession, the notion of climax and resolution is not only fundamental musically, but also metaphorically. The notion of the "crisis" and "the fall" are descriptors that apply at the macro and micro levels. Both Bourguignon[38] and Lewis[39] have noted that possession rituals tend to appear in highly stratified societies with members being among the most marginalized and oppressed. On a broader scale, it is usually a crisis that leads a person into seeking out a possession cult in the first place, or from one being formed. These expressions of the divine, function to provide a cathartic arena wherein members temporarily occupy positions of power and domination. Here the ritual context acts as a "mechanism of compensation, of balancing the neglect they experience in everyday life."[40] The cultural prescriptions for acceptable behavior are momentarily suspended thus allowing individuals the freedom to conduct themselves in ways that would normally be deemed inappropriate without being held accountable. Essentially it "offers alternative roles, which satisfy certain individual needs, and it does so by providing the alibi that the behavior is that of spirits and not of the human beings themselves."[41]

Possession trance is a dissociative state that climaxes with the symbolic death of the individual. While the initiate is in trance the dancer's cognizance of the body, identity, and consciousness is completely transformed. In that sense, it "brings about a transformation in the structure of consciousness, by effectuating a particular and exceptional type of relation of the self to the world."[42] The process culminates with the fall, a resolve being marked by the physical collapse of the individual, the parting of the spirit, and the return of a transformed self.

Like possession trance, the origins of rave and club culture have been associated with the marginalized, specifically women, gay men, and the African diaspora.[43] The predecessors and early influences of rave arose out of music subcultures of the marginalized. Disco's roots, for example, can be traced back to New York's underground club scene frequented primarily by blacks and gays. As disco became mainstream, the genre of disco that remained in the underground evolved into what became "house," a popular category of EDM that continues to dominate today. Through the mainstreaming of EDM, the fringes of society are no longer the dominant population to attend EDM events, but like spirit possession, the EDM space offers dancers a vehicle for catharsis and experimentation with different roles in relation to gender, sexuality, and self-expression. The safety around exploring these different roles without the fear of being judged or labeled is evidenced by the dance floor often being described as a "temporary autonomous zone" (TAZ). With reference to the early British rave scene, Pini notes that the dance floor questions traditional images of femininity by dismantling the "cultural associations between dancing, drugged 'dressed-up' women and sexual invitation, and as such opens up a new space for the exploration of new forms of identity and pleasure."[44] Comfort is prioritized over appearance, as many women wear running shoes and cargo pants over the typical club attire.

MDMA, the club drug most linked with rave and post-rave EDM, can also be a factor in lowering one's inhibitions and facilitate the process of socialization, as it is known to promote interaction with others as well as induce feelings of connectedness. For some, club drugs[45] offer a way of absconding accountability as the drug and associated altered state can be faulted instead of the individual. The very act of dancing as a form of self-expression can provide stress relief and emotional catharsis. With all eyes being on the DJ, there is less pressure around "moves" or how one looks while dancing. The transformations that take place go beyond the intellectual; many report alterations in body, self-knowledge, and worldview. Insiders will often refer to a night out as a much-needed "re-set" button. While possession is not the desired outcome, the theme of dissociation from self suggests similar processes at work. The peak moment of the drop where movements and reactions become synchronized implies a detachment of self for a collective state of oneness.[46, 47]

A co-creation of experience: Musicians and dancers

The participatory nature of EDM and the interdependent relationship the DJ establishes with the dancers is another element that is akin to possession trance. In ritual possession, musicians carefully observe the dancers to look for specific bodily movements and cues suggesting that the onset of possession is near. The musicians react by raising the intensity of the music through volume and tempo increases, as well as changes in rhythm.[48] The dynamic between musicians and dancers is an intimate one where communication occurs at a symbolic, personal, and emotional level.

Like possession trance, the ability to read the crowd is another more subtle and intuitive facet of DJing that is fundamental to the success or failure of the night. It is a common practice for a DJ to arrive early before his set to get a pulse for the crowd. A good DJ needs to be flexible and walks a fine line between giving the dancers what they expect, while adding elements of surprise into the mix. This is where having an extensive archive of music on hand is helpful. Going digital has allowed the DJ to carry his entire music collection with him at once. Tracks can be instantly located with digital files, and many DJs have commented that this allows time for other aspects of performance such as observing the crowd, layering, and creative mixing. Being able to carry one's entire music library offers the DJ flexibility and ease with adaptability; if the crowd isn't responding to the music, one can easily modify accordingly having a larger pool of music to draw from (assuming the set is live and not prerecorded).

Despite more track options to better respond to the crowd, and time saved with song selection allowing more space to interact with the crowd, not all DJs use this to their advantage. I have frequently witnessed DJs who are so involved with their laptops that they hardly look up to engage with the crowd. This reciprocal dynamic between the DJs and dancers is predicated on the assumption that it is a live set. By making decisions on the fly based on the feedback from the dancers, the event becomes a process that is shaped and experienced collectively. Since every crowd comes with its own vibe, this makes each performance unique and effectively customized for that specific event and moment in time. It is a journey that is shared and created together and it is the participatory nature that breaks down the barriers between DJ and dancers. This is reflected by the fact that participants are referred to as the crowd rather than the audience. With EDM going mainstream, combined with a new interface that will support it, DJs are increasingly using prerecorded sets and the feedback loop between the DJ and the dancers is less prevalent. A DJ can easily fake a prerecorded set to make it appear live. There are several YouTube videos of supposed "live shows" by superstar DJs in front of consoles that are set up incorrectly and in some cases not even plugged in. While many renowned DJs have been shamed for "miming" this is less the fault of the DJ, and more a repercussion of the business side of EDM. Ticket prices for EDM events are costly and promoters want to avoid potential snags. A prerecorded set removes the pressures associated with technical issues, distractions, or artistic blocks on the part of the DJ. With the commercialization of events, the focus is less about delivering an experience that the crowd of dancers has a hand in shaping, and more about putting on a choreographed show for a crowd of spectators.[49] Pyrotechnics, lasers, and fireworks are frequently programmed beforehand to coordinate with specific build-up and drop sequences. Dancers and other special effects need to be planned and choreographed ahead of time thus making a prerecorded set more appealing. The subtle aspects of what has been compromised in a prerecorded set is well articulated by one of my informants:

> I feel that the downfall of prerecording a DJ set is inherently spiritual and psychological by nature. For one, it detracts from the unity or oneness where everyone is on a journey together with the music and the DJ is part of that journey. There is an air of hierarchy that prerecording a DJ set creates, where the DJ is more separate from the crowd of dancers and doing something to the dancers, instead of being with the dancers … when a set is prerecorded, it doesn't allow the DJ to be inspired by the moment and by the particular vibe of the crowd to surrender to whatever wants to come through via the channel of the music. Prerecording a DJ set detracts from inspiration from the moment and the particular emotional and energetic state of that time and space, the crowd, and himself.[50]

While those DJs who have been busted for "miming" continue to attract mass crowds where the main concern is the music over whether it's live, one informant describes feeling cheated when he realized a DJ he had paid $100 to see had prerecorded his set:

> When I went to see Offer Nissim, I was excited to see such a legend. The next day when I was having the party blues I went to YouTube to play some of his music. While I was browsing, I found a set from Barcelona realizing it was the exact same set that he played here in San Francisco. I felt cheated and really disappointed that a top-notch DJ would do that. It is imperative that the DJ performing plays from the heart and gives it all to the crowd. Unfortunately, because of that, I don't hold him with the same standard as the other fantastic circuit DJs and might not even support him again.[51]

This raises the issue around the formulaic and scripted nature that mainstream EDM events are often criticized for. Expressed by one informant, these DJs are "using a type of mathematical formula or algorithm when prerecording a DJ set, where it's been figured out how to bring the crowd of dancers up and down and create peak experiences."[52] While this formula works well, the tracks are known and predictable and the former role of exposing the crowd to new sounds is sacrificed. Some participants are so disillusioned with the predictable nature of mainstream events and the music taste of the people who attend them that they prefer to differentiate the music they listen to as being separate from EDM.

Another consequence of the business side of EDM is shortened sets with bigger line-ups and multiple stages operating simultaneously. Promoters use impressive line-ups to push ticket sales as well as justify the exorbitant price. Touring DJs may also have multiple residencies and congested travel schedules preventing them from committing to longer sets. Whereas the extended set of five plus hours used to be the norm, now sets are usually limited to two hours or less. The DJ doesn't have the time to settle in, attune to the crowd, or tell a story. The macro structure of the set's journey becomes lost and the overall experience can feel disjointed due to several line-up changes.

While the business side of EDM can account for many of these developments, the new generation of attendees is also partially responsible. In a study by Microsoft that looked at the impact of digital technology on the attention span, it was found that the average attention span is now eight seconds, a four-second drop from the twelve-second finding in 2000.[53] We are constantly being bombarded with texts, emails, and tweets. While our ability to multitask has improved, the lowered attention span has resulted in reducing content to the minimum. The ability to access information instantly through one's tablet, smartphone, or internet has created a culture of immediate gratification. Catering to the millennial generation, who subscribe to YOLO (You Only Live Once) and FOMO (Fear of Missing Out), DJs are giving the mainstream crowd what they want to hear. Perhaps the shortened sets, the predictability and overuse of the build-up and drop to the point of cliché, are only serving the needs of a generation who expect things right away. The onus of the feedback loop is not just on the DJ, but the dancers have an obligation as well. In the time of raves and the epic extended sets, ravers didn't have the distractions of smartphones to text, tweet, and take "selfies" or post pictures and videos on Facebook, Snapchat, and Instagram. There were fewer distractions and the only thing to focus on was the music and the moment. With FOMO at play, smartphones are constantly being checked and this disrupts the musical journey. Being exposed to new tracks, mixes, re-mixes, and mashups[54] also require active listening skills that aren't as necessary when the tracks are already known.

Possession trance and EDM

Despite the commonalities, possession is an absent part of the trance in rave and EDM events. As Rouget noted, possession trance is learned, expected, and socially acceptable. It is a communal event that must be publically witnessed and physically embodied for the state of consciousness to have any credence. In essence, possession trance is a customized, culturally sanctioned, and learned ritual theater where the actors have room to improvise. It is entrenched in a collective worldview that operates within a cosmological system that is enacted in a framework where the participants have a shared understanding of the sacred.[55] Laughlin, McManus, and d'Aquili apply the hermeneutic model, the "cycle of meaning," to illustrate the interplay of assimilating knowledge, memory, and direct experience from ritual (see Figure 12.1).[56]

In the cycle of meaning, possession ritual is just one of the many examples of a culture's mythopoetic symbolism that is reenacted to evoke direct experience

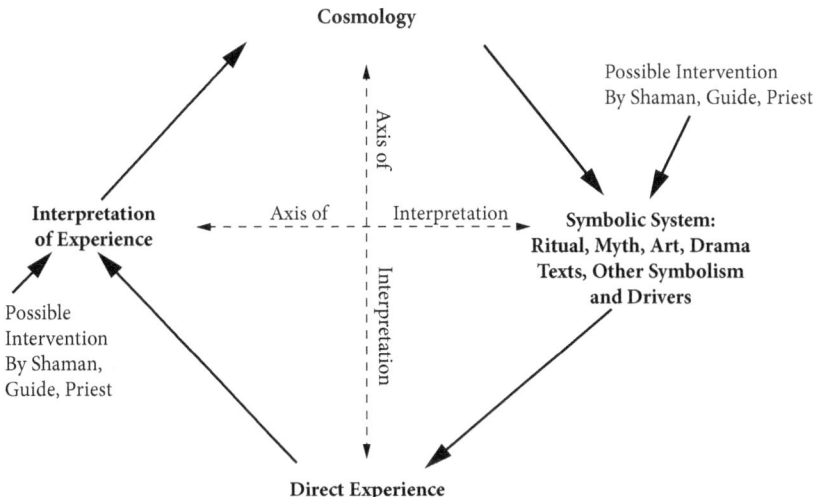

Figure 12.1 The cycle of meaning. The figure is a slightly altered version of the one published in Laughlin, McManus, and d'Aquili, *Brain, Symbol and Experience*, 229. It has been provided by Charles Laughlin and is used with permission.

in a way that authenticates and vivifies that culture's cosmology. Essential to this cycle is what's referred to as the "Shamanic Principle" which highlights the importance of ritual specialists, elders, shamans, or anyone recognized by the initiate as a model for spiritual growth. The role of these specialists becomes apparent at the two points of interjection. The first being the preparatory phase where the ritual training of the initiates, the environment, and the proceedings are overseen by the shaman. There is a second interjection point after the ritual enactment, wherein the shaman interprets the experience for the individual in a way that confirms that culture's worldview and cosmology. Stories and images that are initially understood vicariously through the experiences of others become vivid and real through ritual enactment, and the memories later obtained during these transpersonal experiences will continue to resonate long after the initial encounter. It is the direct experience obtained during an ASC that allows the cycle to continue and complete itself, thus limiting this process to polyphasic societies.[57]

This path of knowledge comprises three stages, with the third being the most critical.[58] The first level of knowledge is referred to as "belief": this represents the most common and rudimentary form of knowing, where awareness is founded on experiences described by others.[59] The second level, "understanding," arises when symbolic expressions of the cosmos transcend the intellectual and begin to become informed through direct experience.[60] It is in the final stage of "realization" that the cycle completes itself as the cosmos is described as "real" and participation in it as "full."[61] In effect, one's experiences start to make sense in relation to the cosmological views that stimulated the experience in the first place.

In the EDM context, the participants are not expecting or seeking out possession, particularly in a culture where this state is associated with mental illness. Even if there was an expectation, if we refer to the cycle of meaning, there is no shared cosmology and worldview underpinning the events and thus agreed-upon spirits to draw from. With the shift toward putting on a show that lacks glitches, the prerecorded sets are beginning to dominate, minimizing the participatory and creative component by assigning dancers a passive role. The generation of EDM goers are also distracted by social media thus making the experience truncated rather than journey oriented. Additionally, the shamanic interjection points are missing; absent are ritual specialists to prepare the dancers and the environment, and following the event, participants are left to their own devices in interpreting any transcendent experiences. Essentially the DJ simply has to show up.

Conclusion

Rave was at one time viewed as a culture void of meaning and content because the rave was never intended to be uncovered, controlled, or pinned down. Yet there was an underlying thread of a storyline that distrusted authority and rejected doctrine over direct experience. The narrative of rave was one that promoted self-exploration through alternative modes of sociality, being, thought, and fashion. It was a subculture that advocated PLUR,[62] connectedness, and consciousness expansion through the primary vehicles of MDMA, dancing, and electronic music. Rave offered an understanding of the varying expressions of spirituality in a postmodern globalizing world. The post-rave EDM storyline, like the current-day DJ set, is now more convoluted than ever. Characterized by overlapping, incomplete storylines that have been spliced, layered, duplicated, and recombined, there is no consistent ethos or worldview in EDM. In contrast, underground music genres intentionally use the dance space to initiate change at the social, cultural, and spiritual levels, while EDM speaks to the importance of dance without any sense of commitment to belief.[63]

My own interest in the ineffable quality of music and its effects on the body and consciousness has been the undercurrent propelling this research. While digital technology has simplified the mechanics of DJing, it still cannot replace taste, read a crowd of dancers, express a mood, or tell a story. It doesn't have the intuition to gauge how much intensity to put into a build-up and drop, and where and how often to place these moments in the set. On the flipside, the underground DJs who play in more intimate locales continue to develop and master the intuitive aspects of engaging with a crowd, building and releasing tension, controlling the energy of the space, and finding the delicate balance of the familiar and exposure to the unknown. This, combined with an extensive library to choose from, ease with locating and mixing tracks, and the ability to perform multiple tasks at once, enriches the content, fluidity, precision, and effects of the music on the body. While many DJs have maximized the creative capacity of digitization, others choose to opt out of these opportunities, and the commercialization of EDM encourages that. The mainstream EDM DJ has been placed at the top of the chain by shifting the direction toward events promising a spectacle over an experience co-created by the DJ and the dancers. As a result, this has also generated two different camps of listeners: the shorter, more predictable sets with a one-way channel from DJ to dancers, versus the listeners who grew up with turntable DJs, or enthusiasts who prefer being exposed to new sounds in a space where the dancers have an active influence on the experience.

One can find these DJs spinning in smaller, less commercialized underground venues, and those associated with these scenes often dissociate themselves from the umbrella "EDM."

As the drive toward prioritizing direct experience over ethos continues to dominate, so does the gap between worldview and this embodied knowledge. Through the build-up and the drop, DJs evoke peak experiences, altered states, and activate parts of the brain associated with pleasure and reward. Technology has enabled events replete with driving mechanisms so numerous and sophisticated for trance that it is not surprising that EDM has a global mainstream appeal. While cell phones, the internet, and social media are intended to connect us, they have also enabled feelings of loneliness and isolation, which have been steadily increasing over the past twenty years.[64] EDM provides a temporary sanctuary from this collective crisis of isolation by allowing people to connect and experience oneness at a deep level, without subscribing to a belief system. As a music lover, classical musician, and piano teacher who grew up with analog technology, there are times when I mourn the loss of the extended sets, the simplicity of a turntable, the intimate venues, active listening, and connection with the DJ. Without a consistent belief system underpinning the experience, one wonders if there is a cost. Churchill once said: "Without tradition, art is a flock of sheep without a shepherd. Without innovation, it is a corpse."[65] Electronic music is without question innovative and the experiences garnered from these events transformative. Yet, without a clear storyline and a shamanic principle to inform and interpret these experiences, EDM remains a flock of sheep without a shepherd whose destination has yet to be determined. I believe we are unlikely to see a change in EDM's trajectory, if our society continues to foster the promotion of self, disembodiment, and separateness. For now, EDM effectively satisfies this void by giving participants a taste of human connectedness and in some instances the divine.

Notes

Introduction

1 See Janne Mäkelä, *John Lennon Imagined: Cultural History of a Rock Star* (New York: Peter Lang, 2004).
2 Michael J. Gilmour, ed., *Call me the Seeker: Listening to Religion in Popular Music* (New York: Continuum, 2005); Thomas Bossius, Andreas Häger, and Keith Kahn-Harris, eds, *Popular Music and Religion in Europe* (London: I.B. Tauris, 2011); Christopher Partridge and Marcus Moberg, eds, *The Bloomsbury Handbook of Religion and Popular Music* (London: Bloomsbury, 2017).
3 H. Richard Niebuhr, *Christ and Culture* (New York: Harper & Row, 1951).
4 Karel Dobbelaere, *Secularization: A Multi-Dimensional Concept* (London: Sage, 1981).
5 This aspect is also very close to what has been called detraditionalization; see Linda Woodhead and Paul Heelas, *Religion in Modern Times: An Interpretive Anthology* (Oxford: Blackwell, 2000), 342–7.
6 Stig Hjarvard, "The Mediatization of Religion: A Theory of the Media as Agents of Religious Change," *Northern Lights* 6, no. 1 (2008): 9–26.
7 Mike Featherstone, *Consumer Culture and Postmodernism* (London: Sage, 1991), 66–8.
8 Woodhead and Heelas, *Religion in Modern Times*, 429–32.
9 Christopher Partridge, *The Re-Enchantment of the West. Volume I. Alternative Spiritualities, Sacralization, Popular Culture and Occulture* (London: T & T Clark International, 2004). Partridge also uses the term "reenchantment," indicating a direct reversal of "disenchantment," which Weber describes as a central aspect of the rationalization of the modern world.
10 Andreas Häger, "Moral Boundaries in Christian Discourse on Popular Music," *Research in the Social Scientific Study of Religion* 11 (2000): 156–71; Andreas Häger, "Seek and You will Find: A Critical Discussion of the Search for 'Christian' Content in Popular Culture," in *Implications of the Sacred in (Post)Modern Media*, edited by Johanna Sumiala-Seppänen, Knut Lundby and Raimo Salokangas (Göteborg: Nordicom, 2006), 217–33.
11 Häger, "Seek and You will Find."
12 Bruce Forbes, "Introduction: Finding Religion in Unexpected Places," in *Religion and Popular Culture in America*, edited by Bruce David Forbes and Jeffrey H. Mahan (Berkeley: University of California Press, 2000), 1–20.

13 Confer Jay R. Howard and John M. Streck, *Apostles of Rock: The Splintered World of Contemporary Christian Music* (Lexington: The University Press of Kentucky, 1999), for their discussion on different grounds of legitimacy for contemporary Christian music (CCM), where (in addition to the more traditional stated purposes, evangelization, or clean entertainment for Christian youth) aesthetic criteria are one possible and perhaps the ultimately legitimate reason for the existence of CCM.

14 For example Michael Jindra, "It's about Faith in our Future: *Star Trek* Fandom as Cultural Religion," in *Religion and Popular Culture in America*, edited by Bruce David Forbes and Jeffrey H. Mahan (Berkeley: University of California Press, 2000), 165–79; and Anja Löbert, "Fandom as a Religious Form: On the Reception of Pop Music by Cliff Richard Fans in Liverpool," *Popular Music* 31, no. 1 (2012): 125–41. For a more critical discussion of such a perspective, see Cornel Sandvoss, *Fans: The Mirror of Consumption* (Cambridge: Polity Press, 2005), 61–3.

Chapter 1

1 See, for instance, Mircea Eliade, *Mephistopheles and the Androgyne: Studies in Religious Myth and Symbol* (New York: Sheed and Ward, 1965).

2 Justin L. Barrett, "Metarepresentation, Homo Religiosus, and Homo Symbolicus," in *Homo Symbolicus: The Dawn of Language, Imagination and Spirituality*, edited by Christopher S. Henshilwood and Francesco d'Errico (Amsterdam: John Benjamins Publishing, 2011), 205–24.

3 Curtis W. Marean, et al., "Early Human Use of Marine Resources and Pigment in South Africa During the Middle Pleistocene," *Nature* 449, no. 7164 (2007): 905–8.

4 Tom Beaudoin, *Virtual Faith: The Irreverent Spiritual Quest of Generation X* (San Francisco: Jossey-Bass, 1998).

5 Alyzandra Vesey, "Putting Her on the Shelf: Pop Star Fragrances and Post-Feminist Entrepreneurialism," *Feminist Media Studies* 15, no. 6 (2015): 992–1008.

6 Vesey, "Putting Her on the Shelf," 996.

7 Adrian-Mario Gellel, "Traces of Spirituality in the Lady Gaga Phenomenon," *International Journal of Children's Spirituality* 18, no. 2 (2013): 214–26.

8 Tania Zittoun, Gerard Duveen, Alex Gillespie, Gabrielle Ivinson, and Charis Psaltis, "The Use of Symbolic Resources in Developmental Transitions," *Culture & Psychology* 9, no. 4 (2003): 415–48.

9 See Adrian-Mario Gellel, "Popular Music as a Resource for the Religious Education Classroom: A Study through Lady Gaga's Judas," *Religious Education Journal of Australia* 29, no. 1 (2013): 28–33.

10 Neil Howe and William Strauss, *Millennials Rising: The Next Great Generation* (New York: Vintage, 2009).

11 Gregory Smith, et al., *America's Changing Religious Landscape* (Washington, DC: Pew Research Center, 2015), at http://assets.pewresearch.org/wp-content/uploads/sites/11/2015/05/RLS-08-26-full-report.pdf (accessed August 28, 2017).
12 Howe and Strauss, *Millennials Rising*.
13 Lisa Robinson, "Katy Perry's Grand Tour. PERRY-GO-ROUND Sidesaddle on the Carrousel de Paris in the Jardins du Trocadéro," *Vanity Fair*, June, 2011, at http://www.vanityfair.com/hollywood/2011/06/katy-perry-full-201106 (accessed August 30, 2016).
14 "The Complete Guide to Katy Perry's Music," *Rolling Stone*, June 22, 2011, at http://www.rollingstone.com/music/pictures/the-complete-guide-to-katy-perrys-music-videos-20110622 (accessed August 30, 2016). Lisa Frank produces colorful stationary, stickers etc. https://www.facebook.com/LisaFrankOfficial/ (accessed May 5, 2017).
15 Vanessa Grigoriadis, "Sex, God & Katy Perry: How did a Fire-and-Brimstone-Preacher's Daughter Become America's Sexiest Pop Star?," *Rolling Stone*, August 19, 2010, at http://www.rollingstone.com/music/news/sex-god-katy-perry-rolling-stones-2010-cover-story-20110607 (accessed September 18, 2016).
16 Claire Hoffman, "Katy Conquers All," *Marie Claire*, December 9, 2013, at http://www.marieclaire.com/celebrity/a8596/katy-perry-interview-january-cover/ (accessed September 18, 2016).
17 Hoffman, "Katy Conquers All." Tolle is a German-Canadian author and "spiritual teacher," at https://www.eckharttolle.com/ (accessed April 7, 2016).
18 "Katy Perry: I Want to Join the Illuminati! 'I Guess You've Kind of Made it When they Think you're in the Illuminati'," *Rolling Stone*, August 20, 2014, at http://www.rollingstone.com/music/news/katy-perry-i-want-to-join-the-illuminati-20140801 (accessed September 10, 2016).
19 I. Weishaupt, "Is Katy Perry Illuminati: ABSOLUTELY". February 7, 2015, at https://illuminatiwatcher.com/katy-perry-illuminati/ (accessed April 7, 2017).
20 Katy Perry, "Katy Announces Release of 'Teenage Dream: The Complete Confection," February 9, 2012, at https://web.archive.org/web/20120215191947/http://www.katyperry.com/katy-announces-release-of-teenage-dream-the-complete-confection (accessed August 30, 2016).
21 Katy Perry, "Katy Perry Talks about Her New Single Wide Awake," *VH1*, November 20, 2012, at http://www.vh1.com/video/interview/katy-perry/793742/katy-perry-talks-about-her-new-single-wide-awake.jhtml (accessed August 30, 2016).
22 Katy Perry, "MTV First: Katy Perry is 'Wide Awake,'" *MTV*, August 19, 2012, at http://www.mtv.com/artists/katy-perry/playlist/1688109 (accessed August 30, 2016).
23 Perry, "MTV First: Katy Perry is 'Wide Awake.'"
24 Tania Zittoun, "The Role of Symbolic Resources in Human Lives," in *The Cambridge Handbook of Sociocultural Psychology*, edited by Jann Valsiner and Alberto Rosa (Cambridge: Cambridge University Press, 2007), 343–61.

25 Tania Zittoun, "Symbolic Resources and Responsibility in Transitions," *Young* 15, no. 2 (2007): 193–211.
26 Zach Johnson, "Katy Perry Reveals What She Learned from Therapy after Russell Brand and John Mayer Breakups," *ENews*, September 10, 2014, at http://www.eonline.com/news/577679/katy-perry-reveals-what-she-learned-from-therapy-after-russell-brand-and-john-mayer-breakups (accessed August 30, 2016); "Katy Perry Talks about Depression after Split from Russell Brand," November 10, 2014, at https://www.youtube.com/watch?v=lydqMCTnbjA (accessed August 30, 2016).
27 Zittoun, "Symbolic Resources and Responsibility in Transitions", 196.
28 Ellie Genower, "'Therapy Keeps Me Pretty Normal': Katy Perry Reveals How She Stays Grounded in 'Difficult' Music Industry," *Mailonline*, August 25, 2016, at http://www.dailymail.co.uk/tvshowbiz/article-3758118/Katy-Perry-reveals-attends-therapy-sessions-stay-normal-music-industry.html#ixzz4KgXTfnkj (accessed September 10, 2016).
29 Perry, "MTV First: Katy Perry is 'Wide Awake.'"
30 Katy Perry, "Wide Awake" (2010), at https://www.youtube.com/watch?v=k0BWlvnBmIE: 0'–12", 4':21"–4':23".
31 Perry, "Katy Perry Talks about Her New Single Wide Awake."
32 Perry, "Wide Awake," 30"–1':09".
33 Perry, "Wide Awake," 59"–1':31".
34 Perry, "Wide Awake," 1':30".
35 Perry, "Wide Awake," 1':27"–1':48".
36 Perry, "Wide Awake," 1':51"–2':07".
37 Perry, "Wide Awake," 2':10"–2':33".
38 The Vigilant Citizen, "Katy Perry's 'Wide Awake': A Video about Monarch Mind Control," *The Vigilant Citizen*, June 24, 2012, at http://vigilantcitizen.com/musicbusiness/katy-perrys-wide-awake-a-video-about-monarch-mind-control/ (accessed September 10, 2016).
39 The Vigilant Citizen, "Katy Perry's 'Wide Awake.'"
40 Perry, "Wide Awake," 2':34"–3':13".
41 Perry, "Wide Awake," 3':15"–3':51".
42 Perry, "Wide Awake," 4':00".
43 Perry, "Wide Awake," 4':03"–4':11".
44 Perry, "Wide Awake," 4':19"–4':23".
45 Perry, "MTV First: Katy Perry is 'Wide Awake.'"
46 Gellel, "Traces of Spirituality."
47 Deftly, "General Comment on Wide Awake," *SongMeanings*, June 24, 2012, at http://songmeanings.com/songs/view/3530822107859428359/?&specific_com=73016153137#comments (accessed September 12, 2016).
48 Gellel, "Popular Music as a Resource."

49 Beaudoin, *Virtual Faith*, 74–7, 81.
50 Andreas Häger, "The Interpretation of Religious Symbols in Popular Music," *Temenos* 33 (1997): 49–62.
51 Anikabritt, "General Comment on Wide Awake," *SongMeanings*, August 2, 2012, at http://songmeanings.com/songs/view/3530822107859428359/?&specific_com=73016160077#comments (accessed September 14, 2016).
52 Spirityvoice, "General comment on Who am I Living For?," *SongMeanings*, November 24, 2011, at http://songmeanings.com/songs/view/3530822107858841122/?&specific_com=73016103053#comments (accessed September 14, 2016).

Chapter 2

1 See Jerma A. Jackson, *Singing in My Soul: Black Gospel Music in a Secular Age* (Chapel Hill: University of North Carolina Press, 2004).
2 Jon Michael Spencer, *Protest and Praise: Sacred Music of Black Religion* (Minneapolis: Fortress Press, 1990), 207–8.
3 CeCe Winans with Renita J. Weems, *On a Positive Note* (New York: Pocket, 1999), 92, 100.
4 Winans, *On a Positive Note*, 84.
5 Winans, *On a Positive Note*, 84.
6 Winans, *On a Positive Note*, 84.
7 Winans, *On a Positive Note*, 115.
8 In CeCe Winans's 1999 autobiography, *On a Positive Note*, she uses the title "Lord, Lift Us Up." *Lord, Lift Us Up* is the title of BeBe and CeCe's debut PTL album. The song, on the other hand, is titled "Up Where We Belong" on the PTL single and on their album.
9 Winans, *On a Positive Note*, 116.
10 *Journeys in Black* [Film], directed by Paul H. Hutchinson (Thousand Oaks: UrbanWorks).
11 Winans, *On a Positive Note*, 116.
12 Winans, *On a Positive Note*, 129.
13 Winans, *On a Positive Note*, 116.
14 *An Officer and a Gentleman* did not win the 1983 Academy Award for Best Picture (Richard Attenborough's *Ghandi* won). However, African American Louis Gossett, Jr. won the Academy Award for Best Supporting Actor and the Golden Globe Award for Best Supporting Actor in the film. Internationally, *An Officer and a Gentleman* won the Japan Academy Prize for Outstanding Foreign Language Film in 1984.
15 Theodor W. Adorno, *Introduction to the Sociology of Music* (New York: Seabury Press, 1976), 25.

16 Pearl Williams-Jones, "Afro-American Gospel Music: A Crystallization of the Black Aesthetic," *Ethnomusicology* 19, no. 3 (Sept. 1975): 380.
17 Williams-Jones, "Afro-American Gospel Music," 381.
18 Winans, *On a Positive Note*, 73.
19 Winans, *On a Positive Note*, 74–5.
20 Winans, *On a Positive Note*, 57.
21 Winans, *On a Positive Note*, 19.
22 Winans, *On a Positive Note*, 60.
23 Winans, *On a Positive Note*, 38.
24 CeCe Winans with Claudia Mair Burney, *Always Sisters: Becoming the Princess You Were Created to Be* (New York: Howard, 2007), 137.
25 Winans, *On a Positive Note*, 159.
26 Winans, *On a Positive Note*, 159–60.
27 Olivier Driessens, "The Celebritization of Society and Culture: Understanding the Structural Dynamics of Celebrity Culture," *International Journal of Cultural Studies* 16, no. 6 (2012): 643.
28 Winans, *On a Positive Note*, 128.
29 Winans, *On a Positive Note*, 99.
30 Winans, *On a Positive Note*, 105.
31 Winans, *On a Positive Note*, 127.
32 Winans, *On a Positive Note*, 127.
33 Winans, *On a Positive Note*, 128.
34 Winans, *On a Positive Note*, 183.
35 Winans, *On a Positive Note*, 185–6.
36 Driessens, "The Celebritization of Society and Culture," 650.
37 Mark Ward, *Air of Salvation: The Story of Christian Broadcasting* (Grand Rapids: Baker Books, 1994), 169.
38 Don Cusic, "The Powerful Medium," *Billboard*, 27 September 1980: 6–10.
39 Winans, *On a Positive Note*, 86.
40 Winans, *On a Positive Note*, 86.
41 Winans, *On a Positive Note*, 151.
42 Interestingly, in the July 5, 1980 issue, *Billboard* included a "Best Selling Spirituals LPs" chart which focused solely on black gospel music (44). Gospel or Christian music albums by white artists were not included. The Spirituals LPs chart actually began in 1974. In an advertisement in the December 24, 1983 issue of *Billboard*, three *Billboard* Spiritual Gospel Chart research packages were available for purchase. Described as the "definitive lists of the best-selling albums year by year, through the entire history of the Top Spiritual Gospel LPs chart," research packages included Number One Spiritual Gospel Albums, Top Ten Spiritual Gospel Albums, and Top Spiritual Gospel Albums of the Year (78). See "*Billboard* Best Selling

Spiritual LPs," *Billboard* SPECIAL SURVEY for Week Ending 7/5/80, *Billboard* July 5, 1980: 44, 78.
43 "'Jesus Freak' Wins Flock of Doves for Trio," *St. Petersburg Times*, 27 April 1996.
44 Winans, *On a Positive Note*, 215.
45 Winans, *On a Positive Note*, 48–9.
46 CeCe Winans with Claire Cloninger, *Throne Room: Ushered into the Presence of God* (Nashville: Thomas Nelson, 2004), 1.
47 Winans, *On a Positive Note*, 195.
48 Winans, *On a Positive Note*, 200–1.
49 "4394. Propheteia." Available online at http://biblehub.com/greek/4394.htm (accessed January 27, 2017).
50 Winans, *On a Positive Note*, 68.
51 Winans, *On a Positive Note*, 68.
52 Winans, *On a Positive Note*, 128.
53 Winans, *On a Positive Note*, 44.
54 Winans, *On a Positive Note*, 141.
55 Winans, *On a Positive Note*, 90–1.
56 Winans, *On a Positive Note*, 117.
57 Winans, *Throne Room*, 12.
58 Winans, *On a Positive Note*, 37–8.
59 Winans, *On a Positive Note*, 172.
60 *Journeys in Black*.
61 *Journeys in Black*.
62 *Journeys in Black*.
63 See Emilie Raymond's *Stars for Freedom: Hollywood, Black Celebrities, and the Civil Rights Movement* (Seattle: University of Washington Press, 2015).

Chapter 3

1 Judas Priest, "Monsters of Rock," *Ram it Down* (Columbia, 1988); Judas Priest, "Deal with the Devil," *Angel of Retribution* (Epic, 2005).
2 "Monsters of Rock"; "Deal with the Devil."
3 "Monsters of Rock."
4 "Deal with the Devil."
5 Ian Christe, *Sound of the Beast: The Complete Headbanging History of Heavy Metal* (New York: itbooks, 2003).
6 *Dream Deceivers: The Story behind James Vance vs. Judas Priest* [Film], directed by David van Taylor (USA: KNPB Channel 5 Public Broadcasting, 1992). See also Martin Popoff, *Judas Priest: Heavy Metal Painkillers* (Toronto: ECW Press, 2007), 197–200.

7 *Dream Deceivers* (1992).
8 Jon Butler, "Magic, Astrology, and the Early American Religious Heritage, 1600–1760," *American Historical Review* 84, no. 2 (April 1979): 318, 320, 322, 345–6; Leigh Schmidt, "From Demon Possession to Magic Show: Ventriloquism, Religion, and the Enlightenment," *Church History* 67, no. 2 (June 1998): 274–304; Mitch Horowitz, *Occult America: The Secret History of How Mysticism Shaped Our Nation* (New York: Bantam Books, 2009), 55; Owen Davies, *Grimoires: A History of Magic Books* (Oxford: Oxford University Press, 2009), 191, 195–6.
9 Scott W. Poole, *Satan in America: The Devil We Know* (Lanham, MD: Rowman & Littlefield, 2009), 125–6; Robin Sylvan, *Traces of the Spirit: The Religious Dimensions of Popular Music* (New York: New York University Press, 2002), 153–4.
10 Poole, *Satan in America*, 127–8; Kelly J. Wyman, "The Devil We Already Know: Medieval Representations of a Powerless Satan in Modern American Cinema," *Journal of Religion and Film* 8, no. 3 (2016); Davies, *Grimoires*, 232–3; Horowitz, *Occult America*, 66–7, 72–5, 115, 250.
11 Bill Ellis, "The Highgate Cemetery Vampire Hunt: The Anglo-American Connection in Satanic Cult Lore," *Folklore* 104, no. 1–2 (1993): 35.
12 Poole, *Satan in America*, 55–182; Robert Wright, "'I'd Sell You Suicide': Pop Music and Moral Panic in the Age of Marilyn Manson," *Popular Music* 19, no. 3 (October 2000): 367.
13 Popoff, *Judas Priest*, 2–5.
14 Christe, *Sound of the Beast*, 27, 32.
15 David Konow, *Bang Your Head: The Rise and Fall of Heavy Metal* (New York: Three Rivers Press, 2002), 135.
16 Konow, *Bang Your Head*, 136; *Dream Deceivers* (1992).
17 *Dream Deceivers* (1992).
18 Popoff, *Judas Priest*, 1. Popoff attributes this observation to both Black Sabbath and Judas Priest.
19 Popoff, *Judas Priest*, 8–12.
20 Konow, *Bang Your Head*, 138.
21 Judas Priest, "Winter," *Rocka Rolla* (Gull, 1974).
22 Judas Priest, "Deep Freeze," *Rocka Rolla* (Gull, 1974); Judas Priest, "Winter Retreat," *Rocka Rolla* (Gull, 1974).
23 Judas Priest, "Last Rose of Summer," *Sin After Sin* (Columbia, 1977).
24 Judas Priest, "Run of the Mill," *Rocka Rolla* (Gull, 1974); Judas Priest, "Let Us Prey," *Sin After Sin* (Columbia, 1977).
25 Popoff, *Judas Priest*, 38.
26 Judas Priest, "Epitaph," *Sad Wings of Destiny* (Gull, 1976).
27 Judas Priest, "Beginning of the End," *Redeemer of Souls* (Epic, 2014).
28 Judas Priest, "Beyond the Realms of Death," *Stained Class* (Columbia, 1978).

29 Christe, *Sound of the Beast*, 20–1.
30 Judas Priest, "Dying to Meet You," *Rocka Rolla* (Gull, 1974).
31 Judas Priest, "Killing Machine," *Hell Bent for Leather* (Columbia, 1978). Songs of war and colonialism that reflect on mortality include: Judas Priest, "Genocide," *Sad Wings of Destiny* (Gull Records, 1976); Judas Priest, "Savage," *Stained Class* (Columbia, 1978); and Judas Priest, "Dissident Aggressor," *Sin After Sin* (Columbia, 1977).
32 Judas Priest, front cover, *Sad Wings of Destiny* (Gull, 1974); Judas Priest, back cover, *Defenders of the Faith* (Columbia, 1984).
33 Popoff, *Judas Priest*, 27, 204; Judas Priest, front cover, *Painkiller* (Columbia, 1990).
34 Judas Priest, back cover, *Painkiller* (Columbia, 1990).
35 Popoff, *Judas Priest*, 345; front cover, *Sad Wings of Destiny*; and, Judas Priest, front cover, *Angel of Retribution* (Epic, 2005); Judas Priest, "Solar Angels" *Point of Entry* (Columbia, 1981).
36 Judas Priest, front and back cover, *Redeemer of Souls* (Epic, 2014).
37 Judas Priest, "Angel," *Angel of Retribution* (Epic, 2005).
38 Judas Priest, "Angel."
39 Luke 13:34, New American Standard Bible.
40 Norman Cohen, *Cosmos, Chaos & the World to Come: The Ancient Roots of Apocalyptic Faith*, 2nd edn (New Haven: Yale University Press, 2001), 42.
41 Cohen, *Cosmos, Chaos & the World to Come*, 65.
42 Conrad E. Ostwalt, Jr., "Hollywood and Armageddon: Apocalyptic Themes in Recent Cinematic Presentation," in *Screening the Sacred: Religion, Myth, and Ideology in Popular American Film*, edited by Joel W. Martin and Conrad E. Ostwalt, Jr. (Boulder, CO: Westview Press, 1995), 56, 61.
43 Elana Gomel, "Mystery, Apocalypse and Utopia: The Case of the Ontological Detective Story," *Science Fiction Studies* 22, no. 3 (November 1995): 343–4; Popoff, *Judas Priest*, 35, 348; Judas Priest, "Tyrant," *Sad Wings of Destiny* (Gull, 1976).
44 Gomel, "Mystery, Apocalypse and Utopia," 352.
45 Judas Priest, "Rapid Fire," *British Steel* (Columbia, 1980).
46 Judas Priest, "Rapid Fire"; Matthew 13:24–30.
47 Judas Priest, "Dreamer Deceiver," "Deceiver," *Sad Wings of Destiny* (Gull, 1976).
48 Judas Priest, "Deceiver."
49 Judas Priest, "Starbreaker," *Sin After Sin* (Columbia, 1977).
50 Judas Priest, "Evening Star," *Hell Bent for Leather* (Columbia, 1978).
51 Judas Priest, back cover, *Screaming for Vengeance* (Columbia, 1982).
52 Judas Priest, "Riding on the Wind," *Screaming for Vengeance* (Columbia, 1982).
53 Judas Priest, "All Guns Blazing," *Painkiller* (Columbia, 1990). For an example of an invasion from above that is all about destruction to humanity, though thwarted by vigilance and ingenuity, such as a "shield ... sealed upon this earth," see Judas Priest, "Invader," *Stained Class* (Columbia, 1978).

54 Judas Priest, "Exciter," *Stained Class* (Columbia, 1978); Acts 2:1–3, New American Standard Bible.
55 Judas Priest, "Exciter," *Stained Class* (Columbia, 1978).
56 Judas Priest, "Painkiller," *Painkiller* (Columbia, 1990).
57 Judas Priest, "Judas Rising," *Angel of Retribution* (Epic, 2005). Little is added by the Dragonaut character, except the demonic moniker, "Father of Sin," in Judas Priest, "Dragonaut," *Redeemer of Souls* (Epic, 2014).
58 Mircea Eliade, *Occultism, Witchcraft, and Cultural Fashions: Essays in Comparative Religions* (Chicago: The University of Chicago Press, 1976), 38–9.
59 Clifford Geertz, *The Interpretation of Cultures: Selected Essays* (New York: Basic Books, 1973), 140.
60 Geertz, *The Interpretation of Cultures*, 127–30.
61 Judas Priest, "Sinner," *Sin after Sin* (Columbia, 1977).
62 Judas Priest, "Saints in Hell," *Stained Class* (Columbia, 1978).
63 Judas Priest, "Demonizer," *Angel of Retribution* (Epic, 2005).
64 Judas Priest, "Night Crawler," *Painkiller* (Columbia, 1990).
65 Judas Priest, "Devil's Child," *Screaming for Vengeance* (Columbia, 1982); Judas Priest, "A Touch of Evil," *Painkiller* (Columbia, 1990);Judas Priest, "A Touch of Evil," *Electric Eye* [DVD] (Sony 2003)."A Touch of Evil" equates strong erotic desire with "evil" and "A dark angel of sin," portrayed visually though snake-handling religion. The story of Judas's betrayal of Christ is found in Luke 22.
66 Judas Priest, "White Heat, Red Hot," *Stained Class* (Columbia, 1978). A similar rewriting of Christianity where "sacrament," "sermon," and "sacrifice" are appropriated for the new metal faith is found in Judas Priest, "Between the Hammer and the Anvil," *Painkiller* (Columbia, 1990). "The Lord's Prayer" is found in Matthew 6:9–13.
67 Raymond J. Rice, "Cannibalism and the Act of Revenge in Tudor-Stuart Drama," *Studies in English Literature, 1500–1900* 44, no. 2 (Spring, 2004): 299.
68 Rice, "Cannibalism and the Act of Revenge," 305.
69 Judas Priest, "Breaking the Law," *British Steel* (Columbia, 1980); Judas Priest, "Wheels of Fire," *Angel of Retribution* (Epic, 2005); Judas Priest, "You Don't Have to be Old to be Wise," *British Steel* (Columbia, 1980).
70 Judas Priest, "Reckless," *Turbo* (Columbia, 1986); Judas Priest, "Heading out to the Highway," *Point of Entry* (Columbia, 1981).
71 Judas Priest, "Hard as Iron," *Ram it Down* (Columbia, 1988); Judas Priest, "Exciter," *Stained Class* (Columbia, 1978).
72 Judas Priest, "Grinder," *British Steel* (Columbia, 1980).
73 Judas Priest, "You've Got Another Thing Comin'," *Screaming for Vengeance* (Columbia, 1982); Judas Priest, "Hell Bent for Leather," *Hell Bent for Leather* (Columbia, 1978).

74 Judas Priest, "Stained Class," *Stained Class* (Columbia, 1978).
75 Judas Priest, "Screaming for Vengeance," *Screaming for Vengeance* (Columbia, 1982).
76 Judas Priest, "The Sentinel," *Defenders of the Faith* (Columbia, 1984).
77 Judas Priest, "The Sentinel."
78 Judas Priest, "Rocka Rolla," *Rocka Rolla* (Gull, 1974).
79 Judas Priest, "Victim of Changes," *Sad Wings of Destiny* (Gull, 1976).
80 Judas Priest, "Victim of Changes."
81 Judas Priest, "Island of Domination," *Sad Wings of Destiny* (Gull, 1976).
82 Judas Priest, "Island of Domination."
83 Konow, *Bang Your Head*, 137–8; Christe, *Sound of the Beast*, 74–8; Popoff, *Judas Priest*, 77.
84 Judas Priest, "Burnin' Up," *Hell Bent for Leather* (Columbia, 1978; released in UK as *Killing Machine*); Judas Priest, "Evil Fantasies," *Hell Bent for Leather* (Columbia, 1978; released in UK as *Killing Machine*).
85 Judas Priest, "Troubleshooter," *Point of Entry* (Columbia, 1981).
86 Judas Priest, "All the Way," *Point of Entry* (Columbia, 1981), Judas Priest, "Pain and Pleasure," *Screaming for Vengeance* (Columbia 1982); Judas Priest, "Jawbreaker," "Eat Me Alive," and "Love Bites," *Defenders of the Faith* (Columbia, 1984).Quote from "Love Bites."
87 Judas Priest, "Locked In" and "Hot for Love," *Turbo* (Columbia, 1986); Judas Priest, "Love You to Death," *Ram it Down* (Columbia, 1988).
88 Judas Priest, "Here Come the Tears," *Sin after Sin* (Columbia, 1977); Judas Priest, "Desert Plains," *Point of Entry* (Columbia, 1981).
89 Judas Priest, "Desert Plains." For a similar use of western American imagery of the heroic journey over barren terrain, here with ghost towns, kerosene and tumbleweeds, to one's lover, see Judas Priest, "Worth Fighting For," *Angel of Retribution* (Epic, 2005).For Vikings, see Judas Priest, "Halls of Valhalla," *Redeemer of Souls* (Epic, 2014).
90 Judas Priest, "Before the Dawn," *Hell Bent for Leather* (Columbia, 1978); Judas Priest, "Don't Go" and "Turning Circles," *Point of Entry* (Columbia, 1981). Similar use of images for the longing of a lover and fear of abandonment are found in Judas Priest, "Night Comes Down," *Defenders of the Faith* (Columbia, 1984).
91 Judas Priest, "(Take These) Chains," *Screaming for Vengeance* (Columbia, 1982).
92 Judas Priest, "Fever," *Screaming for Vengeance* (Columbia, 1982).
93 Judas Priest, "Out in the Cold," *Turbo* (Columbia, 1986).
94 Geertz, *The Interpretation of Cultures*, 89.
95 Judas Priest, *Nostradamus* (Epic, 2008); Judas Priest, "Defenders of the Faith," *Defenders of the Faith* (Columbia, 1984).

Chapter 4

1. "I Love You All," *Scream*, 2010. "Gets Me Through" is another "tribute" to his audience. In the liner notes for *Down to Earth* (2001), he explains he wrote it because "saying thank you doesn't seem like enough. I owe my life to you." I take all song lyrics from liner notes. Osbourne is a collaborative songwriter though I do not list other contributors here.
2. There is significant academic interest in heavy metal and associated subcultures, which inevitably includes discussion of Ozzy Osbourne owing to his seminal influence on the genre. Among many helpful titles representing a range of disciplinary interests, see, e.g., Brenda Gardenour Walter, Gabby Riches, Dave Snell, and Bryan Bardine, eds, *Heavy Metal Studies and Popular Culture*, Leisure Studies in a Global Era (London: Palgrave Macmillan, 2016), and Deena Weinstein, *Heavy Metal: The Music and its Culture*, rev. edn (Boston: Da Capo, 2000).
3. Ozzy Osbourne, "Over the Mountain," *Diary of a Madman*, 1981.
4. E.g., Ozzy Osbourne, "See You on the Other Side," *Ozzmosis*, 1995.
5. See, e.g., Douglas A. Knight and Amy-Jill Levine, *The Meaning of the Bible: What the Jewish Scriptures and Christian Old Testament Can Teach Us* (New York: HarperOne, 2011), 443–4.
6. For introductions to some of the wide-ranging functions of horror, see, e.g., Timothy K. Beal, *Religion and its Monsters* (New York: Routledge, 2001) and W. Scott Poole, *Monsters in America: Our Historical Obsession with the Hideous and the Haunting* (Waco: Baylor University Press, 2011).
7. I distinguish Ozzy Osbourne the artist from "Ozzy Osbourne" as an artistic construct. The two are not synonymous, though a tendency to blur the distinction between on-screen and off-screen, on-stage and off-stage personalities is commonplace. Rock and roll's so-called Prince of Darkness is aware of this. His surprise that some took Black Sabbath's music seriously as a religious statement illustrates the misstep: "I can honestly say that we never took the black magic stuff seriously for one second. We just liked how theatrical it was… I couldn't believe it when I learned that people actually 'practiced the occult'" (Ozzy Osbourne, with Chris Ayres, *I Am Ozzy* ([New York: Grand Central, 2009], 99). Band mate Tony Iommi provides a fascinating example of this confusion of art with reality. He recalls Alex Sanders, the head witch of England, attending early Sabbath shows, and Anton LaVey, the founder of the Church of Satan, throwing a parade in the band's honor when they first performed in San Francisco. "When we turned down an invitation to play [the song] Walpurgis at Stonehenge," he adds, "this sect put a curse on us" (Tony Iommi, with T. J. Lammers, *Iron Man: My Journey through Heaven and Hell with Black Sabbath* [Boston: Da Capo, 2011], 81).

8 Christopher Partridge lists examples of transgressions by popular musicians, among them Osbourne biting off the head of a bat. Such outrageous actions present society "with that which it… shuns as profane and polluting," which explains why it often constitutes the "threat to the sacred centre" that religious conservatives so fear. Christopher Partridge, *Mortality and Music: Popular Music and the Awareness of Death* (London: Bloomsbury, 2015), 42.

9 E.g., "Sanity now it's beyond me there's no choice … Voices in the darkness / Scream away my mental health" (Ozzy Osbourne, "Diary of a Madman," *Diary of a Madman*, 1981); "I'm quite insane" (Ozzy Osbourne, "Denial," *Ozzmosis*, 1995).

10 E.g., "The wreckage of my past keeps haunting me /… The Road to Nowhere leads to me" (Ozzy Osbourne, "Road to Nowhere," *No More Tears*, 1991); "Wine is fine but whiskey's quicker / Suicide is slow with liquor" (Ozzy Osbourne, "Suicide Solution," *Blizzard of Ozz*, 1980).

11 E.g., "Leave me alone don't want your promises no more / 'Cause rock 'n roll is my religion and my law" (Ozzy Osbourne, "You Can't Kill Rock and Roll," *Diary of a Madman*, 1980).

12 In order: "Shot in the Dark," *The Ultimate Sin*, 1986; "Mr. Tinkertrain," *No More Tears*, 1991; "Crucify," *Scream*, 2010; "Ghost Behind My Eyes," *Ozzmosis*, 1995; "No More Tears," *No More Tears*, 1991.

13 "Osbourne, Ozzy," in *The Encyclopedia of Popular Music*, 5th concise edn (New York: Omnibus, 2007), 1066.

14 For discussion of religious themes in this song and album, see Michael J. Gilmour, "'God,' 'God Part II,' and 'God Part III': Exploring the Anxiety of Influence in John Lennon, U2, and Larry Norman," in *Reception History and Biblical Studies: Theory and Practice*, edited by Emma England and W. J. Lyons (London: Bloomsbury T&T Clark, 2015), 231–9.

15 Cf. his reference to the desecration of Mother Earth in "The Almighty Dollar," *Black Rain*, 2007.

16 Ozzy Osbourne, "Goodbye to Romance," *Blizzard of Ozz*, 1980.

17 M. H. Abrams, with Geoffrey Galt Harpham, *A Glossary of Literary Terms*, 8th edn (Toronto: Thomson Wadsworth, 2005), 161.

18 Abrams, *A Glossary of Literary Terms*, 162.

19 Ozzy Osbourne, "Goodbye to Romance," *Blizzard of Ozz*, 1980.

20 Ozzy Osbourne, "Mr. Crowley," *Blizzard of Ozz*, 1980.

21 Comments taken from http://www.cbc.ca/news/canada/saskatchewan/ozzy-osbourne-song-based-on-latimer-case-1.873402 (accessed January 25, 2018).

22 Ozzy Osbourne, "Latimer's Mercy," *Scream*, 2010. Latimer used exhaust fumes from his truck to kill his daughter.

23 Osbourne's introduction to "Miracle Man" (*No Rest for the Wicked*, 1988) on 1993's *Live and Loud*. My transcription.
24 E.g., Ozzy Osbourne, "Facing Hell," *Down to Earth*, 2001.
25 Osbourne is hardly the only artist giving musical expression to such laments, as a single illustration makes clear. Though very different in style, Emmylou Harris's *Red Dirt Girl* (2000) strikes a similar note in vocalizing the agony of an absent God. This album "introduces this haunting divine silence and then dives into the pain and struggle of human existence that fills the resulting space" (Mark McEntire, "Red Dirt God: Divine Silence and the Search for Transcendent Beauty in the Music of Emmylou Harris," in *The Bible in/and Popular Culture*, edited by Philip Culbertson and Elaine M. Wainwright (Atlanta: Society of Biblical Literature, 2010), 38).
26 Ozzy Osbourne, "Black Rain," *Black Rain*, 2007. Cf. the anti-war sentiments in "Thank God for the Bomb," *The Ultimate Sin*, 1986.
27 Ozzy Osbourne, "I Don't Want to Change the World," *No More Tears*, 1991.
28 Ozzy Osbourne, *Black Rain*, 2007.
29 Cf. Ozzy Osbourne, "Goodbye to Romance," *Blizzard of Ozz*, 1980.
30 Robert Walser, *Running With the Devil: Power, Gender and Madness in Heavy Metal Music* (Hanover and London: Wesleyan University Press and University Press of New England, 1993), 151.
31 Pete Ward, "The Eucharist and the Turn to Culture," in *Between Sacred and Profane: Researching Religion and Popular Culture*, edited by Gordon Lynch (London and New York: I. B. Tauris, 2007), 91.
32 Robin Sylvan, *Traces of the Spirit: The Religious Dimensions of Popular Music* (New York and London: New York University Press, 2002), 178.

Chapter 5

1 Matt Hills, *Fan Cultures* (London and New York: Routledge, 2002), 39.
2 Hills, *Fan Cultures*, 67–8.
3 Bruno Latour, *Reflexão sobre o culto moderno dos deuses fe(i)tiches* (Bauru/SP: EDUSC, 2002[1996]).
4 Eloísa Martín, "Seres extraordinarios. Más allá de la devoción y de los fans," *Revista Todavia* 20 (December 2008): 26–31.
5 Jorge Elbaum, "Los bailanteros. La fiesta urbana de la cultura popular," in *La cultura de la noche. La vida nocturna de los jóvenes en Buenos Aires*, edited by Mario Margulis (Buenos Aires: Espasa Hoy, 1994), 181–210; Eloísa Martín, "The History, Trajectory and Consolidation of the Cumbia in the Field of Argentine Music," in

Troubling Gender: Youth and Cumbia in Argentina's Music Scene, edited by Pablo Vila and Pablo Semán (Philadelphia: Temple University Press, 2011), 23–40.

6 Eloísa Martín, "Cumbia Villera and the End of the Work Culture in Argentina in the 90's," in *Youth Identities and Argentine Popular Music: Beyond Tango*, edited by Pablo Semán and Pablo Vila (New York: Palgrave Macmillan, 2012), 59–82. A *cumbiero* is a person who likes cumbia music; *negro* is a common term in Argentina—it does not have the same value as the word in English.

7 Ricardo Vega, *Gilda. Una estrella que aún sigue brillando* (Buenos Aires: Ediciones Utilsen, 1998); Alma Román, *Las milagrosas sanaciones de Gilda* (Buenos Aires: Latinoamericana Editora, 1999); Viviana Pumar and Lili Bivort, *Un milagro llamado Gilda* (Buenos Aires: authors' edn, 1999); Nils Gherardi, *Gilda. La vida de un ángel. Primera Parte* (Buenos Aires: Ediciones Semanario, 2000); Alejandro Margulis, *Santa Gilda. Su vida, su muerte, sus milagros* (Buenos Aires: Planeta, 2016), among many others.

8 Nadia Fink and Pitu Saá, *Gilda para chicas y chicos*. Colección Antiprincesas n. 5 (Buenos Aires: Chirimbote, 2016).

9 Cf. Erika Doss, *Elvis Culture: Fans, Faith, and Image* (Kansas: University Press of Kansas, 1999), 56.

10 Michael Jindra, " 'Star Trek to Me is a Way of Life': Fan Expressions of Star Trek Philosophy," in *Star Trek and Sacred Ground: Explorations of Star Trek, Religion, and American Culture*, edited by Jennifer E. Porter and Darcee L. McLaren (New York: State University of New York Press, 1999), 217–29; Darcee L. McLaren, "On the Edge of Forever: Understanding the Star Trek Phenomenon as Myth," in *Star Trek and Sacred Ground: Explorations of Star Trek, Religion, and American Culture*, edited by Jennifer E. Porter and Darcee L. McLaren (New York: State University of New York Press, 1999), 231–43.

11 Henry Jenkins, *Textual Poachers: Television Fans and Participatory Culture* (London: Routledge, 1992).

12 Names have been changed to protect anonymity.

13 Tim Ingold, *The Perception of the Environment: Essays on Livelihood, Dwelling and Skill* (London and New York: Routledge, 2000).

14 Colleen McDannell, *Material Christianity: Religion and Popular Culture in America* (New Haven and London: Yale University Press, 1995), 272.

15 Doss, *Elvis Culture*, 50.

16 Doss, *Elvis Culture*, 50; Jennifer E. Porter, "To Boldly Go: Star Trek Convention Attendance as Pilgrimage," in *Star Trek and Sacred Ground: Explorations of Star Trek, Religion, and American Culture*, edited by Jennifer E. Porter and Darcee L. McLaren (New York: State University of New York Press, 1999), 245–70.

17 Jindra, "Star Trek to Me is a Way of Life"; McLaren, "On the Edge of Forever."

18 Joli Jenson, "Fandom as Pathology: The Consequences of Characterization," in *The Adoring Audience: Fan Culture and Popular Media*, edited by Lisa A. Lewis (London: Routledge, 1992), 9–29.
19 Roger C. Aden, *Popular Stories and Promised Lands: Fan Cultures and Symbolic Pilgrimages* (Tuscaloosa and London: The University of Alabama Press, 1999).
20 John Fiske, "The Cultural Economy of Fandom," in *The Adoring Audience: Fan Culture and Popular Media*, edited by Lisa A. Lewis (London: Routledge, 1992), 30–49.
21 Stephen Hinerman, "'I'll be here with you: Fans, Fantasy and the Figure of Elvis," in *The Adoring Audience: Fan Culture and Popular Media*, edited by Lisa A. Lewis (London: Routledge, 1992), 107–34.
22 Hanna Skartveit, "An Angel Watching Over Me: Fan Culture and the Formations of Self and Identity in Buenos Aires" (M.A. diss.; Bergen: Department of Social Anthropology, University of Bergen, 2004).
23 Maria Claudia Coelho, *A experiencia da fama: Individualismo e comunicação* (Rio de Janeiro: Editora FGV, 1999); Patricia Baptista Coralis, "Nunca te vi, sempre te amei. Uma análise antropológica da idolatria a Madonna em um fã-clube virtual" (M.A. diss.; Rio de Janeiro: State University of Rio de Janeiro, 2004).
24 Hills, *Fan Cultures*.
25 Camille Bacon-Smith, *Enterprising Women: Television Fandom and the Creation of Popular Myth* (Philadelphia: University of Pennsylvania Press, 1992).
26 Pablo Semán and Pablo Vila, "Rock chabón: The Contemporary National Rock of Argentina," in *From Tejano to Tango: Latin American Popular Music*, edited by Walter A. Clark (New York and London: Routledge, 2002), 70–94.
27 Umberto Eco, *Apocalípticos e integrados* (São Paulo: Perspectiva, 1979).
28 Marc Augè, *El Genio del Paganismo* (Barcelona: Muchnik Editores, 1993), 180.
29 Gilbert B. Rodman, *Elvis after Elvis: The Posthumous Career of a Living Legend* (London and New York: Routledge, 1996).
30 Maria Julia Carozzi, "Carlos Gardel: el patrimonio que sonríe," *Horizontes Antropológicos* 20 (2003): 59–82.
31 Joan Prat, "Los santuarios marianos en Cataluña: una aproximación desde la etnografía," in *La religiosidad popular, vol. III*, edited by Carlos Alvarez y Santaló, Ma. Jesús Buxó Rey, and Salvador Rodriguez Becerra (Barcelona: Antrophos/ Editorial del Hombre/ Fundación Machado, 1989), 211–52.
32 Maria Julia Carozzi, "Antiguos difuntos y difuntos nuevos: las canonizaciones populares en la década del '90," in *Entre santos, cumbias y piquetes. Las culturas populares en la Argentina reciente*, edited by Daniel Miguez and Pablo Semán (Buenos Aires: Biblos, 2006), 97–110.
33 Richard Dyer, with Paul McDonald, *Stars* (London: BFI Publishing, 2002 [1979]), 22.

34 Pablo Alabarces, "Maradona, o la superación del peronismo por otros medios," in *El espacio cultural de los mitos, ritos, leyendas, celebraciones y devociones* (Buenos Aires: Comisión para la Preservación del Patrimonio Histórico Cultural de la Ciudad de Buenos Aires, 2002), 166–91; Karen Anijar, "Selena—Prophet, Profit, Princess: Canonizing the Commodity," in *God in the Details: American Religion in Popular Culture*, edited by Eric M. Mazur and Kate McCarthy (New York and London: Routledge, 2001), 83–101; Jeffrey Richards, Scott Wilson, and Linda Woodhead, eds, *Diana: The Making of a Media Saint* (London and New York: I.B. Tauris, 1999); Coralis, "Nunca te vi, sempre te amei"; Daniel Cavicchi, *Tramps Like Us: Music and Meaning among Springsteen Fans* (Oxford: Oxford University Press, 1998).
35 Dyer and McDonald, *Stars*, 20.
36 Chidananda Das Gupta, "Seeing and Believing, Science and Mythology: Notes on 'Mythological' Genre," *Film Quarterly* 42, no. 4 (1989), 12–18.
37 S. V. Srinivas, "Devotion and Defiance in Fan Activity," *Journal of Art and Ideas* 29 (1996): 67–83.
38 Latour, *Reflexão sobre*, 31.
39 Latour, *Reflexão sobre*, 49.
40 Latour, *Reflexão sobre*, 23.
41 Carozzi, "Carlos Gardel."

Chapter 6

1 I dedicate this chapter to my dad (mom tati).
2 For more on criticism of established religion among popular music artists, see, e.g., Andreas Häger, "Under the Shadow of the Almighty: Fan Reception of Some Religious Aspects in the Work and Career of the Irish Popular Musician Sinead O'Connor," in *Call Me the Seeker: Listening to Religion in Popular Music*, edited by Michael Gilmour (New York and London: Continuum, 2005), 215.
3 Cave published his first book, *King Ink*, in 1988 and since then has published five more. He has also written screenplays for two feature movies, and composed a large number of original film scores. On a few occasions, Cave appeared in movies as an actor or performer, and even lent his voice as a narrator in an animated film. His theatre work includes score collaboration with Warren Ellis for several stage productions in Iceland.
4 It should be noted that Cave's first performance in that region happened three years earlier when he and The Bad Seeds performed in Ljubljana, which was then also a part of socialist Yugoslavia.
5 Novi Sad is the second largest city in Serbia.

6 For more on this topic see Roland Boer, *Nick Cave: A Study of Love, Death and Apocalypse* (Sheffield and Bristol: Equinox, 2012).
7 "The Daily Grind," *Harp Magazine*, May 2007.
8 "Interview: Nick Cave," *The Scotsman*, August 28, 2009, at http://www.scotsman.com/lifestyle/interview-nick-cave-1-1355795 (accessed April 15, 2016).
9 Mick Brown, "Cave's New World," *The Telegraph*, May 2, 1998, at http://www.bad-seed.org/~cave/interviews/98-05-02_telegraph.html (accessed April 15, 2016).
10 "Nick Cave: Dark Star," *The Big Issue UK*, January 15, 1995, at http://www.nick-cave.com/_interviews.php?subaction=showfull&id=1051737923&archive=&cnshow=headlines&start_from (accessed April 16, 2016).
11 "Interview," *Telemostique*, July 1998, at http://www.nick-cave.com/_interviews.php?subaction=showfull&id=1051742955&archive=&cnshow=headlines&start_from= (accessed April 16, 2016).
12 Dave Thompson, "Nick Cave, Alphabetically," *Alternative Press*, April 1997, at http://www.bad-seed.org/~cave/interviews/97-04_ap.html (accessed April 16, 2016).
13 Nick Cave, *The Secret Life of the Love Song & The Flesh Made Word: Two Lectures by Nick Cave* (London: Mute Records, 2000).
14 "Nick Caves in to Religion," *Contact Music*, May 20, 2003, at http://www.contactmusic.net/new/xmlfeed.nsf/mndwebpages/nick%20caves%20in%20to% (accessed April 15, 2016).
15 Nick Cave, "An Introduction to the Gospel According to Mark," in *Gospel According to Mark* (Edinburgh: Canongate Books, 1998), 1.
16 John Payne, "Improvisations with Nick Cave," *Los Angeles Times*, November 29, 2010, at http://articles.latimes.com/2010/nov/29/entertainment/la-et-nick-cave-20101129 (accessed April 17, 2016).
17 "The Resurrection of Nick Cave," *Salon*, November 18, 2004, at http://www.salon.com/story/ent/feature/2004/11/18/cave/index2.html (accessed April 16, 2016).
18 Simon Hattenstone, "Old Nick," *The Guardian*, February 23, 2008, at https://www.theguardian.com/music/2008/feb/23/popandrock.features (accessed April 17, 2016).
19 Hattenstone, "Old Nick."
20 Hattenstone, "Old Nick."
21 Brown, "Cave's New World."
22 *Popis stanovništva, domaćinstava i stanova* 2011. u Republici Srbiji. *Veroispovest, maternji jezik i nacionalna pripadnost* [2011 Census of Population, Households and Dwellings in the Republic of Serbia] (Statistical Office of the Republic of Serbia, Belgrade: Dragan Vukmirović, 2013).
23 Besides, 4.9 percent are Catholic and 3 percent Muslim.

24 For more on this topic, see Sabina Hadzibulic and Mikko Lagerspetz, "The Colonization of a Celebration: The Transformations of Krsna Slava," *Compaso: Journal of Comparative Research in Anthropology and Sociology* 7, no. 1 (2016): 75–90.
25 I found one unsuccessful attempt to establish a conversation about the music and work of Cave on one of Serbian biggest forums (www.ana.rs). The only possibility of establishing online contact with Cave's fans through a private blog dedicated to translations of rock lyrics failed, as the blog had not been active for the past few years, so the administrator never responded to my attempts to start a communication.

Chapter 7

1 Following Henry Jenkins, *Textual Poachers: Television Fans and Participatory Culture* (New York: Routledge, 1992), being an aca-fan describes hating and loving the same fandom object, building a relation which deepens the connection to the fandom object. In the matter of Prince fans, this assumption follows the stance that Prince did not always treat his fans in a positive fashion and and thereby refuted fandom practices and the pleasures of fandom.
2 Jennifer Otter Bickerdike, *The Secular Religion of Fandom* (London: Sage, 2015), 14.
3 Mark Duffet, *Understanding Fandom: An Introduction to the Study of Media Fan Culture* (New York and London: Bloomsbury, 2003), 515.
4 Matt Hills, *Fan Cultures* (New York: Routledge, 2002), 118.
5 The term "para-religiosity" is similar to "neoreligiosity" used by Hills in *Fan Cultures*. In his plenary lecture at the conference, "Holy Crap! Intersections of the Popular and the Sacred in Youth Cultures" in August 2014 in Helsinki, Finland, Hills used the term "para-religiosity."
6 Daniel Cavicchi, *Tramps Like Us: Music and Meaning among Springsteen Fans* (Oxford: Oxford University Press, 1998).
7 Cavicchi, *Tramps Like Us*, 186.
8 Bickerdike, *The Secular Religion of Fandom*, 23.
9 Chris Rojek, *Celebrity* (London: Reaktion Books, 2001), 191.
10 Prince, "Purple Rain," *Purple Rain* (Warner Brothers, 1984).
11 Interviewee names have been changed to protect anonymity.
12 Prince, "The Love We Make," *Emancipation* (EMI, 1996).
13 Prince, *Lovesexy '88 (Dortmund Live)* [DVD] (Eye Records, 2016).
14 Prince, "Darling Nikki," *Purple Rain* (Warner Brothers, 1984).
15 Touré, *I Would Die 4 U: Why Prince Became an Icon* (Washington, DC: Atria Books, 2013), 46.

16 Margaret Rhodes, "The Fascinating Story of Prince's Iconic Symbol," *Wired*, April 2016, at https://www.wired.com/2016/04/designers-came-princes-love-symbol-one-night/ (accessed November 1, 2016).
17 Love4oneanother was a charity organization founded by Prince in the mid-90s.
18 Bettina Fritzsche, *Pop Fans. Studie einer Mädchenkultur* (Opladen: VS Verlag, 2003), 143.
19 Prince, "Paisley Park," *Around the World in a Day* (Warner Brothers, 1985).
20 Prince, "Paisley Park."
21 Hills, *Fan Cultures*, 154.
22 Unsie Zuege, *Paisley Park, Where Fiction becomes Reality*, at http://www.swnewsmedia.com/eden_prairie_news/news/opinion/columnists/zuege_unsie/paisley-park-where-fiction-becomes-reality/article_448e0533-b7e3-5684-9c0f-53857146d51d.html (accessed November 2, 2016).
23 Tournament of Fictional Places. http://b.hpb.com/places/ (accessed April 12, 2017).
24 Email from Unsie Zuege, October 22, 2016.
25 Prince, "Let's Go Crazy," *Purple Rain* (Warner Brothers, 1984).
26 Gilbert Rodman, *Elvis after Elvis: The Posthumous Career of a Living Legend* (New York: Routledge, 1996), 99.
27 *Under the Cherry Moon* [Film], directed by Prince (Warner Brothers, 1986).

Chapter 8

1 If possible, I use English primary sources to make the text more accessible to a non-Russian-speaking audience. All translations are mine unless otherwise noted. I would like to thank Andreas Häger, Anastasia Kozhevnikova, Karsten Mackensen, Andrei Rogatchevski, Yngvar B. Steinholt, Muhittin Kemal Temel, as well as my students from WPF Popmusikgeschichte 2016, for their comments and help.
2 E.g. David Chioni Moore, "Is the Post- in Postcolonial the Post- in Post-Soviet? Toward a Global Postcolonial Critique," *PMLA* 116, no. 1 (2001), 111–28; David-Emil Wickström, "'Drive-Ethno-dance' and 'Hutzul Punk'—Ukrainian Popular Music and Strategies of Localization in a Post-Soviet Context," *Yearbook for Traditional Music* 40 (2008), 60–88; Edith W. Clowes, *Russia on the Edge: Imagined Geographies and Post-Soviet Identity* (Ithaca, NY and London: Cornell University Press, 2011); David-Emil Wickström, *Rocking St. Petersburg: Transcultural Flows and Identity Politics in Post-Soviet Popular Music* (Stuttgart: ibidem Press, 2014).
3 E.g. Svetlana Boym, *The Future of Nostalgia* (New York: Basic Books, 2001); David-Emil Wickström and Yngvar Bordewich Steinholt, "Visions of the (Holy) Motherland in Contemporary Russian Popular Music: Nostalgia, Patriotism, Religion and Russkii Rok," *Popular Music and Society* 32, no. 3 (2009), 313–30.

4   Jardar Østbø, *The New Third Rome: Readings of a Russian Nationalist Myth* (Stuttgart: ibidem Press, 2016), 9.
5   Ivan Gololobov, "There are No Atheists in Trenches under Fire: Orthodox Christianity in Russian Punk," *Punk & Post-Punk* 1, no. 3 (2012), 305–21.
6   Michael J. Gilmour, *Gods and Guitars: Seeking the Sacred in Post-1960s Popular Music* (Waco: Baylor University Press, 2009).
7   Andreas Häger, "Under the Shadow of the Almighty: Fan Reception of Some Religious Aspects in the Work and Career of the Irish Popular Musician Sinéad O'Connor," in *Call Me the Seeker: Listening to Religion in Popular Music*, edited by Michael J. Gilmour (New York and London: Continuum, 2005), 224.
8   Geraldine Fagan, *Believing in Russia: Religious Policy After Communism* (London and New York: Routledge, 2013), 33.
9   Fagan, *Believing in Russia*, 33.
10 Patriarkh Kirill, "Bystplenie Sviateishego Patriarkha Kirilla Na Vstreche Predsedatelia Pravitel'stva RF V.V. Putina S Liderami Traditsionnykh Religioznykh Obshchin Rossii," *Russkaia Pravoslavnaia Tserkov'* (2012), at http://www.patriarchia.ru/db/print/2004759.html (accessed October 15, 2016).
11 Gleb Bryanski, "Russian Patriarch Calls Putin Era 'Miracle of God,'" *Reuters*, February 8, 2012.
12 Fagan, *Believing in Russia*, 32–3.
13 Svetlana Basharova, "Rossiiane Poluchat Besplatnyi Religioznyi Wi-Fi," *Izvestiia*, November 6, 2015.
14 E.g. "Orthodox Activists Crash Radio Station Anniversary Party," *The Moscow Times*, July 5, 2015. For a detailed report cf. Aleksandr Verkhovskii, "Problemy Realizatsii Svobody Sovesti V Rossii V 2015 Godu," *Informatsionno-analiticheskii tsentr "SOVA"* (2016), at http://www.sova-center.ru/religion/publications/2016/03/d34099 (accessed June 27, 2016).
15 Andrew Higgins, "In Expanding Russian Influence, Faith Combines with Firepower," *New York Times*, September 13, 2016.
16 Leningrad, "V Pitere—Pit," at https://www.youtube.com/watch?v=1ugivNRYfjc (accessed July 11, 2016).
17 "Mer Novosibirska Sdelal Preduprezhdenie Gruppe 'Leningrad,'" *Pravoslavie. FM* (2016), at http://pravoslavie.fm/novosti/myer-novosibirska-sdelal-preduprezhdenie-gruppe-leningrad (accessed July 11, 2016); Evgeniia Nazarets and Tat'iana Shtabel', "Ne Pet' Pro Pit," *Radio Svoboda* (2016), at http://www.svoboda.org/a/27772544.html (accessed October 7, 2016).
18 For more examples cf. Aleksandr Verkhovskii, "Freedom of Conscience in Russia: Restrictions and Challenges in 2015," *Informatsionno-analiticheskii tsentr "SOVA"* (2016), at http://www.sova-center.ru/en/religion/publications/2016/04/d34317 (accessed June 27, 2016).

19 Vserossiiskii tsentr izucheniia obshchestvennogo mneniia (VTsIOM), "Majority of Russians Place Feelings of Believers Above Freedom of Speech and Expression—Poll," *VTsIOM* (2015), at http://www.wciom.com/index.php?id=63&uid=1152 (accessed February 1, 2016).
20 Verkhovskii, "Freedom of Conscience in Russia."
21 Richard Wike and Katie Simmons, "Global Support for Principle of Free Expression, But Opposition to Some Forms of Speech," *Pew Research Center* (2015), at http://www.pewglobal.org/files/2015/11/Pew-Research-Center-Democracy-Report-FINAL-November-18-2015.pdf, 56 (accessed July 18, 2016).
22 Dmitrii E. Furman and Kimmo Kääriäinen, *Religioznost' V Rossii V 90-e Gody XX—Nachale XXI Veka* (Moskva: OGNI TD, 2006); "Religioznaia vera v Rossii," *Levada-Tsentr* (2011), at http://www.levada.ru/2011/09/26/religioznaya-vera-v-rossii (accessed September 16, 2016); "Church," *Levada-Tsentr* (2016), at http://www.levada.ru/en/2016/04/05/church (accessed September 16, 2016).
23 Furman and Kääriäinen, *Religioznost' V Rossii V 90-e Gody XX*, 64; VTsIOM, "Koldovstvo, Sglaz, Porcha: Navstrechu Khellouinu-2016," *VTsIOM* (2016), at http://wciom.ru/index.php?id=236&uid=115928 (accessed November 21, 2016).
24 Furman and Kääriäinen, *Religioznost' V Rossii V 90-e Gody XX*, 64.
25 Verkhovskii, "Freedom of Conscience in Russia."
26 Fagan, *Believing in Russia*, 42–4.
27 Fagan, *Believing in Russia*, 26.
28 Due to space constraints I will not go into an in-depth discussion on Pussy Riot since there have been numerous academic publications on the topic. For a musical analysis of the performance cf. Polly McMichael, "Defining Pussy Riot Musically: Performance and Authenticity in New Media," *Digital Icons* 9 (2013), 99–113. For a general overview and context cf. Joachim Willems, *Pussy Riots Punk-Gebet—Religion, Recht und Politik in Russland* (Berlin: Berlin University Press, 2013), 82; Yngvar Bordewich Steinholt, "Kitten Heresy: Lost Contexts of Pussy Riot's Punk Prayer," *Popular Music and Society* 36, no. 1 (2013), 120–24.
29 This is the common translation, however Willems points out that a *moleben* is a thanksgiving service. The Russian word for prayer is *molitva*. Willems, *Pussy Riots Punk-Gebet*, 32.
30 pussy_riot, "Pank-Moleben 'Bogoroditsa, Putina Progoni' V Khrame Khrista Spasitelia," *Livejournal* (2012), at http://pussy-riot.livejournal.com/2012/02/21 (accessed June 27, 2016); Pussy Riot, "Pank-Moleben 'Bogoroditsa, Putina Progoni' Pussy Riot V Khrame," at https://www.youtube.com/watch?v=GCasuaAczKY (accessed June 27, 2016).
31 Willems, *Pussy Riots Punk-Gebet*, 82.

32. Fagan, however, points out that Putin keeps his faith personal and also frequents churches in the Russian regions thus distancing himself from the Moscow centered pomp. Fagan, *Believing in Russia*, 39–40.
33. An online transcription of the verdict can be found here: "Prigovor Pussy Riot," *Snob* (2012), at https://snob.ru/selected/entry/51999?v=1461934677 (accessed June 27, 2016). After appealing the sentence, Samutsevich was released on probation.
34. Østbø, *The New Third Rome*, 71.
35. Østbø, *The New Third Rome*, 2.
36. Clowes, *Russia on the Edge*, 43–45; Østbø, *The New Third Rome*.
37. Andreas Kappeler, *Russische Geschichte* (München: C.H. Beck, 2005), 24; Fagan, *Believing in Russia*, 8–9.
38. The other two were Autocracy (*Samoderzhavie*) and Nationality (*Narodnost'*). Cf. Andreas Kappeler, *Russland Als Vielvölkerreich—Entstehung, Geschichte, Zerfall* (München: C.H. Beck, 1992), 199.
39. Willems, *Pussy Riots Punk-Gebet*, 105.
40. Administratsiia Prezidenta RF, "Konstitutsiia Rossiiskoi Federatsii," *Ofitsial'nye setevye resursy Prezidenta Rossii* (2009), at http://constitution.kremlin.ru (accessed July 18, 2016).
41. "O Svobode Sovesti I O Religioznykh Ob"edineniiakh," *Gosudarstvennaia sistema pravovoi informatsii* (2016), at http://pravo.gov.ru/proxy/ips/?docbody=-102049359 (accessed July 18, 2016).
42. Furman and Kääriäinen, *Religioznost' V Rossii V 90-e Gody XX*, 32f.
43. Furman and Kääriäinen, *Religioznost' V Rossii V 90-e Gody XX*, 32f.
44. Denis Stupnikov, "Lazareva Subbota Russkogo Roka," *Pravaia.ru—pravoslavno-analiticheskii sait* (2006), at http://www.pravaya.ru/dailynews/7420 (accessed February 12, 2008).
45. Valeriia Mikhailova and Igumen Sergii Rybko, "Neformaly I Monakh, Ili Evangelie Na Rok-Kontserte," *Pravoslavie i Mir* (2011), at http://www.pravmir.ru/neformaly-i-monax-ili-evangelie-na-rok-koncerte (accessed September 16, 2016).
46. Mikhailova and Rybko, "Neformaly I Monakh."
47. Igumen Sergii Rybko and Mikhail Tiurenkov, "Igumen Sergii (Rybko): 'Rok—Muzyka Dumaiushchikh Liudei …,'" *Pravaia.ru—Radikal'naia Ortodoksiia* (2006), at http://www.pravaya.ru/ludi/451/6489 (accessed September 16, 2016).
48. Cf. Wickström, *Rocking St. Petersburg*.
49. Gololobov, "There are No Atheists," 318.
50. Iuliia Makoveichuk and Valeriia Mikhailova, "Konstantin Kinchev: Razgovor Po Dusham," *Pravoslavie i Mir* (2011), at http://www.pravmir.ru/konstantin-kinchev-razgovor-po-dusham (accessed January 28, 2016).
51. Quoted in Artur Gasparian and Il'ia Legostaev, "Po Obrazu I Podobiiu Spasitelia," *Moskovskii Komsomolets*, October 28, 2005.

52 *Dormition* commemorates the death of Mary, the mother of Christ. Konstantin Kinchev, "Novosti," *Gruppa Alisa*, at http://www.alisa.net/informaciya.php?action=main (accessed July 20, 2016).
53 Alisa, "Alisa—Rozhdestvo (Alisa—Christmas)," at https://www.youtube.com/watch?v=5Mn3psDH0Jo (accessed July 20, 2016).
54 Kinchev, "Novosti."
55 Cf. "Metropolitan Kirill Meets with Rock Musicians," *Russkaia Pravoslavnaia Tserkov'* (2006), at http://www.mospat.ru/index.php?page=30881 (accessed January 11, 2008); Sergey Chernov, "Chernov's Choice," *St. Petersburg Times*, April 28, 2006; Stupnikov, "Lazareva Subbota Russkogo Roka."
56 "Metropolitan Kirill Meets with Rock Musicians."
57 Alisa, *Solntsevorot* (CD-Land, 2000). The album cover also caused a minor scandal since it depicts swastikas—or sun wheels, depending on how one argues.
58 Alisa, *Izgoi* (Real Records, 2005).
59 Gasparian and Legostaev, "Po Obrazu I Podobiiu Spasitelia."
60 Gruppa Alisa, "Diskografiia [Videografiia]," (n.d.), at http://www.alisa.net/diskografiya.php?action=videografia (accessed November 21, 2016).
61 The time codes given here are based on this YouTube version of the video: Alisa, "Rok [Sic]-En [Sic]-Rol Krest," at http://www.youtube.com/watch?v=WnsqwQJ_ZBE (accessed February 2, 2009).
62 Alisa, "Alisa—Antikhrist" (Alisa—Antichrist), at https://www.youtube.com/watch?v=mPIdCP33Nco (accessed November 21, 2016).
63 Makoveichuk and Mikhailova, "Konstantin Kinchev."
64 For an image, cf. Fagan, *Believing in Russia*, 51.
65 "Federal'nyi Spisok Ekstremistskikh Materialov," *Ministerstvo iustitsii Rossiiskoi Federatsii* (2016), at http://minjust.ru/ru/extremist-materials?field_extremist_content_value=865 (accessed September 12, 2016).
66 Makoveichuk and Mikhailova, "Konstantin Kinchev."
67 Makoveichuk and Mikhailova, "Konstantin Kinchev."
68 Wickström and Steinholt, "Visions of the (Holy)"; Wickström, *Rocking St. Petersburg*; David-Emil Wickström, "Nebo Slavian (Alisa)," *Songlexikon. Encyclopedia of Songs* (2015), at http://www.songlexikon.de/songs/neboslavianalisa (accessed November 9, 2015).
69 Alisa, "Alisa—Nebo Slavian (Alisa—the Sky of Slavs)," at http://www.youtube.com/watch?v=L7CEiSa_6vw (accessed September, 12, 2016). The song was released on Alisa, *Seichas Pozdnee, Chem Ty Dumaesh'* (Moroz M'iuzik, 2003).
70 I compiled a short medley of the concert which can be seen here: Alisa, "Alisa—Klub Kosmonavt (25.12.2015)," at https://www.youtube.com/watch?v=SHFysVQQZXE (accessed October 4, 2016). The sing-along part is at 2:42.
71 The recurring synth melody resembles the opening line and (vocal) interlude of the Soviet *estrada* song "Ridnyi Krai" (Native Land) composed by Nikolai Mozgovoi.

A version recorded in 1980 with Soviet *estrada* singer Sofiia Rotaru singing can be heard at https://www.youtube.com/watch?v=XoiwikRKjdY (accessed December 10, 2016).

72 Timur Blokhin, "'Kosovo Dlia Serbov—Eto to Zhe Samoe, Chto Dlia Rossii—Kulikovo Pole,'" *Radio Golos Rossii* (2014), at https://web.archive.org/web/20140115165326/http://rus.ruvr.ru/2014_01_15/Kosovo-dlja-serbov-jeto-to-zhe-samoe-chto-dlja-Rossii-Kulikovo-pole-6129 (accessed December 10, 2016); Mikhail Margolis, "Lider Gruppy 'Alisa' Konstantin Kinchev: 'Kosovo—Eto Serdtse Serbii, a Krym—Eto Rossiia,'" *Izvestiia*, June 5, 2008.

73 Alisa, "Alisa—Vlast' (Alisa—Power)," at https://www.youtube.com/watch?v=s42ZvgFYhRA (accessed September 12, 2016). The song was released on Alisa, *Puls' Khranitelia Dverei Labirinta* (CD-Maximum, 2008).

74 Alisa, "Ekstsess," at https://www.youtube.com/watch?v=mw5k4p4d438 (accessed August 28, 2017); Iaroslav Zabaluev, "'Predvideniia Koe-Kakie Imeiu,'" *Gazeta.ru*, September 19, 2016. Cf. Alisa, "Alisa—Naebali," at https://www.youtube.com/watch?v=FyQY3KG6D3M (accessed November 21, 2016) for a concert excerpt from 2014 where he sings *khokhli*, and David-Emil Wickström, "'Ukro-Ska-punk'—Band Identity, Surzhik and Language in Post-Soviet Russia," in *Unsichtbare Landschaften—Populäre Musik und Räumlichkeit*, edited by Giacomo Bottà (Münster and New York: Waxmann, 2016) for a discussion of the derogatory term *khokhol*.

75 Blokhin, "'Kosovo Dlia Serbov.'"

76 Mikhail Riabov and Andrei Lubenskii, "Kinchev Prizval Vydat' Dochek Putina Za Britanskikh Printsev I Vossozdat' Stolitsu Rusi V Kieve," *Novyi Region—Kiev*, February 23, 2008.

77 Tat'iana Shugailo, "Kinchev Trebuet Rasstrelivat' Gomoseksualistov: Ekskliuzivnoe Interv'iu Lidera Gruppy 'Alisa,'" *Ezhednevnye Novosti*, February 22, 2007.

78 Fagan, *Believing in Russia*, 39.

79 Fagan, *Believing in Russia*, 40–1.

80 Fagan, *Believing in Russia*, 47.

81 "Patriarshii Sovet Po Kul'ture," *Ofitsial'nyi sait Russkoi Pravoslavnoi Tserkvi* (2016), at http://www.patriarchia.ru/db/text/141942.html (accessed July.29, 2016); Press-sluzhba Patriarkha Moskovskogo i vseia Rusi, "Utverzhden Sostav Patriarshego Soveta Po Kul'ture," *Ofitsial'nyi sait Russkoi Pravoslavnoi Tserkvi* (2010), at http://www.patriarchia.ru/db/text/1231066.html (accessed July 29, 2016).

82 This is also a quote from the mentioned song "Pravoslavnye."

83 Boym, *The Future of Nostalgia*, 66–8.

84 Boym, *The Future of Nostalgia*, 67.

85 "Church," *Levada-Tsentr* (2016), at http://www.levada.ru/en/2016/04/05/church (accessed September 16, 2016).

Chapter 9

1. Ingvar Svanberg and David Westerlund, eds, *Religion i Sverige* (Stockholm: Dialogos, 2008).
2. *Country News* no. 1 (1985), 7. My translation.
3. Christopher Partridge, *The Re-Enchantment of the West. Volume I: Alternative Spiritualities, Sacralization, Popular Culture and Occulture* (London: T & T Clark International, 2004); Thomas Bossius, *Med framtiden i backspegeln. Black metal- och transkulturen. Ungdomar, musik och religion i en senmodern värld* (Göteborg: Daidalos, 2003); Magnus Hagevi, ed., *Religion och politik* (Stockholm: Liber, 2005); Liselotte Frisk and Peter Åkerbäck, *New Religiosity in Contemporary Sweden: The Dalarna Study in National and International Context* (Sheffield: Equinox Publishing, 2015). Frisk and Åkerbäck's study was originally published in Swedish in 2013. The title of the Swedish volume is: *Den mediterande dalahästen. Religion på nya arenor i samtidens Sverige* (Stockholm: Dialogos, 2013).
4. Frisk and Åkerbäck, *New Religiosity in Contemporary Sweden*, 168.
5. Frisk and Åkerbäck, *New Religiosity in Contemporary Sweden*, 170.
6. Owe Wikström, *Om det heliga och dess envisa vägran att försvinna. Religionspsykologiska perspektiv* (Stockholm: Natur & Kultur, 2003), 92. My translation.
7. Thomas Luckmann, "Shrinking Transcendence, Expanding Religion?," *Sociological Analysis. A Journal in the Sociology of Religion* 50, no. 2 (1990): 132.
8. Thomas Bossius, "Varför ska Djävulen ha all den bra musiken? En musikhistorisk översikt över den kristna populärmusikens framväxt," in *Frispel. Festskrift till Olle Edström*, edited by Alf Björnberg, Mona Hallin, Lars Lilliestam, and Ola Stockfelt (Gothenburg: Department of Musicology, University of Gothenburg, 2005), 507–28.
9. Thomas Bossius, "Keep it Country: Negotiations and Re-negotiations in the Swedish Country Music Culture," in *Made in Sweden: Studies in Popular Music*, edited by Alf Björnberg and Thomas Bossius (New York: Routledge, 2017).
10. The lyrics of Hasse Andersson, Christina Lindberg, and Alf Robertson are all written in Swedish; also their biographies, and most of the interviews quoted, are originally written in Swedish. Unless stated to the contrary, all translations are mine.
11. From the album *Änglahund* with Hasse Andersson and Kvinnaböske Band, 1982.
12. Hasse Andersson and Michael Nystås, *Jag har skrivit mina sånger. En bok om Hasse "Kvinnaböske" Andersson* (Malmö: Kira Förlag, 2013).
13. From the album *Tie bilder* [Ten Pictures] with Hasse Andersson and Kvinnaböske Band, 1985.
14. From the cover of *Tie bilder*.

15 From the cover of *Tie bilder*.
16 Andersson and Nystås, *Jag har skrivit mina sånger*, 196.
17 Andersson and Nystås, *Jag har skrivit mina sånger*, 195.
18 Börje Lundberg, *Alf Robertson. Jag lämnade mitt hjärta i Göteborg* (Göteborg: Reverb, 2009), 109.
19 Lundberg, *Alf Robertson*, 108.
20 Lundberg, *Alf Robertson*, 108.
21 Lundberg, *Alf Robertson*, 110–12.
22 "Renat" means "purified," and is one of the most popular brands of Swedish vodka.
23 Lyrics in Swedish by Hans Sidén.
24 Lundberg, *Alf Robertson*, 141.
25 *Country News*, no. 5/6 (1983): 49f.
26 *Country News*, no. 5/6 (1983): 50.
27 Lundberg, *Alf Robertson*, 179.
28 *Country News*, no. 5/6 (1983): 40.
29 Andersson and Nystås, *Jag har skrivit mina sånger*, 196.
30 Frisk and Åkerbäck, *New Religiosity in Contemporary Sweden*, 170.
31 "De sista ljuva åren" charted for 65 weeks during 1989 and 1990. Until then the record was held by Björn Ulvaeus and his pre-Abba group The Hootenanny Singers and their song "Omkring tiggar'n från Luossa" [Around the Beggar from Luossa] which charted for 52 weeks in the early seventies. "De sista ljuva åren" has been included in several compilations and re-recordings by both Christina Lindberg and Lasse Stefanz. Originally it was released on the Lasse Stefanz album *Livets ljusa sida* (The Bright Side of Life, 1988). For more information on Swedish dance bands, see Lars Lilliestam, "Swedish Dance Bands: Danceable, Melodious and Familiar," in *Made in Sweden: Studies in Popular Music*, edited by Alf Björnberg and Thomas Bossius (New York: Routledge, 2017): 79–90.
32 Quoted from a biography of Christina Lindberg: Vesna Maldaner, *De första ljuva åren (och de alltför tjocka låren). Biografin om countrydrottningen Christina Lindberg* (Malmö: Baba Books, 2013), 139.
33 Maldaner, *De första ljuva åren*, 46.
34 Maldaner, *De första ljuva åren*, 217.
35 From the album *Hemma igen* [Home Again] (1997). Lyrics by Marianne Flynner.
36 From the album *Hemma igen*. Lyrics by Christina Lindberg. The song is also included in the album *Back to the Roots* (2015), then with the title changed to "Vågornas vals" [The Waltz of the Waves].
37 Frisk and Åkerbäck, *New Religiosity in Contemporary Sweden*, 14.
38 Maldaner, *De första ljuva åren*, 25.
39 Maldaner, *De första ljuva åren*.
40 Maldaner, *De första ljuva åren*, 36, 39.

41 Thomas Ziehe, "Inför avmystifieringen av världen. Ungdom och kulturell modernisering," in *Postmoderna tider?* edited by Mikael Löfgren and Anders Molander (Stockholm: Norstedt, 1986).

Chapter 10

1 J. Donaghey, "Researching 'Punk Indonesia': Notes Towards a Non-Exploitative Insider Methodology," *Punk & Post-Punk* 6, no. 2 (2017): 291–314.
2 Anselm Strauss and Juliet Corbin, *Basics of Qualitative Research: Techniques and Procedures for Developing Grounded Theory* (London: Sage Publications, 1998), 43.
3 Robin Banks, *The Hardcore Guide to Christianity* (Chico: AK Press, 1999), 30 [square brackets section in original].
4 See: Anthony T. Fiscella, "From Muslim Punks to Taqwacore: An Incomplete History of Punk Islam," *Contemporary Islam* 6, no. 3 (2012): 255–81.
5 *Taqwacore: The Birth of Punk Islam* [Film], directed by Omar Majeed (Canada: Eye Steel Film, 2009).
6 Sanjiv Bhattacharya, "How Islamic Punk went from Fiction to Reality," *The Guardian*, August 4, 2011.
7 For detailed discussion of instances of religiously engaged punk in Indonesia, see H. Saefullah, "'Nevermind the jahiliyyah, here's the hijrahs': Punk and the Religious Turn in the Contemporary Indonesian Underground Scene," *Punk & Post-Punk* 6, no. 2 (2017): 263–89.
8 From the Indonesian Population Census, 2010, carried out by Badan Pusat Statistik. Detailed breakdown of information on religion available at: http://sp2010.bps.go.id/index.php/site/tabel?tid=321&wid=0 (accessed December 4, 2015).
9 Includes other religions, not stated and not asked.
10 Even more stringently, the definition of religion accompanying the 2010 census information is "belief in Almighty God that *must be possessed by every human being*." http://sp2010.bps.go.id/index.php/site/tabel?tid=321&wid=0 [emphasis added]. The emphasis on monotheism provides the grounds to repress Indonesia's indigenous animist religions, such as Dayak Kaharingan.
11 Kate Hodal, "Indonesia's Atheists Face Battle for Religious Freedom," *The Guardian*, May 3, 2012, at http://www.guardian.co.uk/world/2012/may/03/indonesia-atheists-religious-freedom-aan (accessed December 4, 2015).
12 "Atheist Alexander Aan Gets [out] of Prison," *Jakarta Post*, January 31, 2014, at http://www.thejakartapost.com/news/2014/01/31/atheist-alexander-aan-gets-prison.html#sthash.HcbPqkZL.dpuf (accessed December 4, 2015).
13 Under "Article 28(2) of the Electronic Information and Transaction Law for disseminating information aimed at inciting religious hostility and Criminal Code articles 156a(a) and 156a(b)." "Atheist Alexander Aan Gets [out] of Prison," *Jakarta Post*.

14 Hodal, "Indonesia's Atheists."
15 Hodal, "Indonesia's Atheists."
16 Ian Wilson describes the FPI: "Established in 1998, and initially subsidised by the military and police as part of a street-level militia mobilised against the student-led reform movement, the FPI has now for over 15 years expressed 'alarm' and outrage at liberal democracy, representing it as a threat to Islamic practice and belief" ("Resisting Democracy: Front Pembela Islam and Indonesia's 2014 Elections," *ISEAS Perspective*, no. 10 (2014): 2).
17 "Lady Gaga Cancels Indonesia Show After Threat from Muslim Extremists" (Associated Press article), *The Guardian*, May 27, 2012, at http://www.guardian.co.uk/music/2012/may/27/lady-gaga-indonesia-cancel-muslim (accessed December 4, 2015).
18 "Indonesians Protest Over Miss World Contest" (Associated Press article), *The Guardian*, September 5, 2013, at http://www.theguardian.com/world/2013/sep/05/indonesia-protests-miss-world (accessed December 4, 2015).
19 Wilson, "Resisting Democracy," 2.
20 Andre Vltchek, *Indonesia: Archipelago of Fear* (London: Pluto Press, 2012), 189.
21 The enforcement is limited to Muslim citizens, though non-Muslims are expected to show respect to Shariah law in public.
22 Edward Aspinall, "The Politics of Islamic Law in Aceh," paper given to Association for Asian Studies Annual Meeting, March 22–25, 2007, Boston.
23 "Indonesian Province Moves to Ban Women from Straddling Motorbikes" (Associated Press article), *The Guardian*, January 7, 2013, at http://www.theguardian.com/world/2013/jan/07/indonesia-aceh-ban-women-motorbikes (accessed December 4, 2015).
24 "Indonesia Bans Sale of Beer in Small Shops" (Agence France-Presse article), *The Guardian* April 16, 2015, at http://www.theguardian.com/world/2015/apr/16/indonesia-bans-beer-sales-small-shops (accessed December 4, 2015).
25 Kate Hodal, "Female Indonesian Police Recruits Forced to Undergo 'Virginity Tests,'" *The Guardian*, November 18, 2014, at http://www.theguardian.com/world/2014/nov/18/female-indonesian-police-recruits-forced-virginity-test (accessed December 4, 2015).
26 SETARA Institute (Institute for Democracy and Peace), "Toleransi dalam Pasungan: Pandangan Generasi Muda Terhadap Masalah Kebangsaan Pluralisme dan kepemimpinan Nasional" (Tolerance in confinement: Young generations view of the problems of nationhood, pluralism and national leaderships), June 2008.
27 Vltchek, *Indonesia*, 87.
28 Vltchek, *Indonesia*, 185. Interviewee "Nadya" noted the influence of religion in education. "We learn it at school …..these institutions keep telling us that we must be religious ….. pray blah blah blah instead of respect[ing] each other and humanity." Email exchange with interviewee "Nadya," February 25, 2015.

29 Vltchek, *Indonesia*, 185.
30 The international support campaigns for the punks abducted in Banda Aceh were numerous. A compilation CD called *Aceh Revolution* was released by bands and labels from across Europe. In the US, Aborted Society records launched the "Mixtapes for Aceh" campaign, encouraging punks to send CD-Rs to the area (http://abortedsociety.com/2011/12/mixtapes-for-aceh/). Also in the US, the Punk Aid group, in association with Movement Records in Jakarta, put out a benefit release (http://punkaid.bandcamp.com/album/punk-aid-aceh-calling). There were also protests at the Indonesian embassies and consulates in London and LA, and the Indonesian embassy in Istanbul was attacked and daubed with graffiti by Turkish punks (video of the action online here: http://www.youtube.com/watch?v=4dXrG0Rlrwg [all accessed December 4, 2015]).
31 Aspinall argues that, even though Aceh is a particularly observant Muslim area, the extension of Shariah laws was in fact a tactic to undermine support for the local separatist movement GAM (*Gerakan Aceh Merdeka* or Free Aceh Movement). Aspinall, "The Politics of Islamic Law in Aceh," 5.
32 Aspinall, "The Politics of Islamic Law in Aceh," 8.
33 Ian Wilson, "Indonesian Punk: A Brief Snapshot," *Le Banian*, no. 15 (June 2013): 1. President Soekarno himself likened rock'n'roll to a "mental disease" five decades earlier. Wilson, "Indonesian Punk," 2.
34 "'Hard-Line Indonesian Police Shave Punkers' Mohawks" (Associated Press article), *Hurryiet Daily News*, December 14, 2011, at http://www.hurriyetdailynews.com/hard-line-indonesian-police-shave-punkers-mohawks-.aspx?pageID=238&nID=9195&NewsCatID=356 (accessed December 4, 2015).
35 Interview conducted October 4, 2012.
36 Matt Brown, "No Anarchy in Aceh, Indonesia Cracks Down on Punks," *ABC Radio Australia*, May 7, 2012, at http://www.radioaustralia.net.au/international/2012-05-07/no-anarchy-in-aceh-indonesia-cracks-down-on-punks/939342 (accessed December 04, 2015).
37 Interview conducted October 3, 2012.
38 Jim Donaghey, *Goreng Crazy* (DIY zine, 2013), 19.
39 Interview conducted September 25, 2012.
40 Wilson, "Indonesian Punk," 1.
41 Interview conducted September 27, 2012.
42 Irawaty Wardany, "FPI Sets its Eyes on Underground Music," *Jakarta Post*, March 21, 2011, at http://www.thejakartapost.com/news/2011/03/21/fpi-sets-its-eyes-underground-music.html (accessed December 4, 2015).
43 A distro is essentially a shop ("distro" deriving from "distribution"), though functions as a hangout for punks as well. For more on the "distro" phenomenon in Indonesia, see F. A. Prasetyo, "Punk and the City: A History of Punk in Bandung," *Punk & Post-Punk* 6, no. 2 (2017), 189–211.

44 Baban Gandapurnama, "FPI Akui Spontanitas Sobek Spanduk Distro Prapatan Rebel," *detikNews*, July 18, 2012, at http://news.detik.com/read/2012/07/18/155557/1968584/486/fpi-akui-spontanitas-sobek-spanduk-distro-prapatan-rebel (accessed December 4, 2015).
45 Interview conducted September 27, 2012.
46 Interview conducted September 25, 2012.
47 Email exchange with interviewee "Nadya," February 25, 2015.
48 Wilson, "Indonesian Punk," 4.
49 Wilson, "Indonesian Punk," 4.
50 Email exchange with Dominic Berger, January 14, 2014.
51 Berger notes that "Marxist ideology and symbols associated with the former Communist Party (PKI) continue to be banned," as a legacy of Suharto's seizure of power in 1965, which blamed the PKI for an attempted coup and subsequently massacred between 500,000 and 3,000,000 "leftists," and maintained an anti-communist propaganda campaign throughout his dictatorship. (Abstract to a seminar given at Australia National University on September 27, 2013 titled "Repression on the Cheap: Responses to Anti-State Dissent in Post-New Order Indonesia," http://ips.cap.anu.edu.au/cap-events/2013–09-27/repression-cheap-responses-anti-state-dissent-post-new-order-indonesia#.UtTxVMiuFXU) (accessed January 14, 2014).
52 Email exchange with Dominic Berger, January 14, 2014.
53 Prosedur Tetap, *Kepala Keplisian Negara Republik Indonesia, Nomor: Protap/1/X/2010*, Tentang: Penanggulangan Anarki, October 8, 2010.
54 Farouk Arnaz and Dessy Sagita, "Plan for 'Anti-Anarchy' Police," *The Jakarta Globe*, March 2, 2011, at http://www.thejakartaglobe.com/archive/plan-for-anti-anarchy-police/ (accessed December 4, 2015).
55 See Joanna Pickles, "Punk, Pop and Protest: The Birth and Decline of Political Punk in Bandung," *RIMA* 41, no. 2 (2007): 223–46.
56 Punks are also repressed by the army and the police, though more usually with the aim of extorting bribes.
57 Interview conducted February 23, 2013 and March 19, 2013.
58 Interview conducted September 26, 2012.
59 Interview conducted October 2, 2012.
60 This includes anarchist contributors to their regular columns and frequent reviews of anarchist literature, in addition to the expected anarchist punk bands.
61 Including a gig poster that featured an anarchist flag and a Molotov cocktail, and a poster for an Indonesian rap group, Homicide, which imitated the Crass aesthetic. The image included the faces of Gramsci, Marx, and Nietzsche, and the slogans around the edge read: "Organize your community," "Whoever they vote for we are ungovernable," "Empower your surroundings," "Join the resistance: live life to

the fullest." The combination of Marxist, autonomist, situationist, anarchist, and anarcho-punk themes, if not particularly coherent, points to radical politics in general.

62 Donaghey, *Goreng Crazy*, 18.
63 Email exchange with interviewee "Teuku," March 1, 2015 [emphasis added].
64 Interview conducted October 4, 2012.
65 Interview conducted September 29, 2012.
66 Vltchek, *Indonesia*, 186.
67 Vltchek, *Indonesia*, 186.
68 Disabled, "They are Not a Moslem," *Curhat Colongan, Anjing!* (Curhat Colongan, Anjing! records, 2012).
69 Disabled, *Curhat Colongan, Anjing!* (Curhat Colongan, Anjing! records, 2012), CD booklet [translated from Indonesian].
70 Drawn from my collection, so biased by personal taste.
71 An acronym of the Arabic phrase "*Subhanahu Wa Ta'ala*" which roughly translated means "the most glorified, the most high."
72 Injakmati split 7" with Black Sister, *Rotten Conspiracy* (Neverheard distro, Power Negi records, Problem records, Alcoholic Desaster, Subwix, Urgent Freedom, 2009), lyric sheet.
73 Rasululloh is a synonym for the prophet Mohammed.
74 GunXRose, *Anti Dogmanisasi Berhala* (Chey, Battleground, xTerkubur Hidurx, Pastimati, Alternaive, Teriak, Doombringer, Donttalk, 2012).
75 Street Voices, *Kill Me With Your Lips* (Movement Records, 2010), tape inlay [emphasis added].
76 Interview conducted September 27, 2012.
77 Interview conducted September 29, 2012.
78 Who, despite their band name, share the authorities' misinterpretation of anarchism.
79 Interview conducted September 26, 2012.
80 Interview conducted September 30, 2012.
81 Interview conducted September 25, 2012.
82 Interview conducted September 27, 2012.
83 Of course, this is also the case in "secular" states.
84 Nicholas Jay Demerath III, "The Rise of 'Cultural Religion' in European Christianity: Learning from Poland, Northern Ireland, and Sweden," *Social Compass* 47, no. 1 (2000): 136.
85 Jim Donaghey, "Bakunin Brand Vodka: An Exploration into Anarchist-punk and Punk-anarchism," *Anarchist Developments in Cultural Studies* 1 (2013), 138–70, and J. Donaghey, "Punk and Anarchism: UK, Poland, Indonesia," Ph.D. thesis, Loughborough: Loughborough University, 2016.

86   The mural features a blindfolded face with its mouth opened wide, and winged plates carrying a house, a car, a pile of books, and a mosque towards it, symbolizing oppressive aspects of society, which are "shoved down your throat." The inclusion of the mosque is notable, with three mosques in very close proximity to the info-shop.
87   Anonymous interviewee, September 2012.
88   Krass Kepala (live version), from the split 7" with Die Wrecked, *Solidaritas Internasional* (Die Rex, Pyrate Punx, Jobsworth, Mass Prod, Pumpkin, 2013).
89   KontraSosial, *Endless War* (Final Warning, Kontra Kommunique Division, 2009) [translation from Indonesian].
90   KontraSosial, *Endless War*.
91   Zudas Krust, "Perang Agama," *A Loyal Slave to the Apocalyptic Order* (European release distributed by Rauha Turva, 2011) [translation supplied in tape booklet].
92   Zudas Krust, "God System Slavery," *A Loyal Slave to the Apocalyptic Order* (European release distributed by Rauha Turva, 2011) [translation supplied in tape booklet].
93   Zudas Krust, "Percepat Kiamat!" *Here Lies Your Gods* (Rauha Turva, Gusto Rana!, Disparodesire, 2009) [translation supplied in tape booklet].
94   Zudas Krust, "You Call It Moral," *Here Lies Your Gods* (Rauha Turva, Gusto Rana!, Disparodesire, 2009) [translation supplied in tape booklet].
95   Duct Tape Surgery, *Facing Problems* (Stop 'n' Go, Time Up Records, 2012).
96   Donaghey, "Punk and Anarchism: UK, Poland, Indonesia."

Chapter 11

1   *Metallimessu* [Metal Mass] (Warner Music Finland, 2008).
2   The Swedish priest and musician Ingmar Johansson has written several such masses, for example *Mysterium—En mässa om livets insida* (Signatur, 1995).
3   http://u2-charist.com/ (accessed August 15, 2017).
4   https://www.svenskakyrkan.se/goteborgsstift/kultursamverkan/temamassor-som-genomforts (accessed March 2, 2017).
5   http://saintjameslancaster.org/services/ (accessed February 27, 2017); http://livestream.com/saintjameslancaster/saturday (accessed February 27, 2017).
6   Olof Björner, *Mysteriously Saved: Bob Dylan 1979* (2003), at http://bjorner.com/79.htm (accessed December 20, 2016); Olof Björner, *The Same Man: Bob Dylan 1980* (2004), at http://bjorner.com/80.htm (accessed December 20, 2016).
7   Scott M. Marshall, *Restless Pilgrim: The Spiritual Journey of Bob Dylan* (Lake Mary: Relevant Books, 2002); Michael J. Gilmour, *The Gospel According to Bob Dylan: The Old, Old Story for Modern Times* (Louisville: Westminster John Knox, 2011).

8. Stephen Pickering, *Bob Dylan Approximately: A Portrait of the Jewish Poet in Search of God: A Midrash* (New York: David MacKay, 1975); Daniel Maoz, "Shekhinah as Woman: Kabbalistic References in Dylan's Infidels," in *Call Me the Seeker: Listening to Religion in Popular Music*, edited by Michael J. Gilmour (New York: Continuum, 2005), 3–16.
9. For example Mikal Gilmore (2012), "Bob Dylan Unleashed," at http://www.rollingstone.com/music/news/bob-dylan-unleashed-a-wild-ride-on-his-new-lp-and-striking-back-at-critics-20120927 (accessed December 20, 2016).
10. The first of these is the Dylan Mass at St. James's Episcopal Church, March 3, 2013, available at https://www.youtube.com/watch?v=PjndusQEYCk (accessed January 30, 2018).
11. https://www.youtube.com/watch?v=gxEonwUdMGQ (accessed August 15, 2017).
12. Carmen Germino, in her sermon in St. James's, Richmond VA, on March 30, 2014. https://www.youtube.com/watch?v=97HB2IZG2a0 (accessed January 31, 2018).
13. My translation, as all translations from the sermons and media material in Swedish.
14. http://www.thomascervin.se/kyrkapsalm/dylan (accessed October 27, 2016).
15. Email from Virginia Whitmire, November 11, 2016.
16. Email from Virginia Whitmire, November 11, 2016.
17. https://www.youtube.com/watch?v=PjndusQEYCk (accessed December 13, 2016).
18. The comments on Youtube are quoted verbatim, including misprints.
19. I here include the two albums used in the Saving Grace mass, *Slow Train Coming* (Columbia, 1979) and *Saved* (Columbia, 1980), as well as the less gospel-oriented *Shot of Love* (Columbia, 1981), from which the song "Every Grain of Sand" is used in the Richmond mass.
20. Pål Ketil Botvar, "With God on Our Side: Bob Dylan i norsk kirkeliv," in *Fra forsakelse til feelgood: Musikk, sang og dans i religiøst liv*, edited by Pål Repstad and Irene Trysnes (Oslo: Cappelen Damm Akademisk, 2003), 277–96.
21. Email from Virginia Whitmire, November 11, 2016.
22. http://bobdylan.com/songs/watching-river-flow/ (accessed March 31, 2017).
23. This quote is from his email to me, October 26, 2016.
24. The song title is a reference to Revelations 3:2.
25. From my field notes from the Forever Young mass.
26. One interpretation of the identity of Mr. Tambourine Man is that he is a drug dealer. Later, Dylan has claimed that the character is based on a fellow musician who played tambourine. http://www.rollingstone.com/music/news/mr-tambourine-man-bob-dylan (accessed March 27, 2017).
27. Botvar, "With God on Our Side," 277.
28. Leaflet for Dylan mass at St. James's Episcopal Church, Sunday, March 3, 2013. The leaflet was sent to me by the choir director.
29. From my field notes from the Forever Young mass.

30. There are other examples of rock masses in Sweden when the band, playing in front of the audience, are wearing head gear, for example in masses with the band Eldkvarn. https://www.youtube.com/watch?v=9VV3upRhSuA (accessed March 27, 2017).
31. During the period Dylan played only gospel songs, his set lists were quite similar from show to show, with the same songs and usually in the same order. Björner, *Mysteriously Saved*; Björner, *The Same Man*. The Saving Grace mass does not base its order of songs on the concerts of Dylan's gospel tours.
32. http://www.chantcafe.com/2013/11/the-dylan-mass-why-not.html (accessed June 9, 2016).
33. http://loveandtheft.se/smf/index.php?topic=2274.45 (accessed June 15, 2016).
34. Björner, *Mysteriously Saved*.
35. The concert in Toronto on April 20, 1980 was filmed for television and is available at https://www.youtube.com/watch?v=C0J3Y5s_kfo (accessed March 1, 2017). "In the Garden" starts at 1:46:50.
36. https://www.youtube.com/watch?v=KpLdR5GW91o (accessed March 3, 2017).
37. Marcus Moberg, "Popular Music Divine Services in the Evangelical Lutheran Church of Finland: Concept, Rationale, and Participants," *Journal of Religion and Popular Culture* (forthcoming).

Chapter 12

1. While the number of female DJs are on the rise, particularly with the democratization of DJ equipment, most DJs are male. For this reason, I will refer to the DJ using the masculine pronoun.
2. Scott R. Hutson, "Technoshamanism: Spiritual Healing in the Rave Subculture," *Popular Music and Society* 23 (Fall 1999): 53–77.
3. The rave scene developed in Britain in the 1980s from where it then spread to North America and around the world. Originally an underground movement, raves were characterized by their impromptu nature, the clandestine venues, long and late hours of dancing, advertising through word of mouth, the use of the club drug "Ecstasy," and rapid repetitive electronic music ranging from 120 to 200 beats per minute.
4. Hutson, "Technoshamanism."
5. Melanie Takahashi and Tim Olaveson, "Music Dance and Raving Bodies: Raving as Spirituality in the Central Canadian Rave Scene," *Journal of Ritual Studies* 17, no. 2 (2003): 72–96.
6. Commonalities include: the music, the prolonged hours, the use of club drugs, the emphasis on community and belonging, and the focus being on dancing.

7 Circuit parties are large-scale advertised events that usually last for a weekend or several days and are generally frequented by gay men. They typically happen on a yearly basis attracting participants from all over the world.
8 Stephen Heyman, "An Unprecedented Success for Electronic Dance Music and Its D.J.s," *New York Times*, September 9, 2015, at http://www.nytimes.com/2015/09/10/arts/international/an-unprecedented-success-for-electronic-dance-music-and-its-djs.html (accessed August 10, 2016).
9 Melanie Takahashi, "Spirituality through the Science of Sound: The DJ as Technoshaman in Rave Culture," in *Call Me the Seeker: Listening to Religion in Popular Music*, edited by Michael J. Gilmour (New York: Continuum, 2005), 239–66.
10 Gilbert Rouget, *Music and Trance: A Theory of the Relations between Music and Possession* (Chicago: The University of Chicago Press, 1985).
11 The acronym PLUR came to be known as the ethos of rave culture. Ravers prided themselves for embodying and cultivating this philosophy outside of the rave environment with the purpose of making the world a better place.
12 Sarah Thornton, *Club Cultures: Music, Media and Subcultural Capital* (New England: Wesleyan University Press, 1996), 60–1.
13 Hillegonda C. Rietveld, "Journey to the Light? Immersion, Spectacle and Mediation," in *DJ Culture in the Mix: Power, Technology, and Social Change in Electronic Dance Music*, edited by Bernardo Alexander Attias, Anna Gavanas, and Hillegonda C. Rietveld (New York: Bloomsbury, 2013), 80.
14 Jonathan Yu, "Electronic Dance Music and Technological Change: Lessons from Actor-Network Theory," in *DJ Culture in the Mix: Power, Technology, and Social Change in Electronic Dance Music*, edited by Bernardo Alexander Attias, Anna Gavanas, and Hillegonda C. Rietveld (New York: Bloomsbury, 2013), 163.
15 The vibe refers to an energy that is created by the music, the venue, and the participants.
16 Bernando A. Attias, "Meditations on the Death of Vinyl," *Dancecult: Journal of Electronic Music* 29, no. 1 (2011), at https://dj.dancecult.net/index.php/dancecult/article/view/321/315 (accessed August 29, 2017).
17 "Spinning" is an insider term for DJing.
18 A trainwreck occurs when the beats become out of sync causing an immediate kill of the vibe often resulting in an empty dance floor.
19 Bernando A. Attias, "Subjectivity in the Groove: Phonography, Digitality and Fidelity," in *DJ Culture in the Mix: Power, Technology, and Social Change in Electronic Dance Music*, edited by Bernardo Alexander Attias, Anna Gavanas, and Hillegonda C. Rietveld (New York: Bloomsbury, 2013), 24–5.
20 Attias, "Subjectivity in the Groove."
21 Attias, "Meditations on the Death of Vinyl."
22 "Noah," interviewed by Melanie Takahashi, San Francisco, September 2, 2015.

23 While the turntable has been retired from most clubs, it is making a gradual comeback among music aficionados and hobbyists.
24 The genre of hip-hop is one of the exceptions that continues to use turntables.
25 Robin Sylvan, *Traces of the Spirit* (New York: New York University Press, 2002); Takahashi, "Spirituality through the Science of Sound"; Rupert Till, *Pop Cult: Religion and Popular Music* (London: Continuum, 2010).
26 It should be noted that Bourguignon refers to this as "nontrance possession." Whereas possession occurs within the ritual context and is socially sanctioned, nontrance possession is usually considered an illness. Erika Bourguignon, *Possession* (San Francisco: Chandler and Sharp, 1976), 46.
27 Rouget, *Music and Trance*, 96.
28 Rouget, *Music and Trance*, 111.
29 Rouget, *Music and Trance*, 81.
30 Rouget, *Music and Trance*, 82–4.
31 Rouget, *Music and Trance*, 96–7.
32 Rouget, *Music and Trance*, 120.
33 Anne J. Blood and Robert J. Zatorre, "Intensely Pleasurable Response to Music Correlate with Activity in Brain Regions Implicated in Reward and Emotion," *PNAS* 98, no. 20 (2001): 11818–23.
34 Valorie N. Salimpoor, Mitchel Benovoy, Gregory Longo, Jeremy R. Cooperstock, and Robert J. Zatorre, "The Rewarding Aspects of Music Listening are Related to Degree of Emotional Arousal," *PLoS ONE* 4, no. 10 (2009): 11.
35 Ragnhild T. Solberg, "Waiting for the Bass to Drop: Correlations between Intense Emotional Experiences and Production Techniques in Build-up and Drop Sections of Electronic Dance Music," *Dancecult* 6, no. 1 (2014): 66.
36 Takahashi, "Spirituality through the Science of Sound."
37 Joe De Simone, "6 Tips for Better EDM Buildups and Drops," September 26, 2014, at https://theproaudiofiles.com/tips-for-better-buildups-and-drops-in-edm/ (accessed May 12, 2016).
38 Erika Bourguignon, "Suffering and Healing, Subordination and Power: Women and Possession Trance," *Ethos* 32, no. 4 (2004): 557–74.
39 I. M. Lewis, *Ecstatic Religion: A Study of Shamanism and Spirit Possession* (London: Routledge, 1989).
40 Bourguignon, *Possession*, 23.
41 Bourguignon, *Possession*, 40.
42 Rouget, *Music and Trance*, 123.
43 Jeremy Gilbert and Ewan Pearson, *Discographies: Dance Music Culture and the Politics of Sound* (London: Routledge, 1999), 83.
44 Maria Pini, "Women and the Early Bitish Rave Scene," in *Back to Reality? Social Experience and Cultural Studies*, edited by Angela McRobbie (Manchester: Manchester University Press, 1997), 154–5.

45 LSD, ketamine, GHB, speed, and Adderall are, in addition to MDMA, shared common club drugs used by EDM participants.
46 L. A. Becker-Blease, "Dissociative States through New Age and Electronic Trance Music," *Journal of Trauma & Dissociation* 5, no. 2 (2004): 89–100.
47 Solberg, "Waiting for the Bass to Drop," 61–82.
48 Rouget, *Music and Trance*, 112.
49 Kai Fikentscher, "It's Not the Mix, it's the Song Selection: Music Programming in Contemporary DJ Culture," in *DJ Culture in the Mix: Power, Technology, and Social Change in Electronic Dance Music*, edited by Bernardo Alexander Attias, Anna Gavanas, and Hillegonda C. Rietveld (New York: Bloomsbury, 2013), 132.
50 "Alexa," interviewed by Melanie Takahashi, San Francisco, September 9, 2016.
51 "Elliot," interviewed by Melanie Takahashi, San Francisco, October 21, 2015.
52 "Alexa," 2016.
53 Lizette Borreli, "Human Attention Span Shortens to 8 Seconds Due to Digital Technology: 3 Ways to Stay Focused," *Medical Daily*, May 14, 2015, at http://www.medicaldaily.com/human-attention-span-shortens-8-seconds-due-digital-technology-3-ways-stay-focused-333474 (accessed April 22, 2016).
54 A mashup combines the vocals of one track, with the background of another.
55 Judith Becker, *Deep Listeners* (Bloomington: Indiana University Press, 2004), 27.
56 Charles D. Laughlin, John McManus, and Eugene G. d'Aquili, *Brain, Symbol and Experience* (New York: Columbia University Press, 1992).
57 Polyphasic cultures are those that recognize altered states of consciousness as valid, and whose worldview is often informed by these states. In contrast, those cultures that place primary importance on the "waking phase" are monophasic.
58 Laughlin, McManus, and d'Aquili, *Brain, Symbol and Experience*, 228.
59 Laughlin, McManus, and d'Aquili, *Brain, Symbol and Experience*, 228.
60 Laughlin, McManus, and d'Aquili, *Brain, Symbol and Experience*, 228.
61 Laughlin, McManus, and d'Aquili, *Brain, Symbol and Experience*, 228.
62 See note 11.
63 Gordon Lynch and Emily Badger, "The Mainstream Post-Rave Club Scene as a Secondary Institution: A British Perspective," *Culture and Religion* 7, no. 1 (2006): 315–30, esp. 329.
64 Keith N. Hampton, Lauren F. Sessions, and Eun Ja Her, "Core Networks, Social Isolation, and New Media," *Information, Communication & Society* 14, no. 1 (2011): 130–55.
65 http://www.goodreads.com/quotes/84527-without-tradition-art-is-a-flock-of-sheep-without-a (accessed March 1, 2017).

Bibliography

Abrams, M. H., with G. Galt Harpham. *A Glossary of Literary Terms*. 8th edn. Toronto: Thomson Wadsworth, 2005.

Aden, R. C. *Popular Stories and Promised Lands: Fan Cultures and Symbolic Pilgrimages*. Tuscaloosa and London: The University of Alabama Press, 1999.

Adorno, T. W. *Introduction to the Sociology of Music*. New York: Seabury Press, 1976.

Alabarces, P. "Maradona, o la superación del peronismo por otros medios." In *El espacio cultural de los mitos, ritos, leyendas, celebraciones y devociones*, 166–91. Temas de Patrimonio 7. Buenos Aires: Comisión para la Preservación del Patrimonio Histórico Cultural de la Ciudad de Buenos Aires, 2002.

Andersson, H., and M. Nystås. *Jag har skrivit mina sånger. En bok om Hasse "Kvinnaböske" Andersson*. Malmö: Kira Förlag, 2013.

Anijar, K. "Selena—Prophet, Profit, Princess: Canonizing the Commodity." In *God in the Details: American Religion in Popular Culture*, edited by Eric E. Mazur and K. McCarthy, 83–101. New York and London: Routledge, 2001.

Attias, B. A. "Meditations on the Death of Vinyl." *Dancecult: Journal of Electronic Music* 29, no. 1 (2011). https://dj.dancecult.net/index.php/dancecult/article/view/321/315 (accessed February 5, 2018).

Attias, B. A. "Subjectivity in the Groove: Phonography, Digitality and Fidelity." In *DJ Culture in the Mix: Power, Technology, and Social Change in Electronic Dance Music*, edited by A. Gavanas, H. Rietveld, and B. A. Attias, 15–49. New York: Bloomsbury, 2013.

Augè, M. *El Genio del Paganismo*. Barcelona: Muchnik Editores, 1993.

Bacon-Smith, C. *Enterprising Women: Television Fandom and the Creation of Popular Myth*. Philadelphia: University of Pennsylvania Press, 1992.

Banks, R. *The Hardcore Guide to Christianity*. Chico: AK Press, 1999.

Barret, J. L. "Metarepresentation, Homo Religiosus, and Homo Symbolicus." In *Homo Symbolicus: The Dawn of Language, Imagination and Spirituality*, edited by C. S. Henshilwood and F. d'Errico, 205–24. Amsterdam: John Benjamins Publishing, 2011.

Beal, T. K. *Religion and Its Monsters*. New York: Routledge, 2002.

Beaudoin, T. *Virtual Faith: The Irreverent Spiritual Quest of Generation X*. San Francisco: Jossey-Bass, 1998.

Becker, J. *Deep Listeners*. Bloomington: Indiana University Press, 2004.

Becker-Blease, L. A. "Dissociative States through New Age and Electronic Trance Music." *Journal of Trauma & Dissociation* 5, no. 2 (2004): 89–100.

Bickerdike, J. O. *The Secular Religion of Fandom*. London: Sage, 2015.

Björnberg, A., and T. Bossius, eds. *Made in Sweden: Studies in Popular Music*. New York: Routledge, 2017.

Björner, O. *Mysteriously Saved: Bob Dylan 1979* (2003). http://bjorner.com/79.htm (accessed December 20, 2016).

Björner, O. *The Same Man: Bob Dylan 1980* (2004). http://bjorner.com/80.htm (accessed December 20, 2016).

Blood, A. J., and R. J. Zatorre. "Intensely Pleasurable Response to Music Correlate with Activity in Brain Regions Implicated in Reward and Emotion." *PNAS* 98, no. 20 (2001): 11818–23.

Bossius, T. *Med framtiden i backspegeln. Black metal- och transkulturen. Ungdomar, musik och religion i en senmodern värld*. Göteborg: Daidalos, 2003.

Bossius, T. "Varför ska Djävulen ha all den bra musiken? En musikhistorisk översikt över den kristna populärmusikens framväxt." In *Frispel. Festskrift till Olle Edström*, edited by A. Björnberg, M. Hallin, L. Lilliestam, and O. Stockfelt, 507–28. Göteborg: Göteborgs universitet, 2005.

Bossius, T. "Shout to the Lord: Christian Worship Music as Popular Culture, Church Music, and Lifestyle." In *Religion and Popular Music in Europe: New Expressions of Sacred and Secular Identity*, edited by T. Bossius, A. Häger, and K. Kahn-Harris, 51–70. London: I. B. Tauris, 2011.

Bossius, T. "Keep it Country: Negotiations and Re-negotiations in the Swedish Country Music Culture." In *Made in Sweden: Studies in Popular Music*, edited by A. Björnberg and T. Bossius, 91–102. New York: Routledge, 2017.

Bossius, T., and L. Lilliestam, *Musiken och jag. Rapport från forskningsprojektet Musik i Människors Liv*. Göteborg: Göteborgs universitet, 2011.

Bossius, T., A. Häger, and K. Kahn-Harris, eds. *Religion and Popular Music in Europe: New Expressions of Sacred and Secular Identity*. London: I. B. Tauris, 2011.

Botvar, P.K. "With God on Our Side: Bob Dylan i norsk kirkeliv." In *Fra forsakelse til feelgood: Musikk, sang og dans i religiøst liv*, edited by Pål Repstad and Irene Trysnes, 277–96. Oslo: Cappelen Damm Akademisk, 2003.

Bourguignon, E. *Possession*. San Francisco: Chandler and Sharp, 1976.

Bourguignon, E. "Suffering and Healing, Subordination and Power: Women and Possession Trance." *Ethos* 32, no. 4 (2004): 557–74.

Boym, S. *The Future of Nostalgia*. New York: Basic Books, 2001.

Butler, J. "Magic, Astrology, and the Early American Religious Heritage, 1600–1760." *American Historical Review* 84, no. 2 (April 1979): 317–46.

Carozzi, M. J. "Carlos Gardel: el patrimonio que sonríe." *Horizontes Antropológicos* 9, no. 20 (2003): 59–82.

Carozzi, M. J. "Antiguos difuntos y difuntos nuevos: las canonizaciones populares en la década del '90." In *Entre santos y piquetes. Las culturas populares en la Argentina reciente*, edited by D. Miguez and P. Semán, 97–110. Buenos Aires: Biblos, 2006.

Cave, N. "An Introduction to the Gospel according to Mark." In *Gospel According to Mark*, 93–98. Edinburgh: Canongate Books, 1998.

Cavicchi, D. *Tramps Like Us: Music and Meaning among Springsteen Fans*. Oxford: Oxford University Press, 1998.

Christe, I. *Sound of the Beast: The Complete Headbanging History of Heavy Metal*. New York: itbooks, 2003.

Clowes, E. W. *Russia on the Edge: Imagined Geographies and Post-Soviet Identity*. Ithaca, NY and London: Cornell University Press, 2011.

Coelho, M. *A experiencia da fama: Individualismo e comunicação*. Rio de Janeiro: Editora FGV, 1999.

Cohen, N. *Cosmos, Chaos and the World to Come: The Ancient Roots of Apocalyptic Faith*. 2nd edn. New Haven: Yale University Press, 2001.

Coralis, P. "Nunca te vi, sempre te amei. Uma análise antropológica da idolatria a Madonna em um fã-clube virtual." M.A. Diss. Rio de Janeiro: State University of Rio de Janeiro, 2004.

Das Gupta, C. "Seeing and Believing, Science and Mythology: Notes on 'Mythological' Genre." *Film Quarterly* 42, no. 4 (1989): 12–18.

Davies, O. *Grimoires: A History of Magic Books*. Oxford: Oxford University Press, 2009.

Demerath III., N. J. "The Rise of 'Cultural Religion' in European Christianity: Learning from Poland, Northern Ireland, and Sweden." *Social Compass* 47, no. 1 (2000): 127–39.

Dobbelaere, K. *Secularization: A Multi-Dimensional Concept*. London: Sage, 1981.

Donaghey, J. "Bakunin Brand Vodka: An Exploration into Anarchist-punk and Punk-anarchism." *Anarchist Developments in Cultural Studies* 1 (2013): 138–70.

Donaghey, J. "Punk and Anarchism: UK, Poland, Indonesia." Ph.D. thesis, Loughborough University, Loughborough, 2016.

Donaghey, J. "Researching 'Punk Indonesia': Notes towards a Non-Exploitative Insider Methodology," *Punk & Post-Punk* 6, no. 2 (2017), 291–314.

Doss, E. *Elvis Culture: Fans, Faith, and Image*. Kansas: University Press of Kansas, 1999.

Driessens, O. "The Celebritization of Society and Culture: Understanding the Structural Dynamics of Celebrity Culture." *International Journal of Cultural Studies* 16, no. 6 (2012): 641–57.

Duffet, M. *Understanding Fandom: An Introduction to the Study of Media Fan Culture*. New York and London: Bloomsbury, 2003.

Dyer, R., and P. McDonald. *Stars*. London: BFI Publishing, 2002 [1979].

Eco, U. *Apocalípticos e integrados*. São Paulo: Perspectiva, 1979.

Elbaum, J. "Los bailanteros. La fiesta urbana de la cultura popular." In *La cultura de la noche. La vida nocturna de los jóvenes en Buenos Aires*, edited by M. Margulis, 181–210. Buenos Aires: Espasa Hoy, 1994.

Eliade, M. *Mephistopheles and the Androgyne: Studies in Religious Myth and Symbol*. New York: Sheed and Ward, 1965.

Eliade, M. *Occultism, Witchcraft, and Cultural Fashions: Essays in Comparative Religions*. Chicago: The University of Chicago Press, 1976.

Ellis, B. "The Highgate Cemetery Vampire Hunt: The Anglo-American Connection in Satanic Cult Lore." *Folklore* 104, no. 1–2 (1993): 13–39.

Fagan, G. *Believing in Russia: Religious Policy After Communism.* London and New York: Routledge, 2013.
Featherstone, M. *Consumer Culture and Postmodernism.* London: Sage, 1991.
Fikentscher, K. "It's Not the Mix, it's the Song Selection: Music Programming in Contemporary DJ Culture." In *DJ Culture in the Mix: Power, Technology, and Social Change in Electronic Dance Music*, edited by A. Gavanas, H. Rietveld, and B. A. Attias, 124–49. New York: Bloomsbury Press, 2013.
Fink, N., and P. Saá. *Gilda para chicas y chicos.* Colección Antiprincesas no. 5. Buenos Aires: Chirimbote, 2016.
Fiscella, A. T. "From Muslim Punks to Taqwacore: An Incomplete History of Punk Islam." *Contemporary Islam* 6, no. 3 (2012): 255–81.
Fiske, J. "The Cultural Economy of Fandom." In *The Adoring Audience: Fan Culture and Popular Media*, edited by L. Lewis, 30–49. London: Routledge, 1992.
Forbes, B. "Introduction: Finding Religion in Unexpected Places." In *Religion and Popular Culture in America*, edited by B. David Forbes and J. H. Mahan, 1–20. Berkeley: University of California Press, 2000.
Frisk, L., and P. Åkerbäck. *Den mediterande dalahästen. Religion på nya arenor i samtidens Sverige.* Stockholm: Dialogos, 2013.
Frisk, L., and P. Åkerbäck. *New Religiosity in Contemporary Sweden: The Dalarna Study in National and International Context.* Sheffield: Equinox Publishing, 2015.
Fritzsche, B. *Pop-Fans. Studie einer Mädchenkultur.* Opladen: VS Verlag, 2003.
Furman, D. E., and K. Kääriäinen. *Religioznost' V Rossii V 90-E Gody XX—Nachale XXI Veka.* Moskva: OGNI TD, 2006.
Geertz, C. *The Interpretation of Cultures: Selected Essays.* New York: Basic Books, 1973.
Gellel, A.-M. "Traces of Spirituality in the Lady Gaga Phenomenon." *International Journal of Children's Spirituality* 18, no. 2 (2013a): 214–26.
Gellel, A.-M. "Popular Music as a Resource for the Religious Education Classroom: A Study through Lady Gaga's Judas." *Religious Education Journal of Australia* 29, no. 1 (2013b): 28–33.
Gherardi, N. *Gilda. La vida de un ángel. Primera Parte.* Buenos Aires: Ediciones Semanario, 2000a.
Gherardi, N. *Gilda. La vida de un ángel. Segunda Parte.* Buenos Aires: Ediciones Semanario, 2000b.
Gilbert, J., and E. Pearson. *Discographies: Dance Music Culture and the Politics of Sound.* London: Routledge, 1999.
Gilmour, M. J., ed. *Call Me the Seeker: Listening to Religion in Popular Music.* New York: Continuum, 2005.
Gilmour, M. J. *Gods and Guitars: Seeking the Sacred in Post-1960s Popular Music.* Waco: Baylor University Press, 2009.
Gilmour, M. J. *The Gospel According to Bob Dylan: The Old, Old Story for Modern Times.* Louisville: Westminster John Knox, 2011.

Gilmour, M. J. "'God,' 'God Part II,' and 'God Part III': Exploring the Anxiety of Influence in John Lennon, U2, and Larry Norman." In *Reception History and Biblical Studies: Theory and Practice*, edited by E. England and W. J. Lyons, 231–39. London: Bloomsbury T&T Clark, 2015.

Gololobov, I. "There Are No Atheists in Trenches under Fire: Orthodox Christianity in Russian Punk." *Punk & Post-Punk* 1, no. 3 (2012): 305–21.

Gomel, E. "Mystery, Apocalypse and Utopia: The Case of the Ontological Detective Story." *Science Fiction Studies* 22, no. 3 (November 1995): 343–56.

Häger, A. "The Interpretation of Religious Symbols in Popular Music." *Temenos* 33 (1997): 49–62.

Häger, A. "Moral Boundaries in Christian Discourse on Popular Music." *Research in the Social Scientific Study of Religion* 11 (2000): 156–71.

Häger, A. "Under the Shadow of the Almighty: Fan Reception of Some Religious Aspects in the Work and Career of the Irish Popular Musician Sinéad O'Connor." In *Call Me the Seeker: Listening to Religion in Popular Music*, edited by M. J. Gilmour, 215–25. New York and London: Continuum, 2005.

Häger, A. "Seek and You Will Find: A Critical Discussion of the Search for 'Christian' Content in Popular Culture." In *Implications of the Sacred in (Post)Modern Media*, edited by J. Sumiala-Seppänen, K. Lundby, and R. Salokangas, 217–33. Göteborg: Nordicom, 2006.

Hagevi, M., ed. *Religion och politik*. Stockholm: Liber, 2005.

Hampton, K. N., L. F. Sessions, and E. J. Her. "Core Networks, Social Isolation, and New Media." *Information, Communication & Society* 14, no. 1 (2011): 130–55.

Hills, M. *Fan Cultures*. London and New York: Routledge, 2002.

Hinerman, S. "'I'll be here with you: Fans, Fantasy and the Figure of Elvis." In *The Adoring Audience: Fan Culture and Popular Media*, edited by L. Lewis, 107–34. London: Routledge, 1992.

Hjarvard, S. "The Mediatization of Religion: A Theory of the Media as Agents of Religious Change." *Northern Lights* 6, no. 1 (2008): 9–26.

Horowitz, M. *Occult America: The Secret History of How Mysticism Shaped Our Nation*. New York: Bantam Books, 2009.

Howard, J. R., and J. M. Streck. *Apostles of Rock: The Splintered World of Contemporary Christian Music*. Lexington: The University Press of Kentucky, 1999.

Howe, N., and W. Strauss. *Millennials Rising: The Next Great Generation*. New York: Vintage, 2009.

Hulsether, M. "Like a Sermon: Popular Religion in Madonna Videos." In *Religion and Popular Culture in America*, edited by B. Forbes and J. Mahan, 77–100. Berkeley: University of California Press, 2000.

Hutson, S. R. "Technoshamanism: Spiritual Healing in the Rave Subculture." *Popular Music and Society* 23 (Fall 1999): 53–77.

Ingold, T. *The Perception of the Environment: Essays on Livelihood, Dwelling and Skill*. London and New York: Routledge, 2000.

Iommi, T., with T. J. Lammers. *Iron Man: My Journey through Heaven and Hell with Black Sabbath*. Boston: Da Capo, 2011.

Jackson, J. A. *Singing in My Soul: Black Gospel Music in a Secular Age*. Chapel Hill: University of North Carolina Press, 2004.

Jenkins, H. *Textual Poachers: Television Fans and Participatory Culture*. New York: Routledge, 1992.

Jensen, J. "Fandom as Pathology: The Consequences of Characterization." In *The Adoring Audience: Fan Culture and Popular Media*, edited by L. Lewis, 9–29. London: Routledge, 1992.

Jindra, M. "'Star Trek to Me is a Way of Life': Fan Expressions of Star Trek Philosophy." In *Star Trek and Sacred Ground: Explorations of Star Trek, Religion, and American Culture*, edited by J. Porter and D. McLaren, 217–29. New York: State University of New York Press, 1999.

Jindra, M. "It's about Faith in our Future: *Star Trek* Fandom as Cultural Religion." In *Religion and Popular Culture in America*, edited by B. D. Forbes and J. H. Mahan, 165–79. Berkeley: University of California Press, 2000.

Kappeler, A. *Russische Geschichte*. München: C.H. Beck, 2005.

Knight, D. A., and A.-J. Levine, *The Meaning of the Bible: What the Jewish Scriptures and Christian Old Testament Can Teach Us*. New York: HarperOne, 2011.

Konow, D. *Bang Your Head: The Rise and Fall of Heavy Metal*. New York: Three Rivers Press, 2002.

Latour, B. *Reflexão sobre o culto moderno dos deuses fe(i)tiches*. Bauru/SP: EDUSC, [1996] 2002.

Laughlin, C. D., J. McManus, and E. G. d'Aquili. *Brain, Symbol and Experience*. New York: Columbia University Press, 1992.

Lilliestam, L. "Swedish Dance Bands: Danceable, Melodious and Familiar." In *Made in Sweden: Studies in Popular Music*, edited by A. Björnberg and T. Bossius, 79–90. New York: Routledge, 2017.

Löbert, A. "Fandom as a Religious Form: On the Reception of Pop Music by Cliff Richard Fans in Liverpool." *Popular Music* 31, no. 1 (2012): 125–41.

Luckmann, T. "Shrinking Transcendence, Expanding Religion?" *Sociological Analysis. A Journal in the Sociology of Religion* 50, no. 2 (1990): 127–38.

Lundberg, B. *Alf Robertson. Jag lämnade mitt hjärta i Göteborg*. Göteborg: Reverb, 2009.

Lynch, G., and E. Badger. "The Mainstream Post-Rave Club Scene as a Secondary Institution: A British Perspective." *Culture and Religion* 7, no. 1 (2006): 315–30.

Mäkelä, J. *John Lennon Imagined: Cultural History of a Rock Star*. New York: Peter Lang, 2004.

Maldaner, V. *De första ljuva åren (och de alltför tjocka låren). Biografin om countrydrottningen Christina Lindberg*. Malmö: Baba Books, 2013.

Maoz, D. "Shekhinah as Woman: Kabbalistic References in Dylan's Infidels." In *Call Me the Seeker: Listening to Religion in Popular Music*, edited by M. J. Gilmour, 3–16. New York: Continuum, 2005.

Marean, C. W., M. Bar-Matthews, J. Bernatchez, E. Fisher, P. Goldberg, A. I. Herries, et al. "Early Human Use of Marine Resources and Pigment in South Africa during the Middle Pleistocene." *Nature* 449, no. 7164 (2007): 905–8.

Margulis, A. *Santa Gilda. Su vida, su muerte, sus milagros*. Buenos Aires: Planeta, 2016.

Marshall, S. M. *Restless Pilgrim: The Spiritual Journey of Bob Dylan*. Lake Mary: Relevant Books, 2002.

Martín, E. "Seres extraordinarios. Más allá de la devoción y de los fans." *Revista Todavia*, December 20, 2008. http://www.lobianco.com.ar/Clientes/todaviaweb31/20.sociedadesnota.html (accessed August 28, 2017).

Martín, E. "The History, Trajectory and Consolidation of the Cumbia in the Field of Argentine Music." In *Troubling Gender: Youth and Cumbia in Argentina's Music Scene*, edited by P. Vila and P. Semán, 23–40. Philadelphia: Temple University Press, 2011.

Martín, E. "Cumbia Villera and the End of the Work Culture in Argentina in the 90's." In *Youth Identities and Argentine Popular Music: Beyond Tango*, edited by P. Semán and P. Vila, 59–82. New York: Palgrave Macmillan, 2012.

McDannell, C. *Material Christianity: Religion and Popular Culture in America*. New Haven and London: Yale University Press, 1995.

McEntire, M. "Red Dirt God: Divine Silence and the Search for Transcendent Beauty in the Music of Emmylou Harris." In *The Bible in/and Popular Culture*, edited by P. Culbertson and E. M. Wainwright, 29–39. Atlanta: Society of Biblical Literature, 2010.

McLaren, D. "On the Edge of Forever: Understanding the Star Trek Phenomenon as Myth." In *Star Trek and Sacred Ground: Explorations of Star Trek, Religion, and American Culture*, edited by J. Porter and D. McLaren, 231–43. New York: State University of New York Press, 1999.

McMichael, P. "Defining Pussy Riot Musically: Performance and Authenticity in New Media." *Digital Icons* 9 (2013): 99–113.

Moberg, M. "Popular Music Divine Services in the Evangelical Lutheran Church of Finland: Concept, Rationale, and Participants." *Journal of Religion and Popular Culture* (forthcoming).

Moore, D. C. "Is the Post- in Postcolonial the Post- in Post-Soviet? Toward a Global Postcolonial Critique." *PMLA* 116, no. 1 (2001): 111–28.

Niebuhr, H. R. *Christ and Culture*. New York: Harper & Row, 1951.

Osbourne, O., with C. Ayres. *I Am Ozzy*. New York: Grand Central, 2009.

"Osbourne, Ozzy." In *The Encyclopedia of Popular Music*, 5th concise edn. New York: Omnibus, 2007: 1066–7.

Østbø, J. *The New Third Rome: Readings of a Russian Nationalist Myth*. Stuttgart: ibidem Press, 2016.

Ostwalt, C. E. Jr. "Hollywood and Armageddon: Apocalyptic Themes in Recent Cinematic Presentation." In *Screening the Sacred: Religion, Myth, and Ideology in Popular American Film*, edited by J. W. Martin and C. E. Ostwalt, Jr., 55–63. Boulder: Westview Press, 1995.

Partridge, C. *The Re-Enchantment of the West. Volume I: Alternative Spiritualities, Sacralization, Popular Culture and Occulture*. London: T & T Clark International, 2004.

Partridge, C. *Mortality and Music: Popular Music and the Awareness of Death*. London: Bloomsbury, 2015.

Partridge, C., and M. Moberg. *The Bloomsbury Handbook of Religion and Popular Music*. London: Bloomsbury, 2017.

Pickering, S. *Bob Dylan Approximately: A Portrait of the Jewish Poet in Search of God: A Midrash*. New York: David MacKay, 1975.

Pickles, J. "Punk, Pop and Protest: The Birth and Decline of Political Punk in Bandung." *RIMA* 41, no. 2 (2007): 223–46.

Pini, M. "Women and the Early British Rave Scene." In *Back to Reality? Social Experience and Cultural Studies*, edited by A. McRobbie, 152–69. Manchester: Manchester University Press, 1997.

Poole, W. S. *Satan in America: The Devil We Know*. Lanham: Rowman & Littlefield, 2009.

Poole, W. S. *Monsters in America: Our Historical Obsession with the Hideous and the Haunting*. Waco: Baylor University Press, 2011.

Popoff, M. *Judas Priest: Heavy Metal Painkillers*. Toronto: ECW Press, 2007.

Porter, J. "To Boldly Go: Star Trek Convention Attendance as Pilgrimage." In *Star Trek and Sacred Ground: Explorations of Star Trek, Religion, and American Culture*, edited by J. Porter and D. McLaren, 245–70. New York: State University of New York Press, 1999.

Prasetyo, F. A. "Punk and the City: A History of Punk in Bandung," *Punk & Post-Punk* 6, no. 2 (2017), 189–211.

Prat, J. "Los santuarios marianos en Cataluña: una aproximación desde la etnografía." In *La religiosidad popular vol. III.*, edited by C. Alvarez Santaló; Mª J. Buxó Rey, and S. Rodríguez Becerra, 211–52. Barcelona: Antrophos/Editorial del Hombre/Fundación Machado, 1989.

Pumar, V., and L. Bivort. *Un milagro llamado Gilda*. Buenos Aires: authors' edn, 1999.

Raymond, E. *Stars for Freedom: Hollywood, Black Celebrities, and the Civil Rights Movement*. Seattle: University of Washington Press, 2015.

Rice, R. J. "Cannibalism and the Act of Revenge in Tudor-Stuart Drama." *Studies in English Literature, 1500–1900* 44, no. 2 (2004): 297–316.

Richards, J., S. Wilson, and L. Woodhead. *Diana, the Making of a Media Saint*. London and New York: I. B. Tauris, 1999.

Rietveld, H. C. "Journey to the Light? Immersion, Spectacle and Mediation." In *DJ Culture in the Mix: Power, Technology, and Social Change in Electronic Dance Music*, edited by A. Gavanas, H. Rietveld, and B. A. Attias, 79–102. New York: Bloomsbury, 2013.

Rodman, G. *Elvis after Elvis: The Posthumous Career of a Living Legend*. London and New York: Routledge, 1996.

Rojek, C. *Celebrity*. London: Reaktion Books, 2001.

Román, A. *Las milagrosas sanaciones de Gilda*. Buenos Aires: Latinoamericana Editora, 1999.

Rouget, G. *Music and Trance: A Theory of the Relations between Music and Possession*. Chicago: The University of Chicago Press, 1985.

Saefullah, H. "'Nevermind the jahiliyyah, here's the hijrahs': Punk and the Religious Turn in the Contemporary Indonesian Underground Scene," *Punk & Post-Punk* 6, no. 2 (2017): 263–89.

Salimpoor, V. N., M. Benovoy, G. Longo, J. R. Cooperstock, and R. J. Zatorre. "The Rewarding Aspects of Music Listening are Related to Degree of Emotional Arousal." *PLoS ONE* 4, no. 10 (2009): 1–14.

Sandvoss, C. *Fans: The Mirror of Consumption*. Cambridge: Polity Press, 2005.

Schmidt, L. "From Demon Possession to Magic Show: Ventriloquism, Religion, and the Enlightenment." *Church History* 67, no. 2 (June 1998): 274–304.

Semán, P., and P. Vila. "Rock chabón: The Contemporary National Rock of Argentina." In *From Tejano to Tango: Latin American Popular Music*, edited by W. Clark, 70–94. New York and London: Routledge, 2002.

Skartveit, H. "An Angel Watching Over Me: Fan Culture and the Formations of Self and Identity in Buenos Aires." M.A. Diss., Department of Social Anthropology, University of Bergen, Bergen, 2004.

Smith, G., A. Cooperman, B. Mohamed, J. Martinez, B. Alper, E. Sciupac, and J. Ochoa. *America's Changing Religious Landscape*. Washington, DC: Pew Research Center, 2015.

Solberg, R. T. "Waiting for the Bass to Drop: Correlations between Intense Emotional Experiences and Production Techniques in Build-up and Drop Sections of Electronic Dance Music." *Dancecult* 6, no. 1 (2014): 61–82.

Spencer, J. M. *Protest and Praise: Sacred Music of Black Religion*. Minneapolis: Fortress Press, 1990.

Srinivas, S. V. "Devotion and Defiance in Fan Activity." *Journal of Art and Ideas*, no. 29 (1996): 67–83.

Steinholt, Y. B. "Kitten Heresy: Lost Contexts of Pussy Riot's Punk Prayer." *Popular Music and Society* 36, no. 1 (2013): 120–24.

Strauss, A., and J. Corbin. *Basics of Qualitative Research: Techniques and Procedures for Developing Grounded Theory*. London: Sage, 1998.

Svanberg, I., and D. Westerlund, eds. *Religion i Sverige*. Stockholm: Dialogos, 2008.

Sylvan, R. *Traces of the Spirit: The Religious Dimensions of Popular Music*. New York: New York University Press, 2002.

Takahashi, M. "Spirituality through the Science of Sound: The DJ as Technoshaman in Rave Culture." In *Call Me the Seeker: Listening to Religion in Popular Music*, edited by M. J. Gilmour, 239–66. New York: Continuum, 2005.

Takahashi, M., and T. Olaveson. "Music Dance and Raving Bodies: Raving as Spirituality in the Central Canadian Rave Scene." *Journal of Ritual Studies* 17, no. 2 (2003): 72–96.

Thornton, S. *Club Cultures: Music, Media and Subcultural Capital*. Hanover: Wesleyan University Press, 1996.
Till, R. *Pop Cult: Religion and Popular Music*. London: Continuum, 2010.
Touré. *I Would Die 4 U: Why Prince Became an Icon*. Washington, DC: Atria Books, 2013.
Vega, R. *Gilda. Una estrella que aún sigue brillando*. Buenos Aires: Ediciones Utilsen, 1998.
Vesey, A. "Putting Her on the Shelf: Pop Star Fragrances and Post-Feminist Entrepreneurialism." *Feminist Media Studies* 15, no. 6 (2015): 992–1008.
Vltchek, A. *Indonesia. Archipelago of Fear*. London: Pluto Press, 2012.
Walser, R. *Running With the Devil: Power, Gender and Madness in Heavy Metal Music*. Hanover and London: Wesleyan University Press/University Press of New England, 1993.
Ward, M. *Air of Salvation: The Story of Christian Broadcasting*. Grand Rapids: Baker Books, 1994.
Ward, P. "The Eucharist and the Turn to Culture." In *Between Sacred and Profane: Researching Religion and Popular Culture*, edited by G. Lynch, 82–93. London and New York: I. B. Tauris, 2007.
Wickström, D.-E. "'Drive-Ethno-Dance' and 'Hutzul Punk'—Ukrainian Popular Music and Strategies of Localization in a Post-Soviet Context." *Yearbook for Traditional Music* 40 (2008): 60–88.
Wickström, D.-E. *Rocking St. Petersburg: Transcultural Flows and Identity Politics in Post-Soviet Popular Music*. Stuttgart: ibidem Press, 2014.
Wickström, D.-E. "Nebo Slavian (Alisa)." *Songlexikon. Encyclopedia of Songs* (2015): http://www.songlexikon.de/songs/neboslavianalisa (accessed November 9, 2015).
Wickström, D.-E. "'Ukro-Ska-punk'—Band Identity, Surzhik and Language in Post-Soviet Russia." In *Unsichtbare Landschaften—Populäre Musik und Räumlichkeit*, edited by G. Bottà, 127–44. Münster and New York: Waxmann, 2016.
Wickström, D.-E., and Y. B. Steinholt. "Visions of the (Holy) Motherland in Contemporary Russian Popular Music: Nostalgia, Patriotism, Religion and Russkii Rok." *Popular Music and Society* 32, no. 3 (2009): 313–30.
Wike, R., and K. Simmons. "Global Support for Principle of Free Expression, But Opposition to Some Forms of Speech." *Pew Research Center* (2015): http://www.pewglobal.org/files/2015/11/Pew-Research-Center-Democracy-Report-FINAL-November-18-2015.pdf (accessed July 18, 2016).
Wikström, O. *Om det heliga och dess envisa vägran att försvinna. Religionspsykologiska perspektiv*. Stockholm: Natur & Kultur, 2003.
Willems, J. *Pussy Riots Punk-Gebet—Religion, Recht und Politik in Russland*. Berlin: Berlin University Press, 2013.
Williams-Jones, P. "Afro-American Gospel Music: A Crystallization of the Black Aesthetic." *Ethnomusicology* 19, no. 3 (September 1975): 373–85.
Wilson, I. "Indonesian Punk: A Brief Snapshot." *Le Banian*, no. 15 (June 2013): 1–5.

Wilson, I. "Resisting Democracy: Front Pembela Islam and Indonesia's 2014 Elections." *ISEAS Perspective*, no. 10 (2014): 1–8.

Winans, CeCe, with C. Cloninger. *Throne Room: Ushered into the Presence of God*. Nashville: Thomas Nelson, 2004.

Winans, CeCe, with R. J. Weems. *On a Positive Note*. New York: Pocket, 1999.

Woodhead, L. "Diana and the Religion of the Heart." In *Diana, the Making of a Media Saint*, edited by J. Richards, S. Wilson, and L. Woodhead, 119–39. London and New York: I. B. Tauris, 1999.

Woodhead, L., and P. Heelas. *Religion in Modern Times: An Interpretive Anthology*. Oxford: Blackwell, 2000.

Wright, R. "'I'd sell you suicide': Pop Music and Moral Panic in the Age of Marilyn Manson." *Popular Music* 19, no. 3 (October 2000): 365–85.

Wyman, K. J. "The Devil We Already Know: Medieval Representations of a Powerless Satan in Modern American Cinema." *Journal of Religion and Film* 8, no. 3 (2004): Article 7. http://digitalcommons.unomaha.edu/jrf/vol8/iss3/7/ (accessed August 28, 2017).

Yu, J. "Electronic Dance Music and Technological Change: Lessons from Actor-Network Theory." In *DJ Culture in the Mix: Power, Technology, and Social Change in Electronic Dance Music*, edited by A. Gavanas, H. Rietveld, and B. A. Attias, 151–72. New York: Bloomsbury, 2013.

Ziehe, T. "Inför avmystifieringen av världen. Ungdom och kulturell modernisering." In *Postmoderna tider?* edited by M. Löfgren and A. Molander, 345–61. Stockholm: Norstedt, 1986.

Zittoun, T. "The Role of Symbolic Resources in Human Lives." In *The Cambridge Handbook of Sociocultural Psychology*, edited by J. Valsiner and A. Rosa, 343–61. Cambridge: Cambridge University Press, 2007.

Zittoun, T. "Symbolic Resources and Responsibility in Transitions." *Young* 15, no. 2 (2007): 193–211.

Zittoun, T., G. Duveen, A. Gillespie, G. Ivinson, and C. Psaltis. "The Use of Symbolic Resources in Developmental Transitions." *Culture & Psychology* 9, no. 4 (2003): 415–48.

Selected Discography

Aceh Revolution [compilation]. Ronce Records, 2012.
Alisa, *Solntsevorot*. CD-Land, 2000.
Alisa, *Seychas Pozdnee, Chem Ty Dumaesh*. Moroz M'iuzik, 2003.
Alisa, *Izgoy*. Real Records, 2005.
Alisa, *Puls Khranitelia Dverei Labirinta*. CD-Maximum, 2008.
Bob Dylan, *Slow Train Coming*. Columbia, 1979.
Bob Dylan, *Saved*. Columbia, 1980.
Bob Dylan, *Shot of Love*. Columbia, 1981.
Christina Lindberg, *Hemma igen*. Frituna, 1997.
Christina Lindberg, *Back to the Roots*. CL Musik & Term Musik, 2015.
Curt & Roland, *Curt & Roland*. Curol Music, 1983.
Disabled, *Curhat Colongan, Anjing!* Curhat Colongan, Anjing! records, 2012.
Duct Tape Surgery, *Facing Problems*. Stop'n'Go, Time Up Records, 2012.
GunXRose, *Anti Dogmanisasi Berhala*. Chey Clothing, Battleground Records, Terkubur Hidup Records, Pastimati, Alternaive Distribution, Teriak, Doombringer Records, Don't Talk Records, 2012.
Hasse Andersson, *Nära dig*. Slowfox Grammofon, 2004.
Hasse Andersson & Kvinnaböske Band, *Änglahund*. Sonet, 1982.
Hasse Andersson & Kvinnaböske Band, *Tie bilder*. Sonet, 1985.
Ingemar Johansson, *Mysterium—En mässa om livets insida*. Signatur, 1995.
Injakmati [split 7" with Black Sister], *Rotten Conspiracy*. Neverheard distro, Power Negi records, Problem records, Alcoholic Desaster, Subwix, Urgent Freedom, 2009.
Judas Priest, *Rocka Rolla*. Gull Records, 1974.
Judas Priest, *Sad Wings of Destiny*. Gull Records, 1976.
Judas Priest, *Sin After Sin*. Columbia, 1977.
Judas Priest, *Stained Class*. Columbia, 1978.
Judas Priest, *Hell Bent for Leather*. Columbia, 1978.
Judas Priest, *British Steel*. Columbia, 1980.
Judas Priest, *Point of Entry*. Columbia, 1981.
Judas Priest, *Screaming for Vengeance*. Columbia, 1982.
Judas Priest, *Defenders of the Faith*. Columbia, 1984.

Judas Priest, *Turbo*. Columbia, 1986.
Judas Priest, *Ram it Down*. Columbia, 1988.
Judas Priest, *Painkiller*. Columbia, 1990.
Judas Priest, *Angel of Retribution*. Epic, 2005.
Judas Priest, *Nostradamus*. Epic, 2008.
Judas Priest, *Redeemer of Souls*. Epic, 2014.
KontraSosial, *Endless War*. Final Warning, Kontra Kommunique Division, 2009.
Krass Kepala, *Solidaritas Internasional* [split 7" with Die Wrecked]. Die Rex, Pyrate Punx, Jobsworth, Mass Prod, Pumpkin, 2013.
Lasse Stefanz, *Livets ljusa sida*. Frituna, 1988.
Metallimessu. Warner Music Finland, 2008.
Nick Cave, *The Secret Life of the Love Song & The Flesh Made Word: Two Lectures by Nick Cave*. Mute Records, 2000.
Ozzy Osbourne, *Blizzard of Ozz*. Epic, 1980.
Ozzy Osbourne, *Diary of a Madman*. Jet, 1981.
Ozzy Osbourne, *The Ultimate Sin*. Epic, 1986.
Ozzy Osbourne, *No Rest for the Wicked*. Epic, 1988.
Ozzy Osbourne, *No More Tears*. Epic, 1991.
Ozzy Osbourne, *Live & Loud*. Epic, 1993.
Ozzy Osbourne, *Ozzmosis*. Epic, 1995.
Ozzy Osbourne, *Down to Earth*. Epic, 2001.
Ozzy Osbourne, *Black Rain*. Epic, 2007.
Ozzy Osbourne, *Scream*. Epic, 2010.
Prince, *Purple Rain*. Warner Brothers, 1984.
Prince, *Around the World in a Day*. Warner Brothers, 1985.
Robertson, Alf, *Mitt land*. Mariann, 1980.
Robertson, Alf, *Vår värld*. Mariann, 1983.
Robertson, Alf, *Tellus*. Mariann, 1984.
Street Voices, *Kill Me With Your Lips*. Movement Records, 2010.
Zudas Krust, *Here Lies Your Gods*. Rauha Turva, Gusto Rana!, Disparodesire, 2009.
Zudas Krust, *A Loyal Slave to the Apocalyptic Order*. Rauha Turva, 2011.

Contributor Biographies

Thomas Bossius is Associate Professor in Musicology and Assistant Professor in Cultural Studies. He has a PhD in Musicology from the University of Gothenburg, Sweden. His main research interest are the uses and functions of music and religion in people's everyday life.

Jim Donaghey is an anarchist punk and Research Fellow at Queen's University Belfast's School of History, Anthropology, Philosophy and Politics. His PhD, "Punk and Anarchism: UK, Poland, Indonesia," was awarded at Loughborough University in 2016.

Brian Froese is Associate Professor of History at Canadian Mennonite University, Winnipeg, Canada. His main research interests are in Mennonites, evangelicalism, and political conservatism in the North American West, and religion and popular culture. He is the author of *California Mennonites* (2015).

Adrian-Mario Gellel is Associate Professor in Religious Education in both Faculties of Education and Theology (University of Malta). His main areas of interest are symbol literacy, children's spirituality, religious education, and general pedagogy. Together with Michael Buchannan he edited *Global Perspectives on Catholic Religious Education in Schools* (2015).

Michael J. Gilmour is Associate Professor of English and Biblical Literature at Providence University College and has a PhD in New Testament from McGill University, Canada. One of his research interests is the use of the Bible in popular music of the post-1960s.

Sabina Hadžibulić has both a sociological and a musical academic background. She holds a PhD in sociology and is currently Postdoctoral Researcher at the Uppsala Religion and Society Research Centre, Uppsala University, Sweden. Her research interests include religion, music, migration, identity, culture, and nostalgia.

Contributor Biographies

Andreas Häger is Associate Professor in Sociology at Åbo Akademi University, Turku, Finland. He has a PhD in Sociology of Religion from Uppsala University, Sweden. His main research interests are religion and popular culture, and conservative Christianity in a Nordic context.

Eloísa Martín is Associate Professor of Sociology at Federal University of Rio de Janeiro, Brazil, and Secretary-Treasurer of the International Sociological Association Research Committee on Sociology of Religion (RC22). Her main research interests are popular religion, Catholicism in Latin America, theories of religion and the sacred, and the processes of institutionalization of sociology of religion.

Angela M. Nelson is Associate Professor at Bowling Green State University in Ohio. She has a PhD in American Culture Studies from Bowling Green State University. Her main research interests are black popular culture, religion, and genre studies.

Carla Schriever is lecturer in Philosophy and Musicology at the University of Oldenburg in Germany. She has a PhD in Philosophy from Humboldt University of Berlin, Germany. Her main research interests include popular culture, performance, and gender.

Melanie Takahashi received her PhD in Religious Studies from the University of Ottawa in 2004 and was Professor of Anthropology at Heritage College from 2004 to 2008. Her research focuses on the relationship between music and trance and she has published articles on rave and the subset of electronic dance music cultures that evolved from the movement. She has been a dedicated practitioner of meditation and yoga for over 25 years and a piano teacher since the age of 16. She lives in San Francisco, California.

David-Emil Wickström is Professor for Popular Music History at the Popakademie Baden-Württemberg in Mannheim, Germany. He has a PhD in ethnomusicology from the University of Copenhagen, Denmark. His main research interests are post-Soviet popular music, transcultural flows, and music and migration, as well as music and identity.

Index

Note: Page numbers in italics refer to tables and figures; the letter 'n' following locators refers to notes.

Aan, Alex 152–3
aca-fandom 107
Acts of the Apostles (biblical text) 56
aesthetization of religion 4–5, 6
   album art 52–3, 68, 164
   institutional use of popular music 3, 4, 130 (*see also* Dylan masses)
   religious symbols in music videos 5, 15, 17, 18, 19, *20*, 21–2, 23, 25
African American gospel singers. *See* Winans, CeCe (Priscilla)
Åkerbäck, Peter 138, 139, 147, 149
album art 52–3, 68, 90, 164
Aliokhina, Mariia 128
Alisa 2–3, 123, 124–5, 129–36
"All Guns Blazing " (Judas Priest) 56
Allom, Tom 50
Alone in His Presence (CeCe Winans) 29, 34–5, 39, 43
Andersson, Hasse 141–4, 146–7, 150
"En ängel följer i ditt spår" ("An Angel is Following Your Track", Christina Lindberg) 148, 149
Angel of Retribution (Judas Priest) 53
angels
   Gilda's mythification 81, 88, 89
   heavy metal motif 52–4, 56, 67, 68, 71
   KontraSosial's *Endless War* album art 164
   Richmond Dylan mass, bible verse 175
   Swedish country music 142, 148, 149
"Änglahund" ("Angel dog", Hasse Andersson) 141–2
An Officer and a Gentleman 32
"Antikhrist" ("Antichrist", Alisa) 133
antimasques 71–2
apocalypse 15, 54–7, 60–1, 63, 74
apologetics 6

apostillization 30, 40–3, 46
Argentina. *See* Gilda fandom
"Arogansi Agama" ("Religious Arrogance", Krass Kepala) 163
Around the World in a Day (Prince) 116, 119
art. *See* aesthetization of religion
artistic rights 111, 112
atheism 151, 152–3, 157, 161, 162–4, 165

The Bad Seeds 96
Bakker, Jim 31, 32, 37, 38, 73
Bakker, Tammy Faye 31, 32, 37, 73
"Balladen om Birger Bergman" ("The Ballad of Birger Bergman", Alf Robertson) 145
Banda Aceh 154–5, 158, 160
Bandung Pyrate Punx collective 163
Bark at the Moon (Ozzy Osbourne) 73
beatmatching 188
"Before the Dawn" (Judas Priest) 62
"Beginning of the End" (Judas Priest) 51
"Believer" (Ozzy Osbourne) 70
Belknap, Ray 48
Berger, Dominic 157
"Beyond the Realms of Death" (Judas Priest) 51–2
Bianchi, Miriam Alejandra (Gilda). *See* Gilda fandom
biblical references
   Bob Dylan lyrics 168
   Dylan masses 168, 174–5
   Gilda's fan 86
   Judas Priest's imagery from The Revelation 54, 57, 61
   Ozzy Osbourne 66, 67–8, 69, 70, 73, 74, 75
   symbolic understanding of love 12
   "Wide Awake" (Katy Perry) 21–2

Bickerdike, Jennifer Otter 107, 108
Billy Graham Crusades 35
The Birthday Party 96, 97
Black Church 30, 31, 33–4, 36, 42, 45
Black gospel singers. *See* Winans, CeCe (Priscilla)
Black Rain (Ozzy Osbourne) 74
"Black Sabbath" 65
Black Sabbath 65, 68, 71, 74, 75
Blizzard of Ozz (Ozzy Osbourne) 65, 68, 70
"Blowin' in the Wind" (Bob Dylan) 173, 174, 175, 176, 177, 179
blues 48–9
Bogoiavlenskii sobor v Elokhove (Bogoiavlenskii Cathedral) 127, 128
"Bogoroditsa, Putina Progoni" ("Mother of God, Drive Putin Out", Pussy Riot) 127–8
boundaries 1, 6–7. *See also* sacralization
Brand, Russell 17–18, 19, 24
"build-up" and "drop" 187, 190–2, 195, 196, 199, 200
"By the Grace of God" (Katy Perry) 24

carnivalesque 71
Carson, D. A. 29
catharsis 66, 192, 193
Cave, Nick 95–8. *See also* Serbian Nick Cave fans
CCM. *See* Contemporary Christian Music (CCM)
celebritization (CeCe Winans) 29, 30, 36–40
celebrity
 brand culture 13, 14
 friction with faith (*see* Winans, CeCe (Priscilla))
Cerullo, Morris 49
Cervin, Thomas 170–1, 172, 175, 176, 181
chaos 53, 54, 55, 56, 57, 63, 67, 71, 76
Chapman, Gary 39
"Christ and Culture" dilemma 30. *See also* Winans, CeCe (Priscilla)
Christ-Culture typology (Niebuhr) 2, 29, 30–1, 36, 40
Christian apologetics 6
church. *See* institutional religion
Church of Satan 212 n.7
Classical mythology 20, 21, 23

club drugs 186, 191, 193, 199
Cocker, Joe 32
Cohen, Norman 54, 63
communion. *See* Holy Communion
Contemporary Christian Music (CCM) 140, 145, 146
copyright 112
Corazón Valiente (*Braveheart*, Gilda) 90
Corinthians (biblical text) 12, 67, 68, 74
"crisis" and "fall" 187, 189–90, 192
crosses and crucifixes 26, 68, 109, 111, 123, 128, 131, 132–3
crucifixion 57, 58, 68, 132
culture, "Christ and Culture" dilemma 30. *See also* Winans, CeCe (Priscilla)
cumbia 3, 81–2. *See also* Gilda fandom
Curt & Roland 146
cycle of meaning 187, 197–8

Daft Punk 26
Dance Till World Ends (Britney Spears) 15
"Dark Horse" (Katy Perry) 17
"Darling Nikki " (Prince) 110
"Deal with the Devil" (Judas Priest) 47
death
 Gilda's mythification (*see* Gilda fandom)
 heavy metal theme 50–2, 53, 57, 60, 67, 69, 70
 Katy Perry image 21
 of Prince 2, 109, 115, 117, 118, 119
 "Russian-Orthodoxy or Death" motto 133
 Swedish country music theme 137, 142, 144, 147–8
"Deep-Freeze" (Judas Priest) 50, 51
Defenders of the Faith (Judas Priest) 52, 61–2, 64
"Demonizer" (Judas Priest) 58
"Den sista seglatsen" ("The Last Voyage", Hasse Andersson) 142–3
"Desert Plains" (Judas Priest) 62
"Det finns ett träd" ("There is a Tree", Hasse Andersson) 144
devils. *See* Satan and devils
"Devil's Child" (Judas Priest) 58
Diary of a Madman (Ozzy Osbourne) 68, 70
Different Lifestyles (BeBe and CeCe Winans) 34, 39, 40, 45

"Diggin Me Down" (Ozzy Osbourne) 73–4
Disabled 159
DJs
    "build-up" and "drop" 187, 190–2, 195, 196, 199, 200
    crowd skills and feedback loop ("the vibe") 190, 194–6, 199
    digitalization 3, 186, 187–9, 191–2, 194, 199
    evolution of rave music 185–6
    prerecorded sets 188, 194–5, 198
Dobbelaere, Karel 3
"Don't Go" (Judas Priest) 62
Dove Awards 38–9, 40
Downing, K. K. 50
Down to Earth (Ozzy Osbourne) 68, 70
"Dreamer Deceiver" (Judas Priest) 55
"Dreamer" (Ozzy Osbourne) 70
Duct Tape Surgery 164
Dugin, Aleksandr 128, 136
"Dying to Meet You" (Judas Priest) 52
Dylan, Bob 3, 49, 168. See also Dylan masses
Dylan masses 3, 7, 167, 168, 169–70
    Dylan as liturgy 173–7
    performance 177–82, 183
    religious legitimation 170–3, 182

"Eat Me Alive" (Judas Priest) 48
Ecstasy (MDMA) 191, 193, 199
EDM. *See* electronic dance music (EDM)
Ekstsess (*Excess*, Alisa) 134
electronic dance music (EDM) 7
    "build-up" and "drop" 187, 190–2, 195, 196, 199, 200
    co-creation of experience 194–7, 199
    digitalization 3, 186, 187–9, 191–2, 194, 199
    evolution from rave 185–6, 199
    transformation of consciousness 193, 197–8, 200
Eliade, Mircea 57, 63
Ellis, Warren 96
Elvis 79, 83, 88, 90, 117, 118
Endless War (KontraSosial) 164
Entre el cielo y la tierra (Between Heaven and Earth, Gilda) 82
Ephesians (biblical text) 175

"Epitaph" (Judas Priest) 51
Erling, Valle 171, 172, 173, 177, 181
eschatology 15, 54–7, 60–1, 63, 74
Eucharist 58, 167, 174, 178, 181–2
"Evening Star" (Judas Priest) 55
"Everything from Jesus to Jack Daniels" (Tom T. Hall) 145
"Evil Fantasies" (Judas Priest) 61

Fagan, Geraldine 125, 127, 135
"Fallen Angel" (Patrick Woodroffe) 52
fans 1, 3
    Alisa's army 125, 131, 136
    Dylan masses 3, 168, 170, 172, 181, 182
    heavy metal 71, 75–6
    of Katy Perry 2, 3, 22–3, 25–7
    of Nick Cave 2, 4, 99–106
    as religious devotees 5, 7, 107–8 (*see also* Gilda fandom; Prince fans)
    of Swedish country music 137–8, 140
"Fate" (Duct Tape Surgery) 164
Featherstone, Mike 4
"Firework" (Katy Perry) 22, 24
"Forever Young" (Bob Dylan) 176
Forever Young Dylan mass 167, 168, 169
    Dylan as liturgy 173, 175–6, 177
    performance 179–80, 181, 182
    religious legitimation 170, 171
Forsberg, Monica 144
FPI. *See* Front Pembela Islam (Islamic Defenders Front, FPI)
"Frälsningssoldaten" ("The Salvation Army Soldier", Hasse Andersson) 142, 143
"Från religion till renat" ("From Religion to Renat", Alf Robertson) 145
Frisk, Liselotte 138, 139, 147, 149
Front Pembela Islam (Islamic Defenders Front, FPI) 153, 156, 157, 158, 159
front-row phenomenon 114–15

Gaga. *See* Lady Gaga
Galatians (biblical text) 68
Gardel, Carlos 89
Geertz, Clifford 57, 63
Gilda fandom
    becoming a fan 85–7
    Biographical data 81–2, 91–2
    fan practices 82–4, 85, 86, 92

Gilda's personal qualities 87–92
   posthumous fame 79–80, 93
   research methodology 80–1
GMA Dove Awards 38–9, 40
God Bless Ozzy Osbourne 71
"God" (John Lennon) 69–70
Gololobov, I. 124, 130
Gomel, Elana 54, 63
gospel music. *See also* Winans, CeCe (Priscilla)
   Bob Dylan 168, 169, 171, 172, 173–4, 177, 181, 182
   and Swedish country music 140, 144, 146
Gospel Music Association Dove Awards 38–9, 40
Graceland 117, 118
Grebenshikov, Boris 123–4
Greek mythology 20, 21, 23
"Grinder" (Judas Priest) 59
Grinderman 96, 97
Gundyayev, Vladimir Mikhailovich (Patriarch Kirill) 125, 126, 127, 131, 135, 136
GunXRose 159

Halford, Rob 48, 50, 51, 53, 54, 58, 61
"En hälsning till morgonen" ("A Greeting to the Morning", Christina Lindberg) 148–9
"Hard as Iron" (Judas Priest) 59
Harris, Emmylou 168
"Heading out to the Highway" (Judas Priest) 59
heaven
   Alisa 132
   Bob Dylan 175, 176, 177, 179
   CeCe Winans 34
   Indonesian punk music 164
   saviours from the sky 54–7
   Swedish country music 141–2
Heaven (BeBe and CeCe Winans) 34, 39, 40
heavy metal 6–7. *See also* Judas Priest; Osbourne, Ozzy
Hebrews (biblical text) 74
"Hej, Hasse, Hej" (Hasse Andersson) 142
hell
   blues 49

Judas Priest lyrics 52, 53, 57–8, 60, 63
   Katy Perry lyrics 16
Hell Bent for Leather (Judas Priest) 61
"Here Come the Tears" (Judas Priest) 62
Here Lies Your Gods (Zudas Krust) 164
hermeneutic model 197–8
Hill, Ian 50
Hills, Matt 80, 85–6, 107, 117
Hinch, John 50
Hizbut Tahrir 153
Holy Communion 58, 167, 174, 178, 181–2
homosexuality 16, 61, 153, 163
homo symbolicus 11–13
house music 193
Houston, Whitney 37
"How?" (Ozzy Ozbourne) 68–9
Hudson, Katheryn. *See* Perry, Katy
Hutson, Scott 185
hymns 34–5, 141, 144, 167
hypocrisy 73, 75, 144, 147

I am Ozzy (Ozzy Osbourne) 71
"I Believe in You" (Bob Dylan) 175
"I Don't Know" (Ozzy Osbourne) 65
"I Kissed a Girl" (Katy Perry) 16
Illuminati 17, 22
Imagine (John Lennon) 68, 69
"Imagine" (John Lennon) 69, 71
individualism 26–7, 48, 59–60, 76, 187
individualization 4
   Indonesian punk rockers 160–1
   Katy Perry's symbolic repertoire 17, 18, 19–23, 24, 25
   millennial generation 16
   Nick Cave's religious approach 95, 96–8, 100–6
   Ozzy Osbourne's trinity of sex/music/self 69, 70, 71, 76
   Prince's anti-normative ideas 109–11
   Swedish country artists 139, 141–50
Indonesian punk rockers 3, 7
   atheism 151, 157, 161, 162–4, 165
   Muslim practices 151, 157–62
   religion in Indonesia 152–4
   repression of 154–7
"In the Garden" (Bob Dylan) 181
Injakmati 159
Institut A group 163

institutional differentiation 3, 4
institutional religion. *See also*
	individualization; Russian
	Orthodox Church
	Black Church 30, 31, 33–4, 36, 42, 45
	heavy metal's rejection 63, 69, 75–6
	hypocrisy 73
	Islam (*see* Indonesian punk rockers)
	Serbian Orthodox Church 98–9,
	104–6
	using popular music in church 3, 4,
	130 (*see also* Dylan masses)
Isaiah (biblical text) 68, 175
"I shall be released" (Bob Dylan) 175
Islam 129, 134. *See also* Indonesian punk
	rockers
"Island of Domination" (Judas Priest)
	60–1
Izgoi (*Social Outcast*, Alisa) 132

Jackson, Michael 17
"Jag tittar i mitt fönster" ("I look through
	my window", Hasse Andersson) 144
Jenkins, Henry 107
Job (biblical text) 66
John (Gospel of) 29, 73, 75
Johnson, Robert 48–9
Jonson, Ben 72
Journeys in Black 30, 32
"Judas" (Lady Gaga) 15, 25
Judas Priest
	and the cultural ubiquity of Satan
	49–50
	descent into hell 57–8
	eschatology 54–7, 60–1, 63
	Fallen Angel motif 52–4
	lyrics on mortality 50–2
	origin story 47, 50
	revenger/strong loner figure 59–60
	sadomasochism and love 47, 60–2
	Satanic motifs 47–8, 52, 57, 58, 63

"Käre Fader" ("Dear Father", Hasse
	Andersson) 144
Karlsson, Pelle 145
Katy Perry: Part of Me 18
Khram Khrista Spasitelia (Cathedral of
	Christ the Savior) 127, 128
"Killing Machine" (Judas Priest) 52
Kill Me with Your Lips (Street Voices) 159

Kinchev, Konstantin 123, 124, 125, 129–36
King Ink II (Nick Cave) 96
Kirill, Patriarch (Vladimir Mikhailovich
	Gundyayev) 125, 126, 127, 131,
	135, 136
Knight, Michael 152
"Knockin' on Heaven's Door" (Bob Dylan)
	175, 176, 179
KontraSosial 163–4
Kosovo 134
Kountry Korral 140
Krass Kepala 163, 164
Kuraev, Andrei 130, 131

Lady Gaga 14–15, 18, 24, 25, 153, 159
"Last Rose of Summer" (Judas Priest) 51
Latimer, Robert 72
"Latimer's Mercy" 72
Latour, Bruno 81, 91, 93
Leningrad (band) 124, 126
Lennon, John 68–70, 71
"Lenyapkan Zionis" (GunXRose) 159
"Let It Die" (Ozzy Osbourne) 67–8
Letov, Egor 124
"Let's Go Crazy" (Prince) 118, 119
"Let us Prey " (Judas Priest) 51
"Like a Prayer" (Madonna) 25
Lindberg, Christina 141, 147–50
Lopez, Jennifer 13
Lord Lift Us Up (BeBe and CeCe Winans)
	39
Lord's Prayer 58
love
	Bob Dylan 171
	homo symbolicus 11, 12
	Judas Priest theme 51, 53, 62, 63
	Katy Perry's *Wide Awake* video 23
	Nick Cave 97, 100, 101, 102
	Ozzy Osbourne 69, 72
	Prince 110, 111, 112–13
	rave ethos 186
	Swedish country songs 137, 144, 149
Love, Alvin 45
"Love Lift Us Up (Where We Belong)"
	32–3
Love, Priscilla Winans. *See* Winans, CeCe
	(Priscilla)
LoveSexy tour (Prince) 110
"LOVE" statue (New York) 69
"The Love We Make" (Prince) 110

A Loyal Slave to the Apocalyptic Order (Zudas Krust) 164
Luckmann, Thomas 139, 147
Luke (Gospel of) 70, 74
Lundberg, Börje 144, 145

McCrary, Howard 31, 32
Macri, Mauricio 79–80
Madonna 25
Mamonov, Piotr 123
Marchenko, Evgenii 126
Mark (Gospel of) 68, 74, 96
masques 71–2
mass 114. *See also* Dylan masses
Matthew (Gospel of) 67, 68, 69, 70, 73, 74
MDMA (Ecstasy) 191, 193, 199
mediatized religion 4, 5. *See also* Dylan masses
    CeCe Winans's celebritization 29, 38–9
    remembering Gilda 80, 81, 82, 91–2
    Russian orthodoxy 124, 125, 127–8, 129–36
    Serbian fandom 4, 100–6
    using popular music in church 3, 4, 130
Medvedev, Dmitri 123, 135
Michetti, Gabriela 80
millennials 15–16, 186, 187, 196
Minin, Nikita (Patriarch Nikon) 128
"Miracle Man" (Ozzy Osbourne) 73
Miss World Beauty pageant 153
Mitchell, Joni 168
"Mitt land" ("My Country", Alf Robertson) 145
Mitt land (*My Country*, Alf Robertson) 145
Monarch programme 22–3
Monson, Mitch 111
"Monsters of Rock" (Judas Priest) 47
mortality. *See* death
"Mr. Tambourine Man" (Bob Dylan) 176–7, 179
music videos
    aesthetization of religion 5, 15, 17, 18, 19, *20*, 21–2, 23, 25
    Alisa 131, 132–3, 134
    boosting the symbolic power of music 13, 14
    "Dance Till World Ends" (Britney Spears) 15
    "Judas" (Lady Gaga) 15, 25

Katy Perry 2, 3, 7, 18, 19, 21–3, 24
"Like a Prayer" (Madonna) 25
Ozzy Osbourne 69
"Starboy (feat. The Weekend)" (Daft Punk) 26
Muslims. *See* Islam

"Naebali" ("Fucked", Alisa) 134
Nära dig ("Close to You", Hasse Andersson) 144
"När du går över floden" ("When You Cross the River", Alf Robertson) 145
Nashe Radio 133
nationalism
    Post-Soviet Russia 3, 7, 123, 124, 129, 130, 131, 133–4, 136
    Serbian 98–9
"Nebo Slavian" ("Heaven of the Slavs", Alisa) 133–4
"Nepokornye" ("The Rebellious", Alisa) 134
Neumoev, Roman 124, 131
Niebuhr, H. Richard (Christ-Culture typology) 2, 29, 30–1, 36, 40
"Night Crawler" (Judas Priest) 58
Nikon, Patriarch (Nikita Minin) 128
Nissim, Offer 195
"No me arrepiento de este amor" (Gilda) 79–80
No More Tears (Ozzy Osbourne) 68
No Rest for the Wicked (Ozzy Osbourne) 68, 73
"Nostradamus" (Judas Priest) 63–4

occultism 49, 75, 212 n.7
Offer Nissim 195
Oh, Brother, Where Art Thou? 141
1Corinthians (biblical text) 12, 68, 74
One of the Boys (Katy Perry) 22
One More Time with Feeling 96
On a Positive Note (CeCe Winans) 29, 37, 42
Open symbols 25
original sin 21–2, 74–5
Osbourne, Ozzy
    biography 71
    contemplative mood 65
    lyrics of 2, 66
    morality 72–3, 75

outside voice 67, 68–71, 76
theodicy 73–4
Ostwalt, Conrad 54, 63
"Out in the Cold" (Judas Priest) 62
outsider status. *See also* revenger/strong loner figure
  Christina Lindberg 149, 150
  club culture 192, 193
  fandom 83, 85
  as a narrative function 67, 76
  Ozzy Osbourne as 68–71

Painkiller (Judas Priest) 52–3
Paisley Park 112, 115–18, 119
"Paisley Park" (Prince) 116, 117
Palo Monte (Cuba) 190
Paranoid (Black Sabbath) 74
para-religiosity. *See* Prince fans
Parents Music Resource Center (PMRC) 47–8
"Part of Me" (Katy Perry) 18
Partridge, Christopher 5, 138, 139
Pearl Jam 168
"Perang Agama" ("Religious War", Zudas Krust) 164
"Percepat Kiamat!" ("Hasten the Apocalypse!", Zudas Krust) 164
Perry, Katy
  background 15–17
  music videos 2, 3, 7, 18, 19, 21–3, 24
  "Wide Awake" 17–23, 24, 25, 26
Pink Floyd 168
pluralism 4, 5
PMRC. *See* Parents Music Resource Center (PMRC)
Point of Entry (Judas Priest) 62
popular music/rock masses. *See also* Dylan masses
possession trance 186, 187, 189–93, 194, 197–8, 200
Post-Soviet Russia. *See* Russian Orthodox Church
Prapatan Rebel distro raid 156
pravaya.ru 130, 131
"Pravoslavnye" ("Orthodox believers", Alisa) 132
prayer
  and CeCe Winans 37, 41, 42, 45
  Dylan masses 174, 176, 178, 182
  Indonesian punk rockers 157, 158, 160
  Judas Priest's parody of the Lord's Prayer 58
  "Like a Prayer" (Madonna) 25
  Prince 110
Presley, Elvis 79, 83, 88, 90, 117, 118
Prince fans 2, 5, 7
  concerts and metaphysical physicality 2, 113–15
  Paisley Park 115–18, 119
  Prince's anti-normative behavior 108–11
  Prince's attitude towards 107, 111–12, 116
Prism (Katy Perry) 19, 24
privatization of religion. *See* individualization
Psalms (biblical text) 74
The PTL Club 31–2, 33, 36, 38, 39, 44
punk rock 3, 124. *See also* Indonesian punk rockers
"Purple Rain" (Prince) 108, 109
Pussy Riot 124, 127–8
Putin, Vladimir 123, 125

"Quinn the Eskimo (The Mighty Quinn)" (Bob Dylan) 180

"Rapid Fire" (Judas Priest) 54
rave 185, 186, 187, 188, 189, 193, 196, 197, 199
razia jibab (hijab raids) 154
Red Dirt Girl (Emmylou Harris) 214 n.25
Redeemer of Souls (Judas Priest) 53
redemption
  Alisa's lyrics 132, 133
  Judas Priest 48, 53–7, 60, 62, 63
  Prince 110
Relationships (BeBe and CeCe Winans) 38
"Release the Bats" (The Boys Next Door) 96
"Religi Konsumsi" ("Religious Consumption", KontraSoial) 163–4
The Revelation (Apocalypse of John, biblical text) 54, 57, 61, 68, 70, 175
"Revelation (Mother Earth)" (Ozzy Osbourne) 70
revenger/strong loner figure 59–60
Reviakin, Dmitriy 123
Richmond Dylan mass 168, 169
  Dylan as liturgy 173, 174, 175, 176, 177

performance 178, 179, 180, 181, 182
religious legitimation 170, 171, 172–3
"Riding on the Wind" (Judas Priest) 56
ritual trance. *See* possession trance
Robertson, Alf 141, 144–7, 150
Roberts, Oral 73
Rocka Rolla (Judas Priest) 50, 60
"Rocka Rolla" (Judas Priest) 60
"Rock'n'Roll Krest" ("Rock'n'Roll Cross", Alisa) 132, 136
rock/popular music masses. *See* Dylan masses
rock sermons 131
"Rok k Nebu" ("Rock to Heaven") 130
Romans (biblical text) 74, 75, 174
Romeo and Juliet (William Shakespeare) 12
Romin, Ole 146
Rotten Conspiracy (Injakmati) 159
Rouget, Gilbert 186, 189–90, 191, 197
"Rozhdestvo" ("Christmas", Alisa) 131, 132
"Run of the Mill" (Judas Priest) 51
Russia. *See* Russian Orthodox Church
Russian hard rock. *See* russkii rock
Russian Orthodox Church
 historical role 128–9
 mediatization 2–3, 124, 125, 127–8, 129–36
 national identity 129, 136
 politics 123, 125
 religiosity 123, 126–7
russkii rock 2–3, 7, 123–4, 125, 129–36
Rybko, Sergii 130, 131

sacralization 5–6, 56, 63, 125, 138–9. *See also* Gilda fandom; Prince fans
sadomasochism 47, 60–1
Sad Wings of Destiny (Judas Priest) 51, 52, 53, 54, 60
St. James Episcopalian church (Richmond, Virginia). *See* Richmond Dylan mass
saints 2, 57–8, 90, 123, 128, 129, 177
"Saints in Hell" (Judas Priest) 57–8
salvation 23, 53, 56, 132, 171, 175. *See also* redemption
Samutsevich, Ekaterina 128
Satan and devils
 cultural ubiquity 48–50
 Judas Priest 47–8, 52, 57, 58, 63

Katy Perry's use of symbolism 17
 narrative function 66
 Ozzy Osbourne lyrics 66
 worship by heavy metal fans 75–6
Saved (Bob Dylan) 168
"Saving Grace" (Bob Dylan) 176
Saving Grace Dylan mass 168, 169
 Dylan as liturgy 173, 174, 176, 177
 performance 177, 178, 179, 180, 181, 182
 religious legitimation 170, 171, 172
Scandinavia 3. *See also* Forever Young Dylan mass; Saving Grace Dylan mass; Swedish country music
Screaming for Vengeance (Judas Priest) 55
"Screaming for Vengeance" (Judas Priest) 60
Scream (Ozzy Osbourne) 65, 67, 68, 72, 73
secularization 3–4, 5, 6
 celebrity 13, 14
 "Christ and Culture" dilemma (*see* Winans, CeCe (Priscilla))
 Russian Federation 127, 129
 Swedish country music (*see* Swedish country music)
Seichas pozdnee, chem ty dumaesh (*It is Later Now than You Think*, Alisa) 130
"The Sentinel" (Judas Priest) 60
Serbian Nick Cave fans
 method and sample 99
 on Nick Cave and religion 2, 7, 95, 100–4
 Serbia's religious situation 4, 98–9, 104–6
Serbian Orthodox Church 98–9, 104–6
sex
 Gilda 90, 91
 heavy metal bands 48, 49, 60–2, 63, 69
 Katy Perry 19
 Madonna's "Like a Prayer" 25
 Nick Cave 97, 101, 103
 Prince 109–11
 Shariah law 153, 154, 155, 163
Shakespeare, William 12, 71, 75
shamanism 149, 189, *197*, 198, 200
Shariah law 151, 153–4, 155, 163
"Shelter from the Storm" (Bob Dylan) 167, 175
Shevchuk, Iurii 123, 131

Shot of Love (Bob Dylan) 168
Siberian punk rock artists 124
sin 22, 52, 53, 57, 68, 73, 74–5, 110
"Sinner" (Judas Priest) 57
"De sista ljuva åren" ("The Last Delightful Years", Christina Lindberg) 147–8
Slow Train Coming (Bob Dylan) 168
Solntsevorot ("Solstice", Alisa) 132
"Sometimes it Snows in April" (Prince) 119
Song of Songs (Song of Solomon) 12
Spears, Britney 15
Spencer, Jon Michael 31
spirit possession 187, 189–90, 191, 192, 193
"Spotlight, Piano and a Microphone" tour (Prince) 116
"Stained Class" (Judas Priest) 59
standardization 30, 33–6, 46
"Starboy (feat. The Weekend)" (Daft Punk) 26
"Starbreaker" (Judas Priest) 55
stardom, ambivalence for African American gospel singers. *See* Winans, CeCe (Priscilla)
Star Trek fans 83
The Strange Case of Dr. Jekyll and Mr. Hyde (Robert Louis Stevenson) 67
Stupnikov, Denis 129–30
Sudakov, Oleg "Manager" 124
Swaggart, Jimmy 73
Swedish country music 3, 7
  Alf Robertson 141, 144–7, 150
  Christina Lindberg 141, 147–50
  Hasse Andersson 141–4, 146–7, 150
  and US country music 137–8, 139–40
Swedish Dylan masses. *See* Forever Young Dylan mass; Saving Grace Dylan mass
symbolism
  aesthetization of religion 5
  celebrity branding 13, 14
  and the culture of individualism 26–7
  Dance Till World Ends (Britney Spears, music video) 15
  human capacity for 11–13
  Judas Priest's imagery 52–7, 58, 59–61, 62, 63
  Katy Perry 2, 17, 18, 19–23, 24, 25
  Lady Gaga 14–15, 18, 24, 25
  Like a Prayer (Madonna) 25
  Ozzy Osbourne 66, 68, 69, 70, 71, 73, 75–6
  power of 57, 63
  Prince 111, 112
  sacralization 138
  "Starboy (feat. The Weekend)" (Daft Punk) 26
  Swedish country music - Hasse Andersson 142, 144
  "Symphony" ("Simfonia", Alisa) 135

Taqwacore 152
TAZ. *See* "temporary autonomous zone" (TAZ)
technoshamanism. *See* electronic dance music (EDM)
Teenage Dream: The Complete Confection and Prism (Katy Perry) 17, 18, 19, 24
Tellus (Alf Robertson) 145
The Tempest (William Shakespeare) 75
temporary autonomous zone (TAZ) 193
theodicy 66, 73–4
The Secret Life of the Love Songs & The Flesh Made Word: Two Lectures by Nick Cave 96
"They are Not a Moslem" (Disabled) 159
13 (Black Sabbath) 65
Thomas, Keith 36, 45–6
Throne Room: Ushered into the Presence of God (book, CeCe Winans) 30, 41, 45
Throne Room (album, CeCe Winans) 30, 34, 35, 39, 40, 41, 42, 43
Tie bilder (Ten Pictures) (Hasse Andersson) 142–3
"The times they are a-changin'" (Bob Dylan) 174, 176, 179
Tipton, Glenn 50, 53
Tiurenkov, Mikhail 131
Tolokonnikova, Nadezhda 128
Total Anarchy 160, 161
trance 3, 7, 186, 187, 189–93, 194, 197–8, 200
"Troubleshooter" (Judas Priest) 61
turntables and vinyl records 186, 187, 188–9, 191, 200
20,000 Days on Earth (Iain Forsyth and Jane Pollard) 96
"Tyrant" (Judas Priest) 54

U2charist 168
Ukraine 134–5
Ultimate Sin (Ozzy Osbourne) 68, 74
Under the Cherry Moon 119
underground club scene 185–6, 188, 193, 199, 200
"Up Where We Belong" (BeBe and CeCe Winans) 32–3

Vance, James 48
Vår värld (*Our World*, Alf Robertson) 145
"Vår värld" ("OurWorld", Alf Robertson) 145
"Victim of Changes" (Judas Priest) 60
videos. *See* music videos; YouTube
vinyl records and turntables 186, 187, 188–9, 191, 200
"Vlast'" ("Power", Alisa) 134
Vltchek, Andre 154, 158–9
"V Pitere–pit'" ("In Piter, You Drink", Leningrad) 126

Warnes, Jennifer 32
"War Pigs" 74
War of the Worlds (H. G. Wells) 67
Washington Wives. *See* Parents Music Resource Center (PMRC)
"Watching the River Flow" (Bob Dylan) 175
"What Can I Do For You" (Bob Dylan) 176
"When You Gonna Wake Up" (Bob Dylan) 176
"Whiskey woman" (Judas Priest) 60

"Who am I Living For" (Katy Perry) 26
"Wide Awake" (Katy Perry) 17, 18–23, 24, 25
Wide Awake (Katy Perry) 26
Wikström, Owe 139
Wilson, Ian 155, 156–7
Winans, CeCe (Priscilla) 7
   apostillization 41–3
   background 31–3
   celebritization 29, 30, 36–40
   standardization 33–6
   strategies and practices 30, 43–6
Winans, Ronald 35, 42
Winans, The 35
"Winter Retreat" 50, 51
women 153–4, 154–5, 162, 193
Wonder, Stevie 168

"You Can't Kill Rock and Roll" (Ozzy Osbourne) 70
"You're No Different than Me" (Ozzy Osbourne) 73
YouTube
   church services 4, 169, 172
   DJ tutorials 187
   prerecorded DJ sets 195
   Prince concerts 111, 112
   Pussy Riot's punk prayer 127
   "V Pitere–pit'" ("In Piter, You Drink", Leningrad) 126

Zittoun, Tania 18, 19
Zudas Krust 164
Zuege, Unsie 117

www.ingramcontent.com/pod-product-compliance
Lightning Source LLC
Chambersburg PA
CBHW071815300426
44116CB00009B/1333